"Ted Berrigan was a leader of the New York School; his crazy energy embodied that movement and the city itself."

—John Ashbery, author of *Self-Portrait in a Convex Mirror*

"I copied so many of my favorite passages from this splendid collection I almost reproduced the whole book. Then I thought, hey, why don't I just buy a hundred copies of the book when it's published and give it to a hundred people who love Ted Berrigan and then they can buy a hundred copies to give to their friends? I am immensely grateful to Alice Notley, Edmund and Anselm Berrigan, and Nick Sturm for this intimate look. Ted was my mentor, my teacher of America and its poetry, and I often quote him. He was an oral genius and I have regretted not writing down everything he said to me. Now I have this collection of journals, critical writing on art, aphorisms, and correspondence. It makes for a grand portrait of the poet who charmed my whole generation. Ted Berrigan is alive in this book in ways that no one could guess."

—Andrei Codrescu, author of *Too Late for Nightmares*

"The defining bridge from the 'New American Poetry' of the '50s to that poetry now contemporary on both coasts and in all conditions."

—Robert Creeley, author of *For Love: Poems 1950–1960*

"It's always a significant occasion when we have an edition of a poet's prose. *Get the Money!* offers us an important window into Ted Berrigan's laboratory, his no-bullshit attitude, his class awareness, his gorgeous sentimentality, and his disarming anarchic humor. This book is what anyone could hope it would be: funny, tender, brilliant, intimate, original, alive."

—Peter Gizzi, author of *Now It's Dark*

"One of the most influential poets of his generation."

—Joanne Kyger, author of *On Time*

"Ted Berrigan's voice has always been instantly familiar to me so *Get the Money!* feels less like a reading experience and more like taking a long walk with my favorite poet, then buying him a drink someplace and letting him talk. The pieces collected here offer a superhuman range of formal invention. Highlights include intimate, confiding journals from both the sixties and seventies, the infamous 'interview' with John Cage, two pieces on the portraiture of Alice Neel, a notice on the death of Frank O'Hara, a history of Berrigan's own 'C' magazine, Naropa workshop notes, the Arrival Report, and a letter written to Joanne Kyger on her birthday in 1971. There is poetry included as well: haiku translations from Bashō and several book reviews split into verse. Even with such variety *Get the Money!* somehow maintains the emotional dimension of a memoir, perhaps because Berrigan remains consistently revealing throughout. His prose is often loose and lyrical, hovering somewhere between blogging, letter writing, texting, and transcription. His deadpan bravura and sudden dismissiveness are consistently hilarious. Decades after his death Berrigan remains way ahead of his time. I think Robert Creeley said it best: 'The Bell rings / Ted is ready.'"

—Cedar Sigo, author of *All This Time*

"Ted Berrigan was legendary on the streets of the Lower East Side, and for his editing of 'C' Magazine. I always appreciated his devotion and passion about OUR Time. There had never been anything quite like it. We were all entangled! Ted explores this kind of energy in his personal story and writing. He tracks a bunch of artist/poets growing with deliberation in radically changing the Kulchur. *Get the Money!* captures the esprit de corps of the particular community close to Ted's door on St Mark's Place. This book of prose with its nimble lift, tinged with intimacy, wit, and perception is a welcome addition to the second-gen NY School canon. Ted often went hungry but could make a few dollars with the short reviews. One walks the rounds with Ted on his 'beat': Love, poetry, gossip, art. Telling it like it is. Strolling into artist studios, galleries, poets' modest digs, and into our hearts."

—Anne Waldman, author of *Trickster Feminism*

GET THE MONEY!

BRAINARD-

GET THE MONEY!

Collected Prose (1961–1983)

TED BERRIGAN

EDITED BY EDMUND BERRIGAN, ANSELM BERRIGAN,
ALICE NOTLEY, AND NICK STURM

CITY LIGHTS PUBLISHERS

Cover art by George Schneeman with words by Ted Berrigan:
Ted, 1967, mixed media and collage on canvas, 53 x 53 in.
Used by permission of Kathryn Schneeman.

Frontispiece by Joe Brainard: *Ted Berrigan*, 1971, graphite on paper,
14 1/4 x 11 1/4 in. Collection of the Mandeville Special Collections Library
at the University of California, San Diego. Used by permission of the Estate of Joe Brainard.

ISBN: 978-0-87286-895-3
eISBN: 978-0-87286-896-0

Library of Congress Cataloging-in-Publication Data

Names: Berrigan, Ted, author. | Berrigan, Edmund, 1974- editor. | Berrigan,
Anselm, editor. | Notley, Alice, 1945- editor. | Strum, Nick, 1986-
editor.
Title: Get the money! : collected prose (1961-1983) / Ted Berrigan ; edited
by Edmund Berrigan, Anselm Berrigan, Alice Notley and Nick Strum.
Other titles: Get the money! (Compilation)
Description: San Francisco : City Lights Books, 2022.
Identifiers: LCCN 2022011479 | ISBN 9780872868953 (paperback)
Subjects: LCSH: Berrigan, Ted--Diaries. | Literature, Modern--20th
century--Book reviews. | Art criticism. | LCGFT: Diaries. | Essays. |
Reviews.
Classification: LCC PS3552.E74 G47 2022 | DDC 818/.5408--dc23/eng/20220510
LC record available at https://lccn.loc.gov/2022011479

City Lights Books are published at the City Lights Bookstore
261 Columbus Avenue, San Francisco, CA 94133
citylights.com

CONTENTS

GET THE MONEY!

INTRODUCTION

T ED BERRIGAN'S PROSE, written concurrently with his poetry throughout his writing life, makes for a highly idiosyncratic body of work. The writing constantly changes shape while always devoting itself to the situation of a given or self-selected assignment, amusement, or invitation. Berrigan shaped that devotion into an ethos of affable excitability grounded in attention, and not without its own edges and capacity for sentiment. He had a specific notion of what a literary figure, as part of an ongoing self-education never meant to end, should be doing alongside their primary work, including looking out for new forms to inhabit, reinvent, and share. This multifaceted approach to writing-mind and adventure-in-form, combined with constant social activity and conversation, resulted in a considerable array of forms: private journals, journals written for eventual publication, book and magazine reviews, short and longer reviews of art exhibitions, translations, procedural/collage pieces chased by a version of definition that can't catch up, fabricated interviews, reports ranging from satirical letters to birth announcements, and book reviews written in lines from the books reviewed. In all his endeavors Berrigan worked to bypass formality, while making an explicit distinction between formality and form, the latter something to study and inhabit out of pleasure and exploration.

"Get the Money!" is a phrase coined by the early twentieth-century journalist and literary writer Damon Runyon, a particular hero to Berrigan, who used the phrase as a tonally flexible and oddly practical descriptor as needed in conversation and writing. Sprinkled here and there in this selection, "Get the Money!" is also the title of a particularly bonkers-yet-incisive roundup of art reviews and opinions that kicks off the second half of this book. Built into the phrase in Berrigan's usage is the knowing and amused, if arghifying, implication that "Get" will never become "Got" in any permanent sense, but could happen temporarily on the fly, and might be anyone's reason for a particular decision. Art writing, for instance, was a way to Get the Money! That said, Berrigan's interest in art writing was fueled by the fact that some of his most important living poetry models—Frank O'Hara, James Schuyler, John Ashbery—worked as art writers. Edwin Denby and Fairfield Porter were also important influences, the former a poet and sonnet master working as an acclaimed dance critic, and the latter a painter as well as a prolific and influential art critic. Berrigan entered this milieu in the early 1960s after spending the 1950s dropping out from a first go-round with college, enlisting in the U.S. Army, being sent to Korea at the tail end of the Korean War, and eventually landing in Tulsa on the G.I. Bill to further his formal education. In Tulsa, a number of crucial friendships began, in particular with the high-school-aged poets Ron Padgett and Dick Gallup and their artist schoolmate Joe Brainard, as Berrigan plunged himself fully into a life centered on poetry. All four were living in New York City by the early 1960s.

Berrigan immersed himself in collaboration with Brainard, Gallup, and Padgett, and invented his own small magazine and press "C", an editorial space in which he could bring together the works by his heroes and friends. Editing "C" as a younger, working-class out-sider poet also helped Berrigan to socially enter and subtly change the downtown New York City literary and artistic circles he was inspired by but never felt fully comfortable in. His own particular poetic breakthroughs—his much-celebrated book *The Sonnets*, the long open-field poem "Tambourine Life," and the steady development of musical speech infused by collage and common language—were accompanied by a consistent attention to crafting sentences. In New York, Berrigan completed his master's thesis on George Bernard Shaw and took up a kind of shadow job of writing papers for students at Columbia University, where Padgett had enrolled as a student. These "works" are naturally not included here. That said, Berrigan took every writing task seriously, and cultivated for himself a work ethic based on a sense of professional-ism, as in always being ready for the matter at hand. Outward appearances and manner may have belied this readiness to uptight passers-by, but commitment to the work could not manifest as costume. Berrigan's journals from the early 1960s are markedly different at their outset than his later journal-writing. They give off a gradually developed sense of excitement at all the pos-sibilities emerging—making art among friends, marrying Sandra Alper in 1962, beginning to compose *The Sonnets*—but are also wrought with anxiety born from financial and personal des-peration. In the very early 1960s, Berrigan lived with Brainard, and the two spent a lot of time visiting museums and galleries, looking at art and figuring out through endless conversation how to articulate what they were discovering. Their influence on each other in that period was profound. Berrigan's initial published prose writings were mostly freewheeling reviews of books and magazines for *Kulchur*, the magazine and press published by the inimitable Lita Hornick, with indefinable editorial assistance from Amiri Baraka (then LeRoi Jones). These reviews are subversive, funny, and at times opinionated in ways probably unimaginable to anyone today. It also feels unlikely that *Kulchur* demanded its reviewers adhere to a house style. To wit, the final sentence of Berrigan's five-sentence review of a booklet by Jonathan Williams: "The price is absurd but the book is small and thin and slips easily under one's coat."

By the time Berrigan started writing for *ARTnews* in 1965, he'd absorbed the many les-sons accrued from his conversations with Brainard and other artist friends, as well as his own readings of writings by artists—*The Dada Painters and Poets: An Anthology* (1951), edited by Robert Motherwell, being especially important among them. Berrigan wrote paragraph-length reviews for *ARTnews* at a rate of 4–8 per month for about a year. The shorter reviews are written in a house style, but Berrigan's knack for crafting a sentence that can describe, amuse, and when necessary, assess, consistently break through that style. We have chosen to represent his short reviews mainly as a list of selected sentences, akin and in homage to a similar list edited by painter Rackstraw Downes for Fairfield Porter's book of art writings, *Art in Its Own Terms* (1979). Berrigan's longer art pieces focus on three painters: Alice Neel, Jane Freilicher, and Red Grooms—all lifelong points of interest—and it is notable that he was assigned by editor Tom Hess to write at greater length on painters whose work leaned harder towards representation than abstraction, though Berrigan loved many of the abstract painters of the time. The short reviews also coincide with the composition of "Tambourine Life" across 1965 and 1966, and could be read in imaginative conjunction with the expanse and jumping arrangement of detail and feeling that poem spreads out with. When you look at things with the intention of writing sentences out of that looking, then turn around to maintain your own practice of writing poetry, there's going to be unaccountable overlap in both directions. By his own admission, Berrigan didn't want to take up art writing as an ongoing job after his run at *ARTnews*. He'd gotten what he wanted out of the experience and didn't want to devote his attention to artists longer-term, though he did write about his close friend and collaborator George Schneeman's work some years later.

It's also during this period, in 1966, that his "notorious" interview with John Cage was published in Peter Schjeldahl's *Mother* magazine. Schjeldahl invited Berrigan to write something for a particular issue, and Berrigan told him he'd like to do an interview—an interview with John Cage that he would write himself. Schjeldahl gave him the go ahead, and Berrigan constructed the interview as a way to work through his opinions on art and reality at the time, while also paying homage to Cage's experimental methods of musical composition. He collaged the interview together from interviews with a number of people, citing Bob Dylan, Fernando Arrabal, Andy Warhol, and Cage himself as particular sources. Amazingly, some endeavor at the time called *The National Literary Anthology* awarded the interview a $1,000 prize (Get the Money!). The panel handling the award had no sense the interview was made up without Cage's direct participation, as it was published without a disclaimer, leading to some handwringing on their part. After calling John Ashbery to ask, "Is this guy for or against me?" and being told that, yes, Ted was a big fan of his works, Cage acknowledged he had nothing to do with the interview. Therefore, Berrigan should in fact get all the money (he did give $50 to Dick Gallup, who worked on a couple of pages at Berrigan's request).

* * * * * *

I have to be a little less formal now. My father's life changed dramatically in the late 1960s and early 1970s. He left New York to become a kind of traveling teacher, and experienced a painful breakup with Sandy, which meant not regularly seeing their two children, David and Kate. He taught at Yale, Ann Arbor-Michigan, Iowa City, and the University of Essex in England, and began what he thought of as a second life, one that led to his marriage with poet (mom) Alice Notley, the eventual births of my brother Edmund and me, and a need to find poetic renewal, or reinvigoration, as his health slowly started to fail. Around these changes there was time spent in Southampton, Long Island, and Bolinas, California. Poets and artists were regularly moving around these places at the time, and so one could crash for a while. Dad's journals written at these places operate at a different tempo than in the 1960s journals. The feeling space is more itinerant, more amused, and further inside the ongoing complexities of friendships and survival. Much work has already been made. Lines that show up later in poems appear in these journals; poems and situational prose are merging. A consciousness that anything written with care might be published, that the line between writing in private and writing for the public has been dissolved, and that such dissolution might be ordinary, is now in the cards. One still has to get the money. This is also the period in which he was writing the poems that would be part of the sequence "Easter Monday." As he put it during a reading at Naropa Institute in 1976, "On Easter Sunday, you rise from the grave, which is great. But on Easter Monday, you have to go get a job and support yourself, which is not so great."

The order of *Get the Money!* is roughly chronological, but for my father, who used collage and repetition in part to gently, if decisively, disrupt the hinges linear time-based minds attempt to enforce, chronology is a surface that can't maintain purchase. An awareness of precedent, literary or otherwise, can create a sense of where to find the gaps in any history's presentation of continuity. Dad read widely, found things to study and admire in work by minds drastically different than his, and enjoyed trying on the costumes of prosody (poetic music) all kinds of other poets' works offered. Poetry was the primary vehicle for the movement and performance of his studies, but prose created a parallel space—one where opinion could be treated as a handle, i.e., the way a savvy point guard on a professional basketball team is often described as having a strong handle, meaning they control the ball on offense, and therefore direct the tempo of play, using court vision to anticipate movements by and between players just before they happen. I may be leaning on sports writing because, while I was ten when Dad died, I was reading baseball writing by Roger Angell and Red Smith on his recommendation, and beginning to get into basketball writing. I'd deliberately get out of bed late at night to ask him if such-and-such athlete was really great, and he'd always say, "You better believe it," no matter how late it was, and commence telling me why. My father was, by many accounts, a galvanizing presence through talk—a person interested in getting people into conversation with each other, on the page and in the room. His prose reflects a commitment to the arts without putting a barrier between friendship and something like content. Dad encouraged younger writers throughout his life, and especially upon his return to New York City in 1976 with our family, after a number of years teaching in Chicago at Northeastern Illinois University. In these later years of his, Dad was an elder, an encouraging reader and responder, and an occasional life-advisor and self-appointed nag for many poets working on making their way through lives steeped in poetry. The poet Greg Masters, who was Dad's editor at *The Poetry Project Newsletter* in the early 1980s, puts the experience of getting to talk with him as a younger poet thusly in his long poem "My East Village":

> Talking with Ted was easier
> than anything I'd ever done.
> Camaraderie fueled his being
> and set loose his talk show of the
> streets and parlor, a fusillade
> of pertinent data, gossip,
>
> persuasive opinion flowing
> in a way that cursed out no one
> (except the occasional "jack-
> off") and instead discerned what was
> "terrific" in the process of
> being alive at the present
>
> moment or something peculiar
> or laudable, intangible
> or physical, that ensnared his
> focus from another time, we
> valued each word from the
> mom-loving hippie Socrates.

Greg's lines and perspective are important here not just because he describes Dad's presence and hospitality, but because he also invited Dad to write pieces for *The Poetry Project Newsletter* on a variety of subjects. These pieces—which make up a good portion of the last stage of *Get the Money!*—show a side of my father's prose style that had become more elegant and elaborate; the sentences are longer, they make wider circles, and by extension they make space to admit all the movement he can perceive in the works he's reading and witnessing, as well as the dynamics of their present existence in a room or book. These pieces are in the section titled "Longer Works of the More Academic Type." Dad made a folder of these works late in his life, understanding and letting us know they went together, but not leaving any particular instructions beyond their arrangement, and beyond writing "Longer Works of the More Academic Type" on the folder. These works are not especially long, and they are far from academic. As editors we added a few pieces, including the John Cage interview, to that section, since the title seemed exactly inclusive of anything non-academic. This section also includes a handful of introductions to books and readings, an assortment of occasional pieces written for friends that may appear at times to resemble blurbs, but resist conventional blurb logic by blurring the line between description of work and assessment of character. What "academic poetry" was for my father and his peers in the later twentieth century versus what anyone might think it could be today is an interesting conversation, possibly, to have elsewhere. Dad wasn't interested in an allegiance to convention. He was, as far as I can tell, interested in the ways anyone's work might be interesting, and in the ways each person might be interesting, and where those points of interest could merge. How to live, and how to convert the conventions we all socially and culturally absorb into strengths instead of weaknesses.

There's a brief passage in *Get the Money!* I especially love—two sentences in an obituary Dad wrote after Frank O'Hara died in 1966. As many readers of Ted Berrigan's work may know, he loved O'Hara's work, studied it intensely his whole life, and admired O'Hara as an artist and person while not getting too close personally, as many of Dad's peers did. Inside of the widespread grief I understand O'Hara's early and shocking death to have created among his many friends, Dad wrote this: "In one brief poem, 'The Day Lady Died,' he seemed to create a whole new kind of awareness of feeling, and by this a whole new kind of poetry, in which everything could be itself and still be poetry. Simply for this we loved him before we even met him."

Dad also noted somewhere in his early journals, when he was living with Joe Brainard and reading Joe's journals secretly, that Joe had written, roughly: in a collage everything needs to be itself and part of the whole thing at the same time. I'm not sure if I'm imagining that, or if it's actually in Dad's journals somewhere, but I like either version. My hope is that *Get the Money!* (it never stops being funny to type that title) can be a gift to new and long-time readers of Ted Berrigan's poetry and writings alike, and on behalf of my fellow editors, Edmund Berrigan, Alice Notley, and Nick Sturm, I welcome you into this quark-like ride where parts and wholes hopefully blur into a new shape.

ANSELM BERRIGAN
JANUARY 2022

EDITORIAL NOTE

T ED'S USE OF grammar, style, and punctuation was usually being wielded as an artistic choice, and those choices varied over the years and from piece to piece—sometimes varying within a piece itself. The reader may notice intentional typos in "Note on Jim Brodey's Poems & Him"—probably a commentary on Brodey's own stylistic choices. Ted also employs a "drop down" paragraph break in certain pieces, notably in the "Selections from a Journal, 1 Nov 1977 to 17 May 1978." The effect has the immediacy of a poetic line break, as well as perhaps conveying the casual shape of those days, punctuated with friends constantly dropping by. The reader may also notice Ted's prose often manifests as verse, such as in "3 Reviews," in which Ted's reviews take the shape of poems, constructed from lines from the books being reviewed (mostly). It should also be noted that Ted collaged quite liberally. When we reached out to Simon Schuchat for permission to reprint his poem from *Light & Shadow*, that quotation turned out to be entirely collaged. As for the "quotation" attributed to Gaston Bachelard in "Art Chronicle," well, it did not require any permission, as it seems to have come from Ted himself.

* * * * * *

The selection for the "'60s Journals" was made by Larry Fagin and Anselm Berrigan for the occasion of publication in *Shiny* magazine. The selection is from 13 journals housed in Columbia University's Rare Book & Manuscript Library. There are also 7 journals at the Stuart A. Rose Manuscript, Archives, and Rare Book Library at Emory University from which "Selections from a Journal, 1 Nov 1977 to 17 May 1978" was originally culled and from which we transcribed "The Arrival Report." Ted made additions to his selection of the '77–'78 Journal while preparing it for publication in *United Artists* 13. To know where and when individual works were first published, the reader is invited to consult the publication index at the end.

* * * * * *

It should be noted that "The Chicago Report" is a stylized work, drawing on and mimicking a range of tones, is meant playfully, and should not be considered an exact recounting of events. Ted believed in and used exaggeration, and bawdy and even transgressive humor on occasion. He believed it was necessary for the writer that all language be on the table. He also strongly believed in civil rights and he championed women artists and poets, and those of color, throughout his life. Still, this piece runs the risk of offending readers, and perhaps also the risk of being funny in spite of that. Either situation may be uncomfortable. Written in 1968, an extremely challenging and explosive year politically, it is also very much a commentary on class issues, both in and outside of the literary world, as well as Ted's experience of segregation in Chicago at that time.

* * * * * *

This book is a "Collected" but not a "Complete," and does not include two long works of Ted Berrigan's prose. One is the mysteriously proceduralized pulp western novel *Clear the Range* (Adventures in Poetry/Coach House South, 1977), which deserves its own separate republication. The other work is "Looking for Chris," a longer prose piece in five parts that Berrigan described as "an autobiographical sort of portrait of the artist as a young man in gibberish" which was made from a variation on the baffling combustions method. Unfortunately, part three disappeared many years ago, and has remained out of sight. If anyone has any information on part three's whereabouts, please send word.

* * * * * *

We are grateful to Coffee House Press, Raymond Foye, Jane Dalrymple-Hollo, Richard Kollmar, Annabel Lee, the Estate of Joel Oppenheimer, Ron Padgett, Ed Sanders, Aram Saroyan, and Simon Schuchat for providing permissions to reprint the various poems cited in reviews.

We are also grateful to John Brainard, Ron Padgett (again), and Katie Schneeman for use of images and photographs, as well as to the archivists and staff at the Stuart A. Rose Manuscript, Archives, and Rare Book Library at Emory University for their research support.

In addition, the editors also extend thanks to David Berrigan, Todd Colby, Andrew Epstein, Greg Masters, Tenaya Nasser-Frederick, Carrie Lorig, Julien Poirier, and Karen Weiser for help along the way.

Finally, we would like to thank the original publishers of these works. And also grateful thanks to our editor Garrett Caples, our publisher Elaine Katzenberger, and the staff at City Lights for making this book possible.

'60s JOURNALS

SONNET XVII

1 Each tree stands alone in stillness
14 Sensual, solid, still, swaying alone in the wind
2 After many years still nothing
13 Dear, be the tree your sleep awaits
3 The wind's wish is the tree's demand
12 The tree   the ground   the wind   these are
4 The tree stands still
11 There is no such thing as a breakdown
5 The wind walks up and down
10 Letters   birds   beggars   books
6 Scanning the long selves of the shore
9 Its patternless pattern of excitement
7 Her aimlessness is the pulse of the tree
4 It beats in tiny blots

4 May 63

1961

[January]

Whatever is going to happen is already happening.

—Whitehead
Aims of Ed.

Sunday, Feb 5th [Providence]

I suppose this situation is revealing concerning the kind of person I am: at my brother Rick's wedding yesterday, four of my aunts, all about 15 yrs older than I, began to question me about why I am no longer a Catholic. Two of them were very antagonistic; they seemed to be personally offended by my beard and my disaffiliation from the Church. I tried to answer their questions intelligently, but in everything I said I actually had the secret but entirely conscious idea in mind of impressing my beautiful, shy, wide-eyed 14-yr-old cousin, dtr of one of the aunts, who was also sitting in the group.

Feb 6th

At moments when things seem to crystallize for me, when life comes together for a minute, when what I am sensing, thinking, reading, ties together for a magic moment of unity, along with the instant desire I have to tell Chris [Murphy], or Marge [Kepler], or the beautiful girl I met yesterday somewhere, comes the simultaneous thought that I am the only one who can know what *I* mean. My girls must be real—not symbols.

[nd, Providence]

Tonight, standing in the snow on the corner of Potters Ave. & Broad St. I remembered an incident from my childhood. I was about 13 yrs old, and in the mornings before school I sold papers on that corner, to cars driving by. I went out at 6 a.m., went home for breakfast at 7:45, and to school at 8:10. One morning a man about 32 came over to me and asked if I [had] seen twin girls come up the street yet. I said no. He said he wanted to "make" one of them, and was waiting to offer them a ride. He winked at me, and went back to his car and drove off. I didn't know what "make" meant, but my puritan Catholic 13-yr-old mind was outraged, and I resolved not to speak to him, or help him at all. He never returned. Perhaps he sensed my attitude.

[nd]

Books I was most impressed by in late 1960:

> *Science & Sanity* – Korzybski
> *Baudelaire* – Sartre
> *Aims of Ed* – Whitehead
> *Symbolism* – Whitehead
> *Poems of Milton*
> *Poems of Shelley*
> *Don Juan* & *Cain* – Byron
> *Poems of W. Stevens*
> *Agee on Film* vII

Feb 18th

. . . once the barrier of having sex is surmounted, then a partner is no longer necessary.

[nd]

Ron [Padgett] & Harry [Diakov] & I forged a prescription for Desoxyn. Harry stole it from the Columbia dispensary, Ron wrote it out, and I took it to the drug store & had it filled. No trouble.

The pills are like Dex & Bennies, less after effects than Bennies. They make me nervous, awake, "high" if I allow myself to get out of control.

Great to take them, go to movies, pore over the movie like a poem or book. . . Makes for total *involvement* with a consciousness of it.

23 Feb: 5:45 a.m.

. . . wrote a poem last night. I am happy with it so far. Ron & I stayed up all night, took Desoxyn, and I wrote this poem as I was "coming down."

> Poem Today 3
> Note to Margie Kepler
>
> Margie, I would write to you
>
> of Friday in July. John Donne.
> If ever any beauty I did see,
>
> which I desired, and got, 'twas
> but a dream of thee.
> >   Garner.
> Saintly I would say
> Negro wailing blues/
>
>
> >   No
> No
> > They
> >   CAN'T
> > Take   that
> A   Way
> >   bop
> >   from
> >   bop
> Me.

Balance. I sit at my desk
on a day in July, Music in my brain
Books on my desk
                        Donne.   Shelley.
Korzybski.
Shaw.
My subject evades me,
self escapes me.
I see

kitchen. My grandmother peels potatoes.
Last year   three attacks. She
is making my supper. Complaining. My Sister
is not home from school.
                        Rick
reads the paper. The sports. My brother
is twenty-three. We discuss baseball
drink beer.
            The telephone!
            Who?
Bearden is dead.   Owen is dead.   Gallup is dead.
or at least   they are older   and there

I am older and here.

Margie   I would write to you
of beauty

and of love.

but rocks intrude.

Feb 28th – *After reading Nietzsche*

Pat Mitchell is a sentimentalist and her ideal is salvation.

(comment Nov 5/61 – whose isn't?)

4 Mar

Heard Allen Ginsberg read last night at the Catholic Worker Hdqtrs in the Bowery. The reading was on the 2nd floor of the Newspaper office, in a kind of loft. The place was jammed, nearly 150 or 200 there. Ginsberg wore levi's and a plaid shirt, and a grey suitcoat. His hair is thinning on top, and he is getting a little paunchy. He wore thick black rimmed glasses, and looked very Jewish. He is good looking, intellectual appearing, and was quiet and reserved, with a humorous glint in his eyes.

He read Kaddish, a long poem about his family and the insanity of his mother. It was a very good poem, and a brilliant reading. Ginsberg reads very well, writes a very moving driving line; and the poem contained much dialogue. Ginsberg seems to have a perfect ear for speech rhythm. The poem was based on Jewish Prayers and was very impressive in sections, with a litany-like refrain.

There was much humor in the reading, much pathos, and all in all, it was the most remarkable reading I've ever heard, very theatrical, yet very natural. Ginsberg was poised and assured, like a Jazz musician who knows he's good. At the end someone asked him what meter the Poem was in and he replied, Promethean Natural Meter.

[later]

Sitting alone in Ron's room at Columbia.

I make a vow—I will try even harder from now on to be a realist. To see. To penetrate the Personae of the world. To be in harmony with my will. To fully develop both my ability for practical reason, and for speculative reason, the methodologies of the tripartite will.

Tues March 6th

. . . It was one of those nights when it was good to be alive. I had slept all day. Started working at ten. At four I went out for Coffee. The heat goes off in our place at 12, and stays off until six. But it wasn't too bad last night. It was raining slightly outside and the air was cool as

I walked through the dirty, empty streets in the Bowery, to the all-night Cafe, a half mile away. My mind was full of thoughts about my thesis, about Hobbes' four-fold division of Philosophy, about writing to [Dick] Gallup discussing his plans for the next yr. of coming to school here, of Pat getting my letter, of getting a job, enrolling in school, and many others. It struck me that I was happy. Everything, for a brief moment, was amalgamating, and had purpose—

Those moments are rare for me. Much of the moment can be attributed to Desoxyn. I take one or two a day, work fifteen or sixteen hours, reading, typing, planning. And Desoxyn keep[s] me alert, and keep[s] my weight down—in the face of my starchy diet—But it was a spontaneous feeling nevertheless. Even recalling my days in Tulsa, the days in 1959 when I nearly broke down, did not dampen it.

Mar 13th – 9 p.m.

. . . While in Providence [in 1959], doing nothing except reading, writing bad poems, and brooding, I slowly came to the conclusion that the best thing I could do in life was to strive for saintliness—that is, to try to be kind to everyone, to hurt no one, to be humble, and to be as much help to people as I cd, by being sympathetic, a listener, a friend. This attitude was brought on by my observation of everyone's unhappiness.

Monday, 27 march

The biggest single influence in my life was, of course [David] Bearden.
Other important influences were
        Tony Powers: (Perhaps the best influence in some ways)
        Marge Kepler:
        Chris Murphy:
        Lauren Owen:
        Pat Mitchell in a curious way.

March 28th

Some interesting facts about some friends of mine.
        Tony Powers age 28 is in jail.
        Martin Cochran age 23 is dead.
        Jim Sears age 24 takes 12 Bennies a day.

Larry Walker age 24 is married for the second time—unhappily.

Joe Keegan, age 26, whom I used to write poems with in the 6th grade, is in the insane asylum.

Johnny Arthur age 23 is being sued for 50,000 for alienation of affections.

and I'm sleepy.

April 11th

I wrote my first poem when I was 11. It was about my Grandfather's death, and how the family missed him. My mother had it published in the *Providence Bulletin* which printed things like that. It had regular meter, and rhymed, and was four lines. When it was published I remember my dismay over the fact that a line had been omitted. I don't remember any of the lines.

My next poems, as far as I can remember, were written in the 8th grade. One was a collaboration with Joe Keegan. It was about Capt. Kidd. In the ninth grade I wrote many morbid horror poems with titles like, "There's a body in The Casket."

I wrote no poems in High School, none in the Army (until after Korea). In 1956 I wrote "In this Corner," my first real poem, which was later published in *Nimrod*. It came out of my relationship with Jan Hayden. I wrote it around December of 1956.

April 29th

Nothing unsettles my ideas as much as when I hear them repeated by some of my "disciples" who profess to totally agree with them. Then I see that I have omitted much and not seen many things.

[later]

Last week Mrs. Taylor said to me, "I don't want to hurt Wm (her husband), he needs me. A boy like you will find someone else in a short time."

[still later]

Mrs. Taylor called me last night. Said she had come to see me once but couldn't find my house. I am to see her tomorrow at 9 a.m.

Saturday May 7th

I got a letter from Mrs. Taylor today. It said,

> Thanks for the noble act; it showed you for the hypocrite you are.
>   gratefully,
>   Marie Antoinette

She's pretty right, of course. But she couldn't attract my interest, and I had to *end* it. And I took the best way, that the present provided.

May 8th

Listening to Miles Davis' recording of "Bye Bye Blackbird," I got an insight into the relationship between form, like a sonnet, and internal variation, such as rhyme, internal rime, varying length of lines, halting of speeding of lines, etc. Here we have the static and the dynamic imposed on each other, and they may produce that something that is beyond either. . .

May 18th

Sold a pint of Blood to get money for typing paper. Felt weak & lethargic for 2 days—got $5.00.

May 19th 2 a.m.

. . . Saw the Moiseyev Dancers. At the end they did a quadrille for an encore, and everyone sang as the orchestra played "Hail, Hail, the Gang's All Here." It was very corny—I felt so good I almost cried.

. . . I wrote a Psychology Experiment for Ron, because he was having trouble with form. . . He handed it in, saving a copy to use as a model in the future—and received an A. . . At the age of 26, after 4 years of college (no course in Psychology though), I seem to have learned how to write A freshman papers. That's some progress.

May 21

I "discovered" Shaw on Music this morning! Is there no end to the indescribable genius of Bernard Shaw? He is the most inspiring writer I have ever read. His writing moves me to thought and action in every direction.

May 23

. . . I have never kissed anyone in my family. My mother has rarely kissed me—though I think she would if I were not aloof as far as kissing goes. My Grandmother kisses me when I say goodbye, but no one kisses or hugs anyone spontaneously or often. I think this is too bad.

Today, June 18th

. . . Ron, in response to my request that he write me concerning my faults—wrote that the difference between he and me, me and most people, is pace. I'm always running, he said, always burning. . .

June 19th

Our cellar [TB was living with Pat Mitchell and Dick Gallup at 5 Willett Street] is a good home. We have books, records, privacy, quiet. We keep odd hours, shock our habits as often as possible. Everything consequently looks fresher and newer all the time. We haunt the museums, the movies, and are constantly amazed and delighted at the wonder and variety of everything around us.

But this state of being, of living on the heights, is difficult to sustain. When we fall, and we do often, such nausea as overwhelms all of everything hits us very hard. Then we are sick, with uneasiness, boredom, fatigue, and gnawing annoyance at everything, everybody, and each other.

1962

July 9th

A distressing visit with Sandy [Berrigan] today. "Why didn't you tell me that there was going to be so much responsibility?" she said.

I know I am lacking in patience. But I feel like Julius Caesar as he told his troubles to the Sphinx.

Wednesday morning, July 11

Dear Carol [Clifford],

. . . I'm going to read Aristotle's Poetics and try not to think of you. It's 5 a.m. now. I went over and sat on the steps [Low Library, Columbia Univ.] after all. Then I came back and cleaned up the room, swept, dusted, put records away, and tried on Dick's dark suit which fit fine though a little small. With my tab collar striped shirt and a soft black tie and red sox and my beard and hair so long in back I look like a complete well-dressed bastard. The judge will be impressed one way or another, and Mrs. Alper [Sandy Berrigan's mother] won't believe it. Sandy, who has never seen me in anything remotely resembling a suit and tie, will be completely ripped out of her mind.

I'm listening to Bill Monroe, and the next two records are Cisco Houston's RR songs and then Ray Charles which I bought just for you to hear, and then it'll be time to go. And all that I've got is a worried mind.

Thursday, July 12th

Yesterday at the hearing Sandy was ordered by the court to the Euphrasian Home for 15 days while a probation investigation takes place. The Judge indicated that after the 15 days she

12

would be released into my custody. The whole business stinks! but there's nothing Sandy and I can do until she is with me. . .

From May 1st to 3rd I read the complete published works of John Ashbery over & over & over while riding to Miami on the bus. . .

[from Aristotle's Poetics] . . . it is Homer who has chiefly taught other poets the art of telling lies skillfully. . . Accordingly the poet should prefer probable impossibilities to improbable possibilities.

[July 15]

. . . Saw Sandy tonight at the Euphrasian Home. She was in tears. Her parents had been there, lecturing, threatening, raging, finally they left her clothes with her—and indicated they could not keep us apart. Once again Sandy is giving me lectures: "We must do this. We can't do this. I don't ever want to be locked up again." I fear they broke her spirit in Jackson, and are completing the job in New York. She is willing to do anything anyone says, to be with me and free. "Free." *But I'm not willing to do anything anyone says.* I am willing to pretend to do so, until we can run. These people will never let us alone. How can Sandy be put on probation when she has never done anything wrong? What a bunch of shit! Her crime is marrying me and my crime is not having a paying job and/or a proper attitude. Well, we'll see what happens.

. . . Haven't been able to write much lately. Nothing good since "I Was Born Standing Up." However, "Personal Poem #8," which I wrote the morning of the hearing, came out very well—one of the most successful in that series.

. . . Johnny Stanton said to me last night, "You're the first guy I ever met who takes the praise he's due." !!!

July 16th

Went last night to hear Kenneth Koch read. Saw Frank O'Hara and [Bill] Berkson and John Ashbery [TB later added: "It wasn't him"] there. Ashbery is a very powerful person—and looks like Apollinaire. O'Hara is slighter, has a very good face. Koch reminds me of Nijinsky as Groucho Marx. His reading was very fine, very sensitive, and his poems, the ones I hadn't read, were very exciting. He & Ashbery & Koch have launched a massive assault on language and "poetry" in a very stimulating & exciting manner. They remind me of Dadaist & Surrealist practices, but they are very "American." Ashbery is not zany like O'Hara & Koch, but he has plenty of humor. Koch's book *Thank You* comes out this week.

July 17th: 4:00 a.m.

Worked on some of my poems tonight. Threw away four or five old poems. Gude came over and took me out for a hamburger about 9. Came back and finished Fowlie's *The Age of Surrealism* which was very exciting and made my head reel. Read some Henry Miller, but am suffering from a blinding headache and have just been lying on the bed in the dark for the past hour.

. . . Nijinsky and Jesus hang above my desk in queer sympathy with each other. . . Time for me to go out and watch the sun come up from the top of the Library steps at Columbia, take a pill or two, and come back and work on Hesiod & Genesis for Gude.

This date last year I was living with Pat & Dick at Willett Street near the Wmsburg Bridge, and everything was beginning to disintegrate.

In 1960 I was in Tulsa, living with Tony Powers, who is now a jr. executive, and saying goodbye to Margie [Kepler], who changed my life so completely.

And in 1959 I was in Rhode Island, mourning for Chris [Murphy], who had kissed me in the early morning darkness, without shame, and who later refused to talk to me or see me and wouldn't say why.

In 1958 I was living in an apartment in Tulsa with Martin Cochran, now dead.

In 1957 Jan Hayden and I broke our engagement—she later married a boy from Edmond Oklahoma, her home town, whom she'd known all her life. I was working in Jenkins Music Co. & going to Summer School. Met Pat Mitchell that summer.

In 1956 I was in the army, at Summer Training Camp at Ft. Sill, Okla., and reading Thomas Wolfe again.

And in 1955 I was in Yokohama, waiting to go back to Korea after 10 days in Japan.

"No one has a personality these days—everyone is faceless. I can't even call the faces of acquaintances to mind. They're nothing." —Harry Diakov, 1962.

I think so too but not in the same way Harry thinks so. I can call people's faces to mind, but there's rarely any reason to. Except to see who I am.

Anyway. All those who are going to keep going will, all those who aren't—well it isn't important anyway.

Now, out to see morning
    through a pepsi

. . . One day last month I went to the grocery store, bought some bread & pepsis, and shop-lifted a steak, putting it under my belt, in the back and letting my shirttail hang over it. It was for Dick & Carol & Sandy & me for supper. One the way home a tall, thin wino stopped me and asked me for some money. He was in his late thirties with a sensitive face, and was dressed in a gray suit & black shirt, rumpled a little but neat. He was dark, perhaps Spanish. I told him that I was sorry but I didn't have any money—and that I'd had to shoplift food to eat. He was in that state of mild glow winos usually stay in. "No kidding," he said. He offered me a handful of change. I told him I didn't need it now that I'd stolen some food. He asked me if I wanted some wine, and I said "Sure" so he took a pint bottle out of his back pocket, half full, and gravely & politely bade me to drink first. I did, and then passed him the bottle. He took a drink, then handed it back. "Have another," he said. "You know, Jesus was a beggar, too." We finished the bottle, and I told him I had to go. He said his name was Maurice & I told him my name was Ted. He said he'd see me later. As I walked off down the street he called after me, "Don't forget to love me."

10:00 p.m. Slept a few hours. Joe came over to take me to a movie. Saw Chaliapin in *Don Quixote*, a great sad movie, and Chaplin & the great Marie Dressler in *Tillie's Punctured Romance*. A masterpiece, & Dressler was unbelievable. Movies are worse than ever. What decay!

[July 18]

". . . a man or woman is only real when he or she impersonates a god or goddess. . . *An event that does not re-occur is nothing*. The particular, the individual, the secular are nothing." [Auden, Introduction to John Ashbery's *Some Trees*]

July 22nd – Sunday, midnight

. . . Tonight I went with Carol & John Stanton & Lorenz Gude to hear Frank O'Hara read [New School of Social Research]. He was great. His reading of "In Memory of My Feelings" was brilliant, and I learned a lot. He also read "Chinese New Year," and read it very well, and it too was illuminating. O'Hara reads well, and with low intensity. His wit is sharp, brittle, sneering often, yet he is tender, gentle, loving. He can be a virtuoso, and yet is serious & with large scope. It was an inspiring night. I want to write differently, but I want to assimilate O'Hara's virtues. He, Koch, and Ashbery are the most original, most exciting, most talented men writing. From them I will take much.

. . . Finished a Biography of Apollinaire by Marcel Adema. Apollinaire is great. Adema is shitty. Thursday is the 26th—the day of the 3rd hearing.

July 26th: Thursday Morning, 7:30 a.m.

—sitting here in black suit & tie & dress shirt, to go to the hearing in a few minutes. Ray Charles is singing "I would moan, for every one in love"

Saturday Morning, July 28th, 1:45 a.m.

Finished Gude's first paper today. A comparison of the World Picture in Genesis & Theogony, 7 pages. It's bad, but contains one good idea—the absence of ability for true creativity in Genesis' World & its presence in Hesiod's World.

Sunday Morning, One a.m. July 29th

     Style (continued)

Punctuation in poems seems almost entirely unnecessary. The arrangement of lines on the page plus the natural rhythms should be more than sufficient indication of how to speak them. Also, anything that makes people read more slowly is a good thing.
    Sometimes some punctuation seems called for. If so, then o.k.
    Picasso—"when I don't have blue, I use red."
    . . . Harry Diakov comments upon my "good ear" and my "natural symbolism." Lauren praises highly my imitation of Rimbaud's "The Drunken Boat." Carol writes that I seem to have come so far, so fast, these last 2 years. Also that my prose is often ordinary. True. Except "papers" ain't "my prose." Let her read my letters.

Sept 1st

Sandy and I sitting here, she reading *Tropic of Capricorn*, I re-reading *The Natural Philosophy of Love* by Remy de Gourmont. We just finished making love and are listening to Elizabethan & Jacobean Madrigals.

Sept 2nd

"The sonnet occurred automatically when some chap got stuck in his effort to make a can-zone." —Ezra Pound

. . . Wrote a Postcard Sonnet to Bernie, a poem with Joe and another with Dick automatically. Both Sonnets. Seems the sonnet still intrigues me.

Wednesday – Sept. 5th

Quit taking pills today.

Sunday – Sept. 9th

One pill since Tuesday. Feel just as energetic but with less duration of energy. Easy enough to not take pill—but hard not to want to take them.

Am working on studying French forms like Villanelle, also reading Erich Neumann, Spenser, and Baugh's *History of English Literature*.

Carol's a tough kid. But there's more to it than that. To hit with your head up is what's wanted.

Sept. 11th

Went back on pills tonight. Wrote a practice villanelle, a personal poem, made love twice—got away from being sickeningly healthy.

Today (it's 4:30 a.m.) I go to United Parcel to see about . . . . A JOB!!! [TB later added: "Didn't go."]

. . . Sandy and I are better every day, and she is a marvelous girl—but it is so very hard for me to be married. I need solitude, and I need to be patient. If I can learn through Sandy to be patient she will have given me more than I could ask.

Note: Friendship must be dependent on the way one's friend lives up to one's own standards for friendship. I never had a friend til Dick. I've learned a lot from his character and our differences. I would be friend to Lauren, too.

Sept. 13th –

In lieu of today's entry:

Personal Poem #13

It's 3:17 a.m. in New York city, and
I'm waiting in the West End Bar for Dick Gallup
and I'm thinking about Annette
                              who just left
to see about her roommate who is puking
all the time because earlier tonight she had
an abortion
                    she's so frantic and she's
Jewish which somehow means some-
thing and so lovely.
                         "I'm an old man
mad about writing" says Madox Ford
the Chinese distracted the Greeks I believe
it as a matter of course
                                Gallup is 3 hours late
he must be fucking Carol or maybe
he's reading about Erich von Stroheim & Greed
and Méliès' trip to the Moon or else
asleep
        I'm ninety per cent asleep
and ten per cent in a rage because
a forty year old fat man in an ivy-
league weskit keeps screaming in my
ear about the disgrace of The Bay of Pigs.

I haven't written a poem in 15 days at
least – it must be time for a pill, and
return to the March of Literature.

Sept 17th

The papers I wrote for Gude on Mythology received As.

[nd]

Got rid of all my books (about 400) except for about 75. Sold them to pay Joe's rent or gave them to Dick & Carol. Also gave up stealing entirely. We have money and it's a joy to buy something, to save for it, then read it! Too many things make everything less.

Sept. 23rd Sunday 10:30 p.m.

Pat & Ron came back to NY together Friday. Pat lives a block and a half from here. I saw her in the street yesterday, from a distance, with Ron & the Beardens.

How strange that two girls, Pat & Anne, who made love with me, who told me they love me, now do not want to see me. What is "friendship"? And is there any kind of communication between people? How little it takes to make people turn away! I love Pat, and Anne, too. But if I marry Sandy they must either hate me, or ignore & try to forget me. Shit! I don't forget them. Nor Margie nor Chris nor Bernie nor Helen nor Jan nor anyone else I have felt love for. And we would make love or not as we wished, for what has that to do with love anymore than talking? or writing letters? or even dreaming of each other?

They make me think they are small, these girls who "love me."

11 Oct 62

Style (Continued)

Wrote "The Anniversary" 2 days ago. Perhaps my best poem ever although far from being good. It contains only very shallowly a John Ashbery lesson, and is in large part the fruit of my sonnet work of the past 2 yrs. But there is much I know to be assimilated into my papers, and much to learn.

. . . Tomorrow, at Pat Mitchell's advice, I must re-read *The Shephearde's Calendar* by Spenser in conjunction with "Eclogue" [Ashbery].

Read also "The Poems" & "The Minstrel Boy" by Ashbery & "Ode to Willem de Kooning" by O'Hara.

Also Sandy & I are enrolled in Theodore Gaster's course in Mythology of All Times at the YMHA.

Talked for Two Hrs tonight to Pat about J.A.—She very helpful & perceptive—naturally, as always. Unfortunately, she wants to do it all in her mind.

4 a.m. Monday (Tuesday) Oct 23rd

Wrote today an 11-page paper on John Ashbery's poem "The Picture of Little J.A. in a Prospect of Flowers" dealing with its relation to *Hamlet* and its themes of growth and anti-Romanticism. Threw the paper away later, but learned much from writing it.

Met Frank O'Hara downtown near Joe's. Sandy introduced herself to him, and brought him over to talk to Joe & me. Joe said he "talks just like you." We talked about movies, and Orson Welles, and he asked if our problems with Sandy's parents were settled.

31 Oct 3:40 a.m.

Lauren told me once that Dave Bearden had said he thought the reason I disliked him was because when we roomed together he used to come into my room late at night when I was asleep and shout things like "You're going to die!"

This is really fascinating. I always slept with my door locked. Also, I am a very light sleeper, and the sound of anyone's voice always wakes me.

Thursday, 13 Nov 3:40 a.m.

Style (continued)

"Oh, how I wish I could convey the ease and the charm of the unfinished." —Juan Gris

Joe told me tonight that Pat's mother told Pat that Margie has married. I am very sad for her.

. . . Saw *The Connection*, which was great. Jack Gelber reminds me of Shaw.

Yesterday Joe & I did 5 very successful collaborations—two writings by me on paintings of Sandy & 3 spontaneous small works. We talked, worked alternately, drank pepsis, took pills. Stayed up 30 hrs.

Margie is married.
Margie is married.
Margie is married.

Margie is married.

13 Nov 62
Ted Berrigan

Today I took Pat to see the New Realism show during her lunch hour. Then I spent the afternoon in sheer ecstasy reading Frank O'Hara's review of *Some Trees* in *Poetry* Magazine 1956—and the *Green Box* by Marcel Duchamp.

Then I called Anne to find out about Margie—and she coolly told me she'd "forgotten about the past" although she thought it was "a good thing to happen when it did etc." and she ended "that's how it is," with a note of triumph in her voice. Well, Sic Semper Tyrannis.

Thursday Nov 15

Happy Birthday to me!

Style: (continued)

Notes from *The Green Box* by Marcel Duchamp

"By perspective (or any other conventional means) the lines, the drawing, are 'strained' and lose the nearly of the 'always possible'" . . .

Nov. 16th: Fri – 3:30 a.m.

The Sonnets consists of lines from each of my 19 sonnets. I asked Sandy to write down her favorite line or lines or image from each. Then I changed them slightly & arranged them on the page 1 to 19 as were [?]. I had certain themes in mind from reading the lines & knowing my sonnets—but much was by chance—which was my plan. The result was very good for a beginning.

But I am still confused about the AMOUNT of control the writer shld. have over his writing (or CONSCIOUS CONTROL).

20 Nov . . . 5:15 a.m.

Wrote (?) (Made) five sonnets tonight, by taking one line from each of a group of poems, at random, going from first to last poem then back again until 12 lines, then making the final couplet from any 2 poems, in the group, one line at random from each. Wrote by ear, and automatically. Very interesting results.

Groups used

> Sonnet #1 – Six poems 1962
> #2 – Personal Poems
> #3 – Le Bateau Ivre
> #4 – My 14 Selected Poems
> #5 – My 10 Newest Poems

All this was partly inspired by reading about DADA but mostly inspired by my activities along the same line for the past 10 months (or since reading *Locus Solus* Two & seeing the Assemblage Show & Working on Collages with Joe (see our Self-Portrait)
Now back to more Dada.

22 Nov

. . . As for me, I keep going keep worrying, keep feeling alone in a good way, keep keeping my own counsel. I don't know hardly anything, yet I know more than nearly everyone I see or know. It's discouraging. Every sage turns seducer upon close contact.
But I feel good, my hair is very long. I weigh 170, and can whip any man in the house, one way or another.

1963

Jan 3rd 10 a.m.

    I still feel at low level. No drive. Financial problems the main cause & the prospect of going to work. The rent is 3 days overdue today, $13.50. I have $1.00 & [am] faced with selling my *Collected Poems of Wallace Stevens*. God damn it!

    . . . Had a dream that I was in a bakery, when a man pointed a gun at the waitress and tried to hold up the place. She looked at me imploringly, and I calmly disarmed the man w/o violence. He ran out. Later, I was at home, I'd quietly left, when Dick (Gallup) & Johnny (Stanton) ran in excitedly and told me W.H. Auden wanted to see me back at the motel restaurant (the bakery of earlier). They brought me a menu autographed by Auden as an award for my "heroics." I thought the menu was going to be autographed by Rilke, and so was a little disappointed but still excited. However, I remained very calm. At the motel I sat with Auden & his family & Dick and Johnny. Auden called me "Ted" twice and talked excitedly about my heroics, how I'd managed it. He praised me lavishly. I said little, felt less excited about the whole thing. I noticed that at the end of the discussion he called me "Berrigan." Later at home I was thinking I had wanted to talk to him about John Ashbery and not about my "heroics." But he'd only been interested in them.

    A few weeks ago I dreamed that I visited with John Ashbery at his home, which was a farm. He was about my age, and we liked each other. I gained much insight into his poems by seeing him on the farm among his brothers and sisters (all younger) and I realized that his poetry was about his personal life. During a tour of the farm as he was showing me around, a field hand or a neighboring farmer came up and said that one thing that he was unsure of in Ashbery's poem was the meaning of the word "Block" and John (the farmer referred to him as John) answered that he used "block" to mean large, or big. The farmer thanked him and said that this cleared up many things for him. Then he drove away on a tractor.

    I awakened from this dream feeling very elated and good.

[Sunday Feb 10th 8 p.m.]

I want to write poems that cannot be understood until they are felt. They must be read, then must germinate in the brain until they flower. Then they will be apparent—but still they cannot be paraphrased with any meaning for others. Each reader must make something out of them himself, w/o effort.

Monday [Feb 11] 10 a.m. (at work) [TB managed a pool of typists at a company called Dial Dictation.]

Had a dream last week that I was at a dinner party, and was seated across the table from Jackie Kennedy. . . Sandy was with me, but vaguely, also another couple, and Jack K was vaguely with Jackie. Jackie and I were talking intimately in a witty way, leaning close to each other. She said it was a bore to talk to all the old ladies in the reception line, because she always had to say the same thing. I laughed and told her she ought to say next time, "Getting enough lately?" She laughed at this & said it was a good idea but didn't think she would. Then dessert was served to Jackie. It was cheesecake with chocolate frosting, and I looked at it longingly. But it seems that if you had soda earlier, which I had, you didn't get dessert. Jackie saw me looking at the cake, and immediately ordered the waiter to bring "5 more." Presumably, one for me, Sandy, and the other couple (maybe Dick & someone) & Jack. Next I was on a ship, in a white dinner jacket, but still in a dining room. I was standing talking to someone else who was fair skinned with a crew cut, maybe Tom Malone, a boyhood acquaintance. Everyone else was running around in excitement. "Tom" said to me, "I'm going to join the marines." I felt relief at this, as if a problem was solved for me too, and I said, "I am, too. Let's Go." Whereupon we both ran through the folding doors headlong, and jumped into the sea. We knew what we were doing, it was not a surprise. But I woke up then, feeling uneasy, because it wasn't what I wanted after all.

[June]

No fucking makes for many Poems.

[ca. Nov.]

John Wieners told me that the first time his parents had any inkling he was homosexual was when he was 10 or 12 and his father came home one day & found John dressed all in woman's clothes. John said his father just went out, and later he called up & said, "Be a good boy, Jack."

Dec. 2nd

Went to a cocktail party at Larry Rivers Studio at the Chelsea Hotel given by Larry for Frank O'Hara's return from Europe—talked to Kenneth Koch & Frank about Poetry, and to Edwin & later went to eat with Barbara Guest & Joe Brainard & Barney Newman & his wife. . .

"C" is a big success, altho everyone (except me) hated Andy's cover for the E.D. issue. Hmmmm! Also—it seems that Barbara is primarily responsible for John Myers getting "C" a hundred dollars from James Merrill, & the possibility of more later.

Barbara also said "Ted, you can count on me for at least 20 for any issue, or anytime." She's great! . . .

"C" #5 to be run off today—a "gold-plate" issue with poems by Ashbery, Schuyler, Guest, Jones, Wieners, Richard White, Me, Ron, & Joe Ceravolo, Kenward Elmslie & John's NEW REALISM essay. . .

Joe Ceravolo's 80-page poem [*Fits of Dawn*] is great & I hope to use it all! Must call him soon.

1964

Sunday May 10th

Harry [Fainlight] & I read [Café La MaMa, 82 Second Ave], nice reading. I came across great especially with
Open the Door (story)
&
Dancing
Invention
The Upper Arm

Jonas Mekas was there,
Allen Ginsberg
Bob LaVigne
Peter Orlovsky
Shep Sherbell
Carol Bergé
Al Fowler

Dick Gallup, Ron Padgett,
Ellen & Lorenz Gude, John
Stanton, Dennis Shea,
Tom Veitch, Kate Heliczer,
Mike Steiner, John (?)
& lots of others I didn't
know. We made $10.00
by collection.

Fri Night May 15th

Went to Folk Music Concert at Hunter w. Ron & Pat & Sandy & David to hear Sonny & Brownie & Muddy Waters & Rev. Gary Davis & others & Mississippi John Hurt.

Saturday night [May 16]

Went to cocktail party & reading by Ungaretti at Mario Schifano's. Frank & Allen & LeRoi & Barbara also read. Ceravolo was there, & [Jim] Brodey & Ron & Dick & Aram Saroyan & all the young poets. . . Meanwhile, Thurs the 14th I went to hear Robt. Duncan read at The Poets Theatre and then to Diane di Prima's where Allen Ginsberg & I had a big talk about Tulsa & Wichita & the "old days."

(Allen said he was mostly responsible for Ashbery being published in *Big Table*. He said he sent voluminous letters to Paul Carroll . . . with lists of who to publish. . . He also said he hadn't "picked up on Burroughs," but just "had faith in Bill whatever he did." We talked about Jack Kerouac & Allen asked me if I thought about Jack's poetry. I told him I thought Jack's prose had influenced us all a lot. Allen said that *Howl* & *On the Road* had both been written on benzedrine—I told him my sonnets had been done on desoxyn, & we mentioned [Edward] Marshall's "Leave the Word Alone" as another poem done on pills.)

1966

[n.d.]

> What a poet
> "does" is like
> what a yo-yo
> champ does—
>
> But what is that
> called?

Sat. (ha-ha) Friday, June 3rd

[TB fabricated an interview with John Cage, which was published in *Mother* magazine, all without Cage's knowledge.]

Joe told me that Kenneth told him that John Cage called up John Ashbery and asked him who I was, and if I was putting him down or what in the interview!!! John told him no, that I admired him very much!!

*

Hah! If he had any brains he wd have seen that *he* actually wrote that interview!!

Sat/Sun [June 4] 5 a.m.

    Worked on Chapter 29
of *Clear the Range*
        &
    translated
      CORONA DI CAZZ
    & IN VASE PROEPOSTERO
     by Apollinaire

    Sandy & I went to see Bo Diddley last night at the Cafe Au Go-Go & then to the Fugs (on McDougal Street).
  Gave Aram 4 *Fits of Dawn* for Clark Coolidge & himself & others.

       Di-ethyl-tryptamine
       Hash
       Cocaine
       Di-methyl-tryptamine

1969

[June]

[crimson flower pressed into journal with note: "from Apollinaire's Grave"]

SOME NOTES ABOUT "C"

C

A
Journal of
Poetry

EDITOR   PUBLISHER
Ted Berrigan   Lorenz Gude

"The bachelor grinds his own chocolate"

Marchand du Sel

I

Dick Gallup . . . . .Five poems
Ron Padgett . . . . .Four poems
Joe Brainard. . . . . .A PLAY & DIARY
Ted Berrigan. . . . . .Poems

Manuscripts should be sent to Lorenz Gude,
319 West 100th St., New York City. C will
print anything the Editor likes, and will
appear monthly.

COVER DESIGN BY JOE B-RAINA-

I T'S 6:15 A.M. May 22nd, 1964, just about a year since "C" magazine first appeared, and just as at that time I was scrounging around for money to buy stencils, stamps, paper, etc. (not to mention pay the rent buy food pepsis etc.), so today I'm rushing to finish this so I can scrounge up some money to buy the paper for the issue (number 8) that Lorenz and I are going to pick up thirty dollars' worth of paper for today.

* * * * * *

Last May (1963) I was living at 510 West 113th Street (NY) with my wife, and until a couple of weeks earlier had been working (for a few months) as head proofreader for DIAL DICTATION, inc., proofreading insurance case files and stock market reports. Sandy (my wife) was working as a cashier at Columbia University, and we were saving a lot of money to go to Europe in June or July or sometime. (Meanwhile Sandy got pregnant and we didn't go (later that is) after all.) Ron Padgett was living a few blocks away on the other side of Broadway, and Dick Gallup lived on the floor below us.

Ron was editor of, or rather one of the editors of the *Columbia Review*, and in general disgust over the insipidity of the review he decided to compile an entire issue himself and present it to the rest of the editors. He asked me for a poem, and I told him to take whatever he wanted out of a group of poems I'd written in the preceding six months, and he took a poem called "I Was Born Standing Up," a kind of Apollinairean poem about self-development with particular reference to a young girl we both knew. Ron also got poems from Dick Gallup and from Dave Bearden, a poet friend of ours now living in California, and some writings by Joe Brainard, who was living down on 1st Avenue and 6th Street. When he presented all this to the other editors they of course didn't like the stuff, but after much deliberation decided to use the poems by me and Bearden. Ron had to bully them into it, but somehow he managed to. To make a long story short, the issue went to the printers, and when the proofs came back to Columbia the Dean's office got hold of them and immediately brought in the editors (Padgett, Mitchell Hall, Jon Cott, and Richard Tristam, I think) and told them that my poem and Bearden's poem had to be removed. The editors immediately resigned in protest, and a furor of activity commenced. There were TV appearances by editors, statements to newspapers like the *Post*, daily diatribes in the student newspaper, etc. etc., until finally the student committee called ACTION decided to put out the censored issue. So, they ran off a few thousand copies of the banned issue on legal sized mimeo paper, and sold them to the students for twenty-five cents. This issue was called *The Censored Review*. (Padgett later infiltrated the Review again and this year managed to publish me, Brainard and Gallup in the final issue, including cover by me and Brainard, right under the noses of Trilling and the rest of the pricks there. Then he wrote a letter to the school paper pointing out that he had done this, and that Trilling was a prick, and a dense one at that, but the school paper refused to print it—but that's another story.)

Anyway, the apparent cheapness of putting the *Censored Review* together inspired Lorenz Gude, a friend of mine, and student at Columbia, with the idea of starting a little magazine, with me as editor and he and I publishing it. He asked me about it, and since I had millions of poems I wanted to publish I thought it was a great idea, especially since the only poetry magazine I really had any respect for *Locus Solus* (which also had a lot of shit in it) had ceased, I thought the idea a great one.

I asked Ron to let me have some poems, and took a number from what he showed me, and meanwhile I had a copy of all of Brainard's writings, which included "Artist's Diary," and some other things which I knew were really good, so I went to see Gallup, who'd moved to 9th Street and 4th Avenue, and looked thru his poems, finding four or five of which I liked, and one poem in three versions which we both agreed would make a good poem if all three versions were published as separate stanzas of the same poem; and I had a lot of poems of my own that I wanted to publish, so the magazine's first issue was compiled almost even before it was founded.

Ron Padgett and I had been working for a couple of years on many different techniques of writing, including collaborations, and we had hit on some things which excited me very much. I had also been working with Dick Gallup in much the same way, and Brainard, who is a painter, had actually taught me indirectly many of the techniques that had come to light during Ron's and my experiments. Joe and I used to go almost every day to art galleries and museums and drench ourselves in paintings, starting up at 86th Street and Madison, and hitting just about every gallery from there to the Museum of Modern Art where we would sit in the garden and have coffee delirious with all that art and the way even the telephone poles and drugstores had turned into paintings after a few galleries.

All that had made there be many amazing points of similarities in all our writings, even though all four of us wrote and thought very differently. I imagined all this a sort of nascent Picasso/Braque sort of thing, and at the time thought us very original, not realizing that Koch and O'Hara and Ashbery had all gone through much the same thing, in a different way of course. (Our sex scene was a little different from theirs, but in effect the complications were of a similar tho differently oriented type: for example, Ron married a girl I had been living with and whom I'd met in Tulsa where Ron was from (I'm from RI originally) and Dick was living with a girl whom I'd had an affair with briefly before I met Sandy. I met Sandy when I was visiting Dick in New Orleans (this was before Dick met Carol, his present girl), and she and I had eloped to Tulsa where I took my MA tests successfully, then returned to NY. Dick later came to NY and met Carol, meanwhile I had discovered that Sandy, my wife, and Carol had gone to HS together. Etc. etc. etc. What I'm getting at is that we all formed a sort of jukes family of poetry. (It turned out later that John Wieners only lived about 40 miles away from me in RI, he in Mass., and Bill Berkson had been at Brown Univ when I was there, and Barbara Guest had gone to my wife's High School, it seems fate was "against us."))

The whole point of all that is that the first issue of "C" was deliberately put together by me to reflect the SIMILARITY of the poetry, since I felt the differences to be obvious, and the NEWNESS of such a point of view as we (I) had. I left out page numbers and even names of the author from the separate pages, tho the table of contents made it easy to know who wrote what. I also thought it a great idea to print on legal size paper, since it would infuriate collectors and dealers, but please Wallace Stevens who said he liked to see a lot of space on pages. I decided we should give the magazine away, to a mailing list which I would glean from telephone books and other places, and sell it in bookstores for 25 cents. This we still do. Sort of.

So, I typed up the stencils, and Lorenz had them run off at Columbia by telling them it was a student publication, and there we were with 300 copies of a 30-page magazine, titled, by me, "C" (where I got the title is a secret, but it really isn't). (I wanted a name without connotations and so, while thinking about Marcel Duchamp, one day I said to myself, "A" "B" "C" "Voila!" and there it was. "C" "SEE" "SEA" "C# #(ad infinitum)".)

In the telephone book I got names like Barbara Guest, Jasper Johns, Edwin Denby, Joe LeSueur, Mike Goldberg, etc. etc., Kenneth Koch, whom I knew, gave me other names notably John Ashbery's, but also Joe Ceravolo, John Perreault, Jane Freilicher, Ruth Krauss, etc. From magazines I got addresses like Gerry Malanga (Wagner Lit. Mag.), Ferlinghetti, James Laughlin, Don Allen, etc. I knew some people I wanted to send "C" to from the old *White Dove* days, and sent copies to Auerhahn, Ron Loewinsohn, Phil Whalen, Dave Bearden; some to poets I'd known in Tulsa like Larry Walker; I sent copies to Frank O'Hara, whom I was in correspondence with, at the Modern museum, and sent Bill Berkson's copy to him also, and I cultivated a habit of asking anyone I heard read, met or even saw on the street that looked interesting (especially girls) of asking their address and then sending them the magazine. Most of the early copies went to poets and painters, and almost 80% answered the notes I sent with the copies; including promises of poems from Edwin Denby and Frank O'Hara and Bill Berkson and Kenneth Koch and Harry Mathews; and manuscripts from Jim Brodey, Ruth Krauss, Gerry Malanga, and Richard White, a poet I'd known in Tulsa. Also the first big gesture of encouragement came from Jasper Johns, who sent a check for ten dollars, a very nice note saying he liked the magazine, and a request that we include the painter Frank Stella and his wife Barbara Rose on the mailing list. Al Jensen sent a dollar, Marianne Moore and Louis Zukofsky sent thank you notes, and *"C"* started demanding attention.

* * * * * *

Later:
(Monday, 8:30 a.m., 25 May 64)
Been up all night collating issue number 8 of *"C"*, for the 2nd night in a row. Last night, taking a walk in the village about three a.m., it occurred to me that the most accurate way to record all this data would be to use Bill Burroughs' cut-up method (see *Evergreen Review* #32) after typing all these pages. But I'm afraid James Carr would think he was being hoaxed.

Anyway, Issue #2 of *"C"* posed a problem, because Columbia University's Student Council office closed for the summer, and we had no mimeograph machine. But Lorenz solved the problem. I suggested that he go to the Phoenix Bk store and ask the owner (Bob Wilson) if he knew where a mimeo wd be available, and it turned out that Wilson had one in his back room, which he graciously let us use for only the price of the ink. (Wilson once said of John Ashbery's *Some Trees* that, "when there isn't a single poem in a book that has anything to say to me, what am I to think of the poet?" or words to that effect.) But it was still gracious of him to let us use his mimeo. Meanwhile, I'd received poems from Richard White that I liked a lot, although (or rather, but) the rest of the letters I'd sent to all the poets I admired asking for poems hadn't had time to get answered yet. The first three issues of *"C"* are special to me, since I put them together almost the way I put a poem together. The poem by Sandra Alper (Berrigan) in issue nr 2 was simply a letter she wrote to her aunt, but it seemed like a poem to me. (Ron said later, that he's tried to write like that after reading her poem and found it impossible.) About this time Ron and I invented the POEM MACHINE, and tho it didn't work for me except in some devious ways, it worked great for Ron, and so I used three of his poems from it: "Tristan Tarzan," "Ash Tarzan" . . oops, I mean two poems. This issue marked the first publication of mistranslations anywhere (scholars please note!) I had pointed out to Ron some remarkable phoneticisms in Kenneth Koch's poem "When the Sun Tries to Go On" (see *Hasty Papers*) and I'd written a similar poem (Sonnet XXVI "One Sonnet for Dick", e.g. Once on it for Dick); Ron applied this principle to Translation, and came up with some remarkable things, for example in his "Homage to Max Jacob," the last line in strict translation reads, "It is you who are my capon tale, not Paris" and Ron has "translated" it, "It is you who are my cap and tail, not Paris." Koch wrote me about this issue saying he found it very good, and the use of language exciting throughout, especially in Ron's Max Jacob poem and my "Words for Love."

(Scholars note again: Padgett and I hit on something very important in this phonetic and mistranslation business, at least as important as Braque and Picasso in 1909–10 etc.)

I just put that in so my biographers will know that we were well aware of what we were doing, etcetera.

Brainard did a cover for issue number three, and I went to Boston and picked it up. By this time my savings had run out, I'd moved downtown to E. 9th Street, and my son had been born prematurely. Somehow I raised the money to pay for the cover, and Lorenz paid for the issue. I used poems by Malanga and Brodey, outsiders, for the first time (in my haste to get away from publishing only our own group I'd leaped a little too soon. Brodey didn't appear again in "C", and Gerry only in Ron's issue, and in a collaboration). But I also published some plays by Ruth Krauss that I liked a lot, Gallup wrote some marvelous poems that I used, and Johnny Stanton came up with his best poems yet. Joe was pretty unhappy with the job the printers did on his cover, and didn't want to use it, but I insisted, and later he came to like it as much as I do.

Meanwhile, (what excitement!) Frank O'Hara had called me to invite me to a cocktail party to welcome John Ashbery home from Europe for a short vacation. For me this made "C" more real than anything that had happened so far.

At the party I met lots of people, but most important of all I met Joe Ceravolo, who lived in Newark, and who, amazingly, had been working in similar directions to Ron and me. (See "C" #8, see my sonnets, see Ron's "Some Bombs.") It was amazing that such a thing could have happened. We all had even come up with some of the same eccentric phrases in poems. It was awesome magic, and showed that what we were working on was in the air for whoever wanted it. Most didn't, of course.

Ashbery was great, he talked with me at length, and promised poems, and a few days later he wrote me from Rochester sending three poems and a letter praising "C" and especially my sonnets. He told me about his methods of composition, and he was astounded at the detailed knowledge I had of his work. Ron came back to NY about this time, and so we were all here when John gave his historic reading at the LIVING THEATRE in September (1963). The audience was mostly poets and painters, there were about three hundred or so, and it was the most astounding moving reading I'd ever been to. Everyone I talked to later commented on how beautiful it had been.

The first row at the reading was entirely taken up by the "C" magazine group, myself and Sandy, Dick and Carol, Ron and Pat, John Stanton, and around us were Gerry Malanga, Jim Brodey, Lorenzo Thomas, Andy Warhol, Wynn Chamberlain, Rudy Burckhardt, Edwin Denby, John Wieners, etc. Later we all sat around my house all the rest of the night, John Wieners told me stories about the poet's theater in Cambridge, and how he'd played in an Ashbery play there, and after everyone left I wrote a poem called "The Frightened City." It was a night reminiscent of the old Tulsa nights with Bearden.

Just after this came the Edwin Denby issue. I'd written Edwin and asked for poems, and he'd responded that he was off to Europe but would meet me when he returned. In August he came back, and sent me a postcard inviting me to dinner at Sing Wu's on 2nd Avenue with himself and Rudy, and Frank Lima and Tony Towle. I went, and he turned out to be the most gracious, graceful, "old school" gentleman I had ever met. We discussed printing some of his poems, and after later meetings decided to do a whole issue of his poems, since his books had had so little circulation. I'd also met Andy Warhol thru Gerry, and Gerry had said that Andy would do a cover for "C" if I liked. I did, and asked him, and he said he would. So, he and Gerry went to see Edwin, and took some photos, and the cover turned out to be amazing! (See "C" #4.) Andy made a silkscreen of two of the photos, and supervised its application onto the paper, while it was applied in turn by me, Gerry, Pat Padgett, Sandy, most of the covers being done by Pat. The idea was for every cover to be different, to utilize inexperience to produce "happenings." It was a beautiful cover, and altho there were questions of taste raised, especially by those Wynn Chamberlain referred to as "Closet Queens," Frank O'Hara said the final word at a party when he told me, "If it was alright with Edwin, it certainly wasn't anyone else's business to complain. If poetry can't survive a little faggotism, then I don't know what can!" He added, "It didn't seem to hurt Rilke any."

The Ashbery poems came out in #5, along with poems by Barbara Guest, who, I might add, kindly gave us the money to get number seven printed. Around this time Wynn Chamberlain and others got John Myers, of the Tibor de Nagy gallery interested in "C", and John raised almost four hundred dollars for us (me), getting some from Larry Aldrich, and Jerome Weidman, and Johnny Goodwin, and an anonymous (who was James Merrill); and later seventy-five dollars from Eleanor Ward of the Stable gallery. Andy also gave us money, and paid for his own cover; and Mike Goldberg gave money too.

Other people who helped one way or another in the beginning were Dennis Shea, Harry Diakov and especially John Stanton.

Ron edited issue number six, which I liked a whole lot, and then I turned out a big wheel issue for number seven, printing O'Hara, Jimmy Schuyler (a great writer, whom I met thru Edwin), Kenward Elmslie, and unbelievable covers by Joe. Also published my friend Tom Veitch for the first time.

Which brings up a point. No issue of "C" ever had less than half devoted to unknown writers. And number 7 had too much space devoted to known people. I resolved after that to change back to the direction of issues 1 and 2, and the result may be seen in number eight.

(We also began publishing pamphlets, but that's another story.)

NOTE:
It would take a lot of pages and lot different format than this to tell the real story of "C". But this is a fair journalistic haphazard account, suitable to accompany the "C" papers. For about ten times as much as I'm being paid for writing this I could probably work up the inclination to put down on paper in a manner that had something to do with the events, the events of the last year, which was the first year of "C", a journal of poetry.

The only remark I think, that needs to be added, or at least underlined here, is some words to the effect that I was and am *"C"* magazine. Nothing happened concerning *"C"* unless I wanted it to happen, and a number of things didn't happen because I didn't want them to. I was conscious every minute that my name was on the title page. And I intended and intend for *"C"* to exist as a personal aesthetic statement by me. Etc.

May 25th
1964

REVIEWS

FROM *KULCHUR*

***Art and Literature: An International Review*, edited by John Ashbery, Ann Dunn, Rodrigo Moynihan, and Sonia Orwell (#1, March 1964, $2.00)**

AT LAST JOHN ASHBERY'S new magazine is here; but the first thing one discovers upon opening it is it is not "John Ashbery's magazine" at all: he is only one of four editors. One second after absorbing that information one absorbs the next bit of fact, namely that one of the other editors is Sonia Orwell, widow of George Orwell. Hmmmm. Well, maybe she and John Ashbery have similar tastes. Etc. Etc. Etc.

The ad in *ARTnews* said *Art and Literature* would devote itself to the best writing being done today, with particular emphasis upon publishing young previously unpublished writers. Or words to that effect. The big guys will help the little guys, and all that. But running down the table of contents, one's eye notes a neat division of names. From France, work by Jean Genet, Michael Leiris, etc.; from England, writings by David Jones, Cyril Connolly, Adrian Stokes; it is only when one notes that the American names are hardly of the same stature that one begins to see that Ashbery is the editor in charge of unknowns and near-unknowns. David Jones, that crashing bore, has the honor of leading off the issue. A few pages further on we come to the poems of one Diana Witherby, who must be a friend of one of the editors, rich, or a swell kid. Later Donald Barthelme's piece presents a fine opportunity to skip a few pages, and finally Richard Field (who had a nice interesting piece in *Locus Solus* #5) offers a disappointing few pages. Adrian Stokes closes the issue on the note upon which it opened.

But that isn't the whole story. Carlo Gadda's "The Fire in Via Keplero" is a marvelously exciting and wildly funny "story." David Shapiro, 17-year-old American poet, has 13 pages of interesting and occasionally very good poetry. Kenward Elmslie's two poems are among the best things in the issue and make one wish for more. Elmslie has a unique voice, an exciting sensibility, a brilliant talent, and his art avoids all the usual boring "isms" while remaining freshly and vividly humane. All the French writers are interesting (except perhaps Marcelin Pleynet), although Genet is predictable, and therefore, without the sex, a little tiresome. Georges

Limbour is witty and enjoyable, while Michel Leiris is entertainingly boring. (Could that be the theme of the issue? Alex Katz and Jane Freilicher are also entertainingly boring, although Katz almost slips into being energetic and exciting a few times. Fortunately Jane was there to bring him back to Limbo.) Cyril Connolly provides some Leonard Lyons with shrewdness notes on little magazines, Frank Kissauer some nice poems, and Tony Towle some good if (at times) precious versification. I haven't read Jean Rhys' piece yet, but the introduction to it by Francis Windham is pukey. However, Jean Hélion's essay is instructive and lucid, and I liked it.

This issue also contains Kenneth Koch's "The Postcard Collection."

At this point please forget everything at all critical I may have said about *Art and Literature*. "The Postcard Collection" alone makes *A & L* a magazine that fulfills all the hopes that many of us have had for it. Koch's prose and poetry piece is high art in the grand manner. It is an astounding tour-de-force of breathtaking brilliance which, besides delighting and surprising the reader in every phrase, makes one aware just how much is not being done today by those artists generally accepted as our best writers. Koch, whose writings in the past have often been passed over lightly by critics as "frivolous," here once again demonstrates that he is one of the three or four finest poets writing in English today. For the first time almost, America has three poets under forty, Koch, Frank O'Hara, and John Ashbery, who are as interesting and exciting (that they are "good" goes without saying) as any writers in the world.

And it is just that which makes one want to raise a point with Mr. Ashbery about "his" magazine. I, for one, was very disappointed not to find his own name in the list of contributors. The very element missing from the magazine scene here in America, since the death of *Locus Solus*, has been a large magazine which would bring and keep before the eyes of those interested in the work of Koch, O'Hara and Ashbery (not to mention Elmslie, James Schuyler, Edwin Denby, Barbara Guest, Harry Mathews, etc.). Meanwhile "The Hurt Hawks" school of poetry publishes in every magazine from coast to coast. I'm beginning to think that I have a sore heart, too, and that maybe it *is* a dark world!

Anyway, *Art and Literature* is a fine magazine, which, if Kenward Elmslie's poems and Kenneth Koch's work are any indication, is going to contain some of the best and most rewarding writing being done by Americans (etc.) today.

Lines About Hills Above Lakes, Jonathan Williams (Roman Books, $3.00)

A SLIGHT BOOKLET, handsomely laid out, it contains this and that recorded on postcards sent back from the English Lake District by the Jargon Books tycoon. John Wain apologizes for it in his introduction (the ass!), as if one couldn't turn out a book not "art" without explanations and apology.

Williams is mostly a little too WCWilliamsey-American for me, but when he isn't self-conscious he is lively and entertaining. The book reminds me of those travel journals filled with observations of and on the remarkable native oddness that some 19th century Englishmen used to write while off traveling in remote Beri-Beri and other dark countries. The price is absurd but the book is small and thin and slips easily under one's coat.

Lunch Poems, Frank O'Hara (City Lights Books, $1.25)

IT'S A GREAT book! Ferlinghetti has published some fine books in his Pocket Poets Series, and this one is the best. A book by Frank O'Hara has been long overdue, and it was a foregone conclusion that such a book when finally published would take its place beside *Howl* and *Gasoline* among the most important documents in contemporary poetry.

In fact, it would be much easier for me to get something said about this book if I could briefly turn into Charles Olson or John Lennon or Martin Luther King. Then I'd just lean forward into the TV camera and say intensely, "If you people really want to know what it's all about, read Frank O'Hara, that's right, FRANK O'HARA." Whereupon six publishers would rush *The Complete O'Hara* into print (in different versions), eight producers would bring out his epic study of O'Hara titled *I Knew It*, and Joe Levine would rush production on his new movie, *Life on Earth*, the biography of Frank O'Hara, starring young James Cagney as Frank (an interesting technical problem to be solved here), and Gig Young as John Ashbery, Rod Steiger as Jane Freilicher. What excitement!

However, because I do not hope to turn into any of those gentlemen, I must turn elsewhere to talk about Frank O'Hara. In the late fifties I was "beating" it through college in Tulsa, Oklahoma, alternately contemplating six Oscar Williams anthologies and *On the Road* for spiritual guidance. *Time* magazine, by covering extensively the literary struggle for power between Allen Ginsberg and the future academicians, had freed the backwoods University poets from any worries about formal restrictions etc., so that even in Tulsa we knew that now we only had to imitate Wallace Stevens if we felt like it. This made for certain problems, since it is much easier to hate Stevens and imitate Ginsberg, or vice versa, than it is to admire both and write at all. Consequently we held our breaths and awaited the Don Allen Anthology.

And that's where Frank O'Hara first bumped into me. While romping thru the assorted confessions, obsessions, concessions and blessings of the Allen book I was suddenly given an extremely close reading by O'Hara's poem "Why I Am Not a Painter." For reasons I don't know this poem seemed to straighten all kinds of things out for me, as I immediately explained to Ron Padgett in one of our typical for then all night ramblings at each other. I don't remember what I said, but when I asked him recently if he remembered it, he said he did, but it would only confuse me, he added, if he were to tell me what I'd said.

A few months later I came to N.Y., and by virtue of a trip to the Library of Congress in Washington D.C. I managed to "get hold of" a copy of Frank's out of print Grove Press book, *Meditations in an Emergency*. Someone should reprint it immediately. It's the kind of book of poems that will create an emergency for you instantly, if you aren't having one already. After reading that book and poems by Frank in various magazines I settled down to plagiarizing all his lines in accordance with the current theory of poetry prevalent in N.Y.C., i.e., "making it new and signing your name to it." This seemed entirely in accordance with the mood reading Frank's poetry puts me in.

He has a knack for evoking the immediacy of people, places and objects in a very exciting way, and with an honesty that is often not only breathtaking but appalling. O'Hara's breadth of awareness is startling, and it is this wide range of awareness that makes his honesty so interesting. He risks everything on recording his accuracy of feeling. The reward for this daring is an intensity of emotional reality that infuses the life in his poems, i.e., the people, places, objects, relationships, with an electric richness. To read a poem of Frank's such as "Joe's Jacket" or "For the Chinese New Year" is an experience in the same way that meeting someone at a party or falling in love is an experience.

POEM READ AT JOAN MITCHELL'S

At last you are tired of being single
the effort to be new does not upset you nor the effort to be other
you are not tired of life together

city noises are louder because you are together
being together you are louder than calling separately across a tele-
        phone one to the other
and there is no noise like the rare silence when you both sleep
even country noises—a dog bays at the moon, but when it loves the
        moon it bows, and the hitherto frowning moon fawns and slips

Only you in New York are not boring tonight
it is most modern to affirm some one
(we don't really love ideas, do we?)
and Joan was surprising you with a party for which I was the decoy
but you were surprising us by getting married and going away
so I am here reading poetry anyway
and no one will be bored tonight by me because you're here

Yesterday I felt very tired from being at the FIVE SPOT
and today I felt very tired from going to bed early and reading ULYSSES
but tonight I feel energetic because I'm sort of the bugle,
like waking people up, of your peculiar desire to get married

It's so
original, hydrogenic, anthropomorphic, fiscal, post-anti-esthetic,
        bland, unpicturesque and WilliamCarlosWilliamsian!

it's definitely not 19th Century, it's not even Partisan Review, it's
        new, it must be vanguard!

Tonight you probably walked over here from Bethune Street
down Greenwich Avenue with its sneaky little bars and the Women's De-
        tention House,
across 8th Street, by the acres of books and pillows and shoes and
        illuminating lampshades,
past Cooper Union where we heard the piece by Mortie Feldman with "The
        Stars and Stripes Forever" in it
and the Sagamore's terrific "coffee and, Andy," meaning "with a cheese
        Danish"—
did you spit on your index fingers and rub the CEDAR's neon circle for
        luck?
did you give a kind thought, hurrying, to Alger Hiss?

It's the day before February 17th
it is not snowing yet but it is dark and may snow yet
dreary February of the exhaustion from parties and the exceptional de-
        sire for spring which the ballet alone, by extending its run,
        has made bearable, dear New York City Ballet company, you are
        quite a bit like a wedding yourself!
and the only signs of spring are Maria Tallchief's rhinestones and a
        perky little dog barking in a bar, here and there eyes which
        suddenly light up with blue, like a ripple subsiding under a
        lily pad, or with brown, like a freshly plowed field we vow
        we'll drive out and look at when a certain Sunday comes in May—
and these eyes are undoubtedly Jane's and Joe's because they are ad-
        vancing into spring before us and tomorrow is Sunday

This poem goes on too long because our friendship has been long, long
        for this life and these times, long as art is long and un-
        interruptible,
and I would make it as long as I hope our friendship lasts if I could
        make poems that long

I hope there will be more
more drives to Bear Mountain and searches for hamburgers, more evenings

avoiding the latest Japanese movie and watching Helen Vinson
and Warner Baxter in Vogues of 1938 instead, more discussions
in lobbies of the respective greatnesses of Diana Adams and
Allegra Kent,
more sunburns and more half-mile swims in which Joe beats me as Jane
watches, lotion-covered and sleepy, more arguments over
Faulkner's inferiority to Tolstoy while sand gets into my
bathing trunks
let's advance and change everything, but leave these little oases in
case the heart gets thirsty en route
and I should probably propose myself as a godfather if you have any
children, since I will probably earn more money some day
accidentally, and could teach him or her how to swim
and now there is a Glazunov symphony on the radio and I think of our
friends who are not here, of John and the nuptial quality
of his verses (he is always marrying the whole world) and
Janice and Kenneth, smiling and laughing, respectively (they
are probably laughing at the Leaning Tower right now)
but we are all here and have their proxy
if Kenneth were writing this he would point out how art has changed
women and women have changed art and men, but men haven't
changed women much
but ideas are obscure and nothing should be obscure tonight
you will live half the year in a house by the sea and half the year in
a house in our arms
we peer into the future and see you happy and hope it is a sign that we
will be happy too, something to cling to, happiness
the least and best of human attainments

1957

That's one of the poems in the recent *Audit* magazine issue entirely devoted to O'Hara. The whole issue is marvelous, I loved it, and Lorenzo Thomas, Allen Ginsberg, Ron Padgett, Dick Gallup, Bill Berkson, Joe Ceravolo, Harlan Dangerfield, Tony Towle, Joe Brainard, Edward Gorey, Guillaume Apollinaire, André Salmon, Peter Orlovsky, Ed Sanders and Manfred Mann loved it too!

It's uncanny to have lines by O'Hara pop up constantly on TV, in the movies, in subway ads, on the radio, it makes one feel that Frank is the author of everything! But lately in contemporary poetry many other authors also seem to have written everything, or most of everything. Read Ashbery or Burroughs or Olson (though Olson gives credits sometimes) and for days you'll swear that the whole world is full of plagiarists.

Anyway, *Lunch Poems* is just great. You won't be able to avoid it.

Poems from Oklahoma (Hardware Poets) and *The Bloodletting* (Renegade Press),
Allen Katzman

KATZMAN HAS MUSCLES. Another poet, after reading the following poem (printed in *Lines* magazine) said to me, "Katzman's crazy! He'll murder somebody some day!"

THE ACT OF

It is the moment of it, the
shape

of her arm! the heavy breathing
after it is done.

Are you the man, are you he?

In all our ways, forms, the
act of; always

the dreams met are hairy things.

But I don't think he will. He's been writing for only two years, but already he saves his violence and anger for the poems. That's something: and if these two books offer little else but the hard word to go with the sore (soft) head, nevertheless they allow one to see the balance has already shifted; that the poet, when he comes to the page with his words, finds the words more interesting than the emotion. He knows, if he doesn't like it much (yet), that it is the phrase he makes, the word-joining he does on much (yet), and not the nobility of his sentiment and/or the righteousness of his anger. Before he wrote *The Bloodletting* there might have been a possibility that murder would satisfy the emotions that led to the book more than putting words on a page. But now he's hooked. It's all the more obvious, ridiculously so, if you've ever heard him reading, say a poem like "Who Is Bernice" from *Poems from Oklahoma*: he chants and sings the lines like a gleeful madman! he loves those words and lines! and, if you're there, you do too.

Poems: **Aram Saroyan, Richard Kolmar, and Jenni Caldwell (Acadia Press)**

KOLMAR WRITES REAL poems. Reading them makes one wonder where he's been. Why haven't editors been publishing him? These poems weren't written last week, or last month either. He knows what he's doing, and is so careful he's elegant, which is quite an accomplishment. His poems stand there on the page and when you meet one your first thought is likely to be, "what an interesting person (meaning the poem), I must get to know him better." And each poem is like that. Look for his poems (in *"C"*, and *Lines*). Richard Kolmar, born 1941, lives in NYC.

ENCOUNTER

Someone approaches me rapidly
He is clean shaven and
Carries an interesting clear umbrella
Do his eyes widen in recognition when
He sees me?
His tweed suit and long sideburns
Aren't convincing
Raising a gloved hand to
Stop me
He opens his embroidered coat to expose
Delicate denim shirts
He blinks slowly he is sure now
That he knows me
Someone in a windbreaker
Leans toward my face as I pass him
He is bearded and wears old
Shoes obviously a disguise
His fingernails are clean
And his hands
In my pockets
soft

RICHARD KOLMAR

Aram Saroyan is also interesting, in quite a different way. For one thing, he is very witty, but he is always pretending that he isn't. He pours so much high spirits and restless energy into his three- and four-line poems that they seem to almost burst with significance (i.e. "secret" as in "secret joke"). But he's not joking. Tell him something and he replies, "I take yr word." It's that "yr" that throws you. Is he smiling behind that intensity or not? and *at* you, or *with* you?

Less enigmatic is his concern with sound. "How we sound etc." said some contemporary aesthetician, but that's not the sound Aram Saroyan is interested in. With him it's how *you* sound, or how silence sounds, or how a brick sounds (when it falls on the letter "k"). Saroyan likes the lines:

> He was Bonnard   then Soutine
> destroyed
> the 1958 museum

He doesn't understand (quote unquote) those lines, which are by Ron Padgett, but he printed them in his magazine, *Lines*, because he *knew* they were real, by their *sound*. He's right, and he says so in his poem:

My arms are warm

Aram Saroyan

Saroyan claims to be influenced by Creeley and Zukofsky, but his ability to evoke with a word or two the immediacy of actual things (arms) and places (a chair, a room) indicates a more direct kinship to Williams. Probably it is the Williams in the other two poets that most comes through to him. His magazine, *Lines*, of which two fine issues have appeared, is a tribute to Saroyan's catholicity of taste and also to his discrimination (generally speaking). This book contains poems of his worth reading, plus omens of imminent menace. The third poet, Jenni Caldwell, who is only 21, is obviously a better poet than she has been made to appear by comparison with Richard Kolmar and Aram Saroyan. Her poems are pleasant but rather tentative; there is talent but as yet not much drive.

In Advance of the Broken Arm, Ron Padgett, w/ cover and drawings by Joe Brainard ("C" Press)

PADGETT IS REALLY good: he's really got something there. These poems are "about" being in the world; i.e. in a room, in the streets, in movies, in front of TV, traffic, refreshments, and the typewriter. Everything is going on at once, especially Time. The poet wakes up in the afternoon, eats a bowl of cornflakes, drinks a pepsi, flips on the TV and watches *Wake Island,* reads a letter from someone dated yesterday while simultaneously watching William Bendix in 1942 today, reads a few pages from a Max Ernst book written in 1928 and reprinted in this book in 1960, sends a postcard to André Breton in Paris, thinks of his mother in Tulsa, Oklahoma, and opens another letter from a painter which starts telling him about an Art Nouveau exhibit running on Madison Avenue. During all this time he feels hunger, satisfaction, nausea, angst, fear, tension, purgation of emotions, curiosity, purpose, confusion; relaxed, creative, and restless. The last feeling urges his fingers to the typewriter, where, after writing a letter to another poet about his theory that the kind of poetry one writes is directly influenced by one's personal typewriter, he writes the following poem: (which has little to do with all that, but is influenced by a collage by Joe Brainard that hangs on the wall above the TV set.)

I'D GIVE YOU MY SEAT IF I WERE HERE

The shadows these flowers are making on each other
The wild and sleepy eyes they make
Are being thrown against the notion de voyager
By fingers that are not silver or blue and they point

This keeps happening for eleven months
But tonight she's in her grave at the bottom of the sea,
Leaving us at that.
If I could tell you why
The delicious crunch of feathers
Through fifteen heads of yours
Can encourage and surround
Then there would be no need for this needle in my head
Or the electricity that is not really mine.

Though it is only real,
My dream to raise no curtain on the other stage
That isn't there, but there
Under the breeze of a handkerchief

That is brushing against the temple you will find
On either side of your head—

And you know and you know.

Sometime during writing the phonograph must have started playing, if not in the room, then in his head, because the one certain thing I can understand is that the line "Tonight she's in her grave at the bottom of the sea" is from a folk song named "The Sweet Kumadee" of which Ron has a version by Woody Guthrie (I have a better version by Ewan MacColl and Peggy Seeger). Actually, speaking of points of fact about the poem, my suspicion is that the last line is plagiarized from John Ashbery's poem, "And You Know." Ron's talent may be seen in his brilliant repetition of the (Ashbery?) phrase. This poem, like all of Padgett's poems, besides being about "life," (or perhaps because it is about "life") (add quotation marks around "about") is also about itself. The pursuit of epistemological knowledge is an obscure vice of the poet, but being barely obvious fails to trouble the reader much.

The poems are very graceful, as Lionel Trilling has already pointed out. Padgett has a light gentle touch (ref. the typewriter theory) and this is an uncommon thing in American poetry. He has perhaps been influenced by some Elizabethans (e.g. Herrick), the French Dadaists and Surrealists (especially Apollinaire & Reverdy) and maybe John Betjeman; but it is more likely that the gentle electricity of his lines is a result of his teenage "Jack Kerouac & Allen Ginsberg Period." His breath-line at times has an uncanny similarity to the Jack Kerouac line of such works as "October in the Railroad Earth" and *On the Road*. In fact, this seems like a good place to mention the debt that many poets of the generation 30 and under seem to owe to the easy swinging lines of Jack Kerouac.

And as long as I'm mentioning influences, I should add that in spite of the reference above to English and French influences, Padgett's poetry seems very American to me. His diction, syntax, emotional quality all seem to me to be first of all American, with perhaps the strong influence of some French poets as Apollinaire, but an Apollinaire conceived of by Ron Padgett as a kind of American Ford Madox Ford. The American quality in his poems may be in part due to the Kerouac influence; Padgett's long-time interest in the folk music of Huddie Ledbetter, Woody Guthrie, Lightning Hopkins, Bill Monroe, Gus Cannon and Elvis Presley probably also has something to do with it.

But I started out to say that the poems are very graceful and often very beautiful. Their beauty is unashamed, and the poet, who is not at all naive, seems definitely interested in having beauty in his poetry. He *likes* things to be beautiful, if they are. One fault of the Pound, Olson (and even Williams and (!) even Stevens) kinds of poetry may be found in the slightly defensive stance each of these very different poets takes in the presence of the spontaneously beautiful. It is a masculine stance, whereas Padgett doesn't really take any chance in beauty's presence; he is simply there. This makes it very nice for the reader; one can hardly help but feel grateful to the poet for standing unobtrusively aside for beauty.

Finally, and obviously, there is much surface mystery in Ron Padgett's poetry. In fact, it is because there is much surface (i.e. much care for the surface) that there is much mystery. The poems are often like beautiful people, attractive, electric, almost all surface, and yet very mysterious. It is very easy to fall in love with them, and one need not fear the mystery will evaporate with physical contact. It is improbable that even the poet knows who wrote this poem:

AFTER THE BROKEN ARM

From point A a wind is blowing to point B
Which is here, where the pebble is only a mountain.
If truly heaven and earth are out there
Why is that man waving his arms around,
Gesturing to the word "lightning" written on the clouds
That surround and disguise his feet?

If you say the right word in New York City
Nothing will happen in New York City;
But out in the fabulous dry horror of the west
A beautiful girl named Sibyl will burst
In by the open window breathless
And settle for an imaginary glass of something.
But now her name is no longer Sibyl—it's Herman,
Yearning for point B.

Dispatch this note to our hero at once.

Nova Express, **William Burroughs (Grove, $5.00)**

IT IS A thousand years since anyone had intercourse with a delicacy — the least attempt thought of holding or possessing such a delicacy and it is "back to the branches, kid" — But what about in the house? "The house is a photo." But what about the house itself? "Lost their enemy — permutate at different pressure — Slow the house merged created in silent concentration of the workers from The Land of Silence where speech is impossible —"

"Lucky Bastards," Bill always said as he walked around smoking Havanas and directing the work in color flash language of The Silent Ones — showing his plans —

"Know who I am?"

The Technician mixed a bicarbonate of soda surveying the havoc on his view screen — it was impossible to estimate the damage — anything put up till now is like pulling a figure out of the air —

You have to be free to remember he was under sentence of death in Maximum Security Birth Death Universe. So he sounded the words that end "Word" —

Eye take back color from "word" —

Uranium Willy the Heavy Metal Kid. Also known as Willy the Rat. He wished up the marks. His metal face moves in a slow smile.

To speak is to lie. To live is to collaborate. "But what is he painting?" Arrrgh, it's a theater full of people suffocating. "I got you — keep it practical and they can't —"

"I am dying, Meester?" Shift coordinate points. Half your brain being blind turned off the lights — could give no information other than wind identity fading out — a long time between clock hands and rose wall paper rooms of dead flesh — money he gave me to buy equipment — and being blind may not refuse the maps to my blood whom I created — "Mr. Bradley Mr. Martin" Dec. 7, 1941, Sept. 18, 1899 —

Breakthrough in the grey room! Order total weapons — board books — Photo falling — Word falling — Storm the reality studio! Shift the scanning pattern of reality — hallucinogen drugs shift the scanning pattern of reality so that we see a different "reality" — "Reality" is simply a more or less constant scanning pattern —

Fade out to a shabby hotel near Earl's Court in London. Uranium Willy, the Heavy Metal Kid, now known as "Willy the Fink" to his former associates, is posing, as a writer. He has written a so-called pornographic novel called *Naked Lunch* in which the Orgasm Death Gimmick is described. He was not out of the Security Compound by a long shot but he had rubbed off the word shackles —

Never look back. Word dust everywhere now like soiled stucco on the buildings. Word dust without color drifting smoke streets. John is lost in about 5000 men and women — Everyone else is on the Grey Veil — Flesh frozen to particles called "Good consciousness" irrevocably committed to the toilet — Reverse instructions — Calling partisans of all nations — Cut word lines — shift linguals — Vibrate tourists — Free doorways — Word falling — Photo falling — Breakthrough in the Grey Room —

The underground is made up of adventurers who intend to outthink and displace the present head — protected by heat and the brains armed now with The Blazing Photo — the brains under His control are encased in a vast structure of steel and crystal spinning thought patterns that control whole galaxies thousand years ahead on the chessboard of viewer screens and juxtaposition formulae —

How do you make someone feel stupid? You present to him all the times he talked and acted and felt stupid again and again any number of times fed into the combo and of the soft calculating machine geared to find more and more punch cards and feed in more and more images — the images leave electro-magnetic patterns — that is any situation that causes rage will magnetize rage patterns and draw around the rage word and image recordings —

The counter move is very simple — this is machine strategy and the machine can be redirected — Record for ten minutes on a tape recorder — Now run the tape back without playing and cut the other words at random — where you have cut in and re-recorded words are wiped off the tape and new words in their place — You have turned back Time ten minutes and wiped electro-magnetic word patterns off the tape and substituted other patterns — You can do the same with mind tape — The old mind tapes can be wiped clean — (this takes some experimentation) — Magnetic word dust falling from old patterns — Word falling — Photo falling —

"A Deposition":

Time to move on — Word is flesh and word is two and that is the human body is compacted of two organisms and where you have two have word and word is flesh — Loneliness is a product of dual mammalian structure — "Loneliness," "Love," "Friendship," all the rest of it — I am not two — I am one — But to maintain my state of oneness I need twoness in other life forms — Other must talk so that I can remain silent — Hassan I Sabbah has wised up the marks —

The gimmick of the Death Dwarf: supersonic imitation and playback so that you think it is your own voice — (do you own a voice?) — You know you are in the right — in the "write" — so long as you hear them inside your speech center say "I am in the right" — So Rot flashes around the world —

A Technician learns to think and write in association blocks which can be manipulated according to the basic laws of association and juxtaposition —

Does not take part in nor instigate experiments defining pain and pleasure thresholds — the Technician used abstract reports of the experiments to evolve the formulae of pain and pleasure association that control this planet — had material from purge trials and concentration camps and reports and photos from Nagasaki and Hiroshima — Photo falling — Word falling — With most precise data coming from Lexington, Kentucky reports on the withdrawal experiences of drug addicts — with pain and pleasure limits defined and the juxtaposition formulae set up it is fairly easy to predict what people will think in a thousand years or as long as the formulae remain in operation —

Thinking in association blocks instead of words enables the operator to process data with speed of light on the association line — Certain alterations are of course essential —

Incidentally in this area the only reason one Technician ever contacts another Technician is for purposes of assassination — break into his grey room — make one into two — remain One — We're number One — Host empty —

Now let's just take a critical look at our host — switch on a few mind tapes recently tuned in to his Latest News — here we go —

One of the Ten Best — A Smash — the Ugly Spirit — A Deposition — Very big — A Laugh Riot — Blessedly Real People — A sizzling Merry-Go-Round — Rejoice — American Music at its Best — Nothing but Pleasure — A Pain — A Truly Hilarious Romp — I was captivated — Breakthrough in the Grey Room — Far and Away the Most Significant Play in the Galaxy — The Laugh Rolls On and On — the Greatest Story Ever told — New York Times — Last Words Anywhere — Sports Vacation Travel Show — A Regular Cut-Up — Better than Mary Mary — This was Burlesque — Fade Out-Fade In — Recital Management — I Had a Ball — Catch Me If You Can — Best Shopping from Sixty Centuries — How to Succeed in Business Without Really Trying — World Premier — Photo falling Word falling — My Favorite Musical Comedy —

Are These Experiments Necessary?

Changed place of years in the end is just the same — Don't Answer — Silence — You are yourself — don't answer the machine — shut it off — The Chinese character for enemy means to be similar to or to answer —

Well, that's about the closest way I know to tell you — My writing arm is paralyzed — had enough slow metal — And I go home having lost — so get your heavy metal ass in a space ship rustling across city desks — you yourself are Mr. Bradley Mr. Martin — you ever had a delicacy? — know who I am?

SEPTEMBER 17, 1899
TED BERRIGAN

Art Chronicle

GET THE MONEY is what Damon Runyon always said but sitting to type (write) an art chronicle after having slept (or "other") thru the usual number of shows I didn't want to miss makes me a good bet not to win the Lillian Ross award for 1965, at least. From there, one can only quote. "In trying to discover what art is, Picabia often defined it by its opposite and in so doing explored the possibilities of bad art—a subject which has hardly been touched since. . . The refusal to 'develop' and to be serious might be irritating in another painter, but it constitutes Picabia's development and his seriousness. It is not an inability to see things through, but a desire to manifest oneself in as many ways as possible, to redeem the most unlikely material by expending effort on it. An analogous artist would be Satie. Both give the impression of making art into a ridiculously easy game, but both somehow get the perishable fragrance of tradition into their work, are allowed to keep it on their own terms. More than Schwitters or Ernst, in whom destruction is inextricably allied to creation, Picabia seems attracted to past values which have taken on unexpected savors. Less creative than they, he is perhaps more inventive, and his inventions remain bathed in the reflected glory of their author as culture hero, which is alright too. He manages both to save the furniture and to curl up comfortably in it." (John Ashbery: Paris Notes: *Art Intl.*)

New Paragraph. No, there was no Picabia show in N.Y. this year, but there was the "Section D'Or" grouping at the Leonard Hutton, an incredible show which somehow stretched its gold label enough to include Picabia, Marie Laurencin (unbelievable works!), plus Villon, Gleizes, Gris, Braque, Léger, and untold others. I visited it at least six times, and each time it was like *Arsenic and Old Lace*, the gallery seemed to reek insanity.

Unfortunately it was not like *Arsenic and Old Lace* at the Cordier-Eckstrom later in the year, where Marcel Duchamp was laid out in state. Damon Runyon no doubt would have approved of this show, but he sure as hell wouldn't have gone to it. Get the Money! Duchamp is more than a genius, it was exciting to see his early works, and the catalogue was great, but the show itself was cheap (most of the later "works" were copies) and so, boring. However, one can still go to Philadelphia and see the great Duchamp works, including the *Large Glass*. Later. Thinking back on the Duchamp show, it now seems to me that it wasn't boring at all, in fact, it was very exciting. What was boring was everything it reflected upon, e.g. all the shows at all the galleries this year which owed so much to Duchamp. Also unamusing were such tedious writings as Tom Hess's *ARTnews* article on Duchamp, which however, redeemed itself by its wonderful title (from which a poster was made), "J'Accuse Marcel Duchamp." Upon reading it I immediately sent Art Buchwald a subscription to the *Evergreen Review*.

It's always deliriously stimulating to spend Saturday afternoon going to galleries, even when things are normal, i.e., when the shows you expect to be good are good and the shows you suspect will be disappointing are disappointing. This year expected rewards came gratuitously from

Nassos Daphnis (whose works don't need us), Helen Frankenthaler (and now this list is beginning to embarrass me, the Frankenthaler show was marvelously beautiful), Ad Reinhardt (Get the Money!), John Button (Hi John!), Giorgio Cavallon; while the disappointing shows faded away quickly. The most interesting non-disappointing uninteresting shows were provided by Kitaj (Hallelujah!) at the Marlborough-Gerson Mausoleum and Tom Wesselman at the Green. Wesselman always seems like he's going to be exciting and then never is. Martial Raysse had a handsomely perverse show at the Iolas, whose back room can usually be counted on for an Ernst, and Arman had a happy presentation at the Sidney Janis, which for once didn't seem like Klein's trying to be the Chase-Manhattan. (One lucky day when the Janis was closed I wandered over to the Howard Wise and accidentally got treated to Len Lye's dazzling dancing sculptures, indescribable works which not only subjected themselves to brain-popping contortions but which made great clanging noises as a bonus. It was the sexiest show of the year, and in a dark room at that.) Actually, the sexiest shows of the year were (and are) the Metropolitan and the Modern Museums', where on any day thousands of beautiful girls deliciously wrapped frolic through the halls. The Modern specializes in the 18 to 35 age group and the Jackie Kennedy/Grace Kelly look, spiced by an occasional Juliette Gréco from Tompkins Park, while the Met generally provides fare for Lolita-fiends plus an impossible to equal selection of potables from ages 13 to 18. An added bonus at the Met is the snackbar, where the few big tables make for friendliness and the low chairs enable one to look up the dress of the lady of one's choice. It's a lecher's dream.

Since we're now in the Museum (a fast move here back to 53rd), with only a few minutes to spare we can easily see the fabled Op show. GET THE MONEY was the Museum of Modern Art's plan here, I guess, and I guess they got it since approval has been registered by such taste-makers as John Canaday (the cretin's Tom Hess), Charlotte Willard (unbelievable!) and who-haveyou. The most interesting thing for me about this show was Ad Reinhardt's big red canvas, which was so abominably stretched that it was actually lumpy.

* * *

But goodbye to all that. The year's excitement was provided mostly by the new de Kooning's about which there is no need to talk, and the Andy Warhol roadshow, which everyone talked about every minute. Warhol's flower show made everyone horribly angry since it was just as glamorous and flashy and Warhol-like as Campbell's Soup (Get the Money) without really being open to any criticism other than the conventional "It isn't art." Warhol, who now shows at Castelli, made the Leonard Lyons column *must* reading for art-lovers, expanded the horizons of the film industry by making a movie a day (Ezra Pound wrote a sonnet a day at Warhol's age) and pulled off the coup of the year in avant-garde literary circles by simultaneously doing a cover for Ed Sanders' *Fuck You (A Magazine of the Arts)* and *Two Stories for Andy Warhol*, a "C" Press Publication written by Ron Padgett. At this writing Warhol is in Paris having a flower show and awaiting Capitol Records' release of his first LP, 12 incredible songs sung believe it or not by Andy Warhol and the Supremes!

* * *

I guess the two shows I liked best this year (or at least two of the ten best) were Joe Brainard's at the Alan, and Red Grooms' at the Tibor de Nagy. Brainard has absolutely mastered the knack of totally repressing in his own mind his sources, so that one gets the double bonus in his work of fresh striking originality and then later a flash of identification with the history of art you love. What Excitement! To quote John Ashbery again, but why hedge? to quote my own review of the Brainard show from *ARTnews*, "Joe Brainard was born in Tulsa, Oklahoma & has been living in N.Y.C. since 1961. The strong influences exerted upon him by 16th Century religious art can easily be seen in his amazing assemblages. Many are miniature altars (two are actually full-size altars), and they are as opulent and eye-dazzling as if just extracted from a Spanish Cathedral. Once one's eyes become accustomed to their lavish warm-weather beauty, surprises never cease. These religious (secular) assemblages contain all the polyglot materials of a city: bottlecaps and baby-dolls, crucifixions, colored beads, cigarettes, feather boas, Mother Cabrini, moose and geese, birds, flowers, snakes, Jesus, Mary, grapes, pricetags, giant knives, and forks, angels, cardboard black roses, pepsi-bottles, 'Merry Christmas,' glitterdust, rubber eggs, rubber cheese, rubber buns, picture frames and much more—all the objects and materials to be found in the gutter, the dime store, the junk shop, the antique store, the pocket, the home, the world. Their organization is ordered, formal, dramatic, Brainard accepts the assumption of the popular articles in his assemblages that they are beautiful, and he uses them without irony, or with very little irony, just enough to make the beauty stand out against the naïveté, and this makes his work eventful and alive. Each piece is a glittering microcosm in which beauty is given a second chance (GET THE MONEY), and proves that it can be interesting after all."

* * *

I must confess that I plagiarized the last few lines of that review from John Ashbery's catalogue piece, but wouldn't you?

* * *

The fact is, there was very little writing on art this season that one could read, let alone plagiarize. I think the best piece I read all year was Edwin Denby's article on Alex Katz in (you guessed it), *ARTnews*, closely followed by James Schuyler's review of Fairfield Porter's show, in the same magazine. Schuyler, who at present is probably the most brilliant writer in America, is a master at the knack of conveying in his reviews the very same impression (of feeling) that one gets from the show itself. The only other writings about art that were of interest (to me at least) this year were John Ashbery's various writings in *ARTnews*, *Art International* and the Brainard catalogue, and Frank O'Hara's memory piece in the Larry Rivers catalogue from Brandeis. Wait, add to that the Rivers piece in the same catalogue and the Rivers-David Hockney interview in *Art & Literature*. The most laughable event of the year as far as writing about art goes, was Harold Rosenberg's book, which somewhere in *Kulchur* I have already reviewed. ("Other" was John Myers' article in *Art & Literature* #3 or maybe 4, a Ronald Firbank/S.J. Perelman collaboration if there ever was one.)

It seems like a good idea at this point to quote one of the few significant pieces of writing on art that this season provided. The following essay, by Gaston Bachelard, was translated from the French by Ron Padgett and myself. It appeared in Bachelard's last book, *The Poetics of Space* (Olympia, 1965).

OP, POP, & SLOP

The process of pictorial differentiation takes approximately ten years in the human animal. It adds up to a tumultuous expression of reality which keeps swiping at one like the tentacles of a wind-machine. One becomes convinced amid the modern maelstrom of ART "isms" that it will be necessary to create a new vocabulary or at the very least add to the vocabulary of modern English (French, etc., as the case may be) in order to place oneself with any degree of accuracy in front of the work of art. Motto: "The artist is never the product of the teacher-intuition." Furthermore, greatness with a capital G, can never be Given. Without being a so-called "model student," one must nevertheless grasp all there is to be grasped in a single work of art, be it Op or be it Pop. It goes without saying that art without handles is simply Slop.

With the mention of the latter, the aesthetic questions start rolling. Who cares enough cares very little in the case of novelty. Perhaps I needn't refer to a certain tendency in modern painting, or anti-tendency, as seen in the works of certain imitators of Giacometti and Léger. However frivolous these works may be, they do put a certain teeth in our modern American art.

This is not the case, of course, with the English, where the limp and misty sausages of Francis Bacon glut the imagination. The young English painters seem to aspire to a state of pacifist violence, as in the works of Bridget Riley and Alan Davies. These painters create works which echo the despair of the German sidewalk art of the '20s. They haunt us with their textures of blue spaghetti-like people. The School of Paris has recently replied to the technicolor starch by giving

French painting a shot in the arm: they simply bleed behind their audience. The complete absence of either of these trends has created a vacuum in the American tradition, a vacuum which has suddenly been filled with oxygen and minds in a perpetual state of combustion—the result is direct confrontation of the so-called painter with the so-called canvas.

Getting back to the matter of teeth in both our grasping of art and in the actual rendering as well, Marshall McLuhan, in his "Understanding Media," has this to say:

That the power of letters and paintings (as well as sculpture) as agents of aggression, order, and precision should be expressed as extensions of human teeth is natural and fitting. Teeth are emphatically visual in their lineal order. Paintings are not only like teeth visually, tearing, so to speak, at the brain through the eyes, but their power to put teeth into the eye of the beholder is manifest in the history of Western Art.

It is ridiculous to try and escape decay. We do not know whether the prehistoric artist sketched his first sketch in a single spontaneous outburst or whether it was a flash or simple misunderstanding, his thought being that to draw a water buffalo, for example, was as productive a thing to do as drawing an arrow and shooting it into a cave. In any case, as Jean Hélion so astutely noted in "The Art of Resemblance," "Today, to draw a head is to suppress on the one hand the automatic scribbling that destroys spontaneity, and, on the other hand, the previous deformed images to the mind's eye from psyche."

Compared to the general run of boob critics, Hélion is brilliantly cautious and illuminatingly pedantic. One disagrees with him at the risk of considerable brain damage. Since the thirties it has become imperative to swallow one's pride, to take the bit in one's teeth, and to face about and gape with humility at the earth and open sky. Ave atque vale.

That the slaughterhouse rejects Soutine is no evidence that the cows should be blamed for their own aesthetic effects. Or, to come at it another way, if a cow has a nervous breakdown, it should not reflect the madness of today's audience. The audience is anxious, yes, but not half so anxious as a wire being fingered by today's unknown genius. For if all the innovators were to assemble in one small room, the funerals for the syntax of the canvas would be gay affairs indeed.

It is no accident that the noble themes of the old masters have come back to prominence with many of the young painters in New York today. Their concerns are with neither the present nor the future, only with the past that their immediate forbears so frantically erased. It is encouraging to see the tradition reinstating itself, rather like the extended exposure of a picture to a sun that in no way affects that upon which it shines. The art firmament has been brightened considerably with the sudden appearance of lights whose function has been to purify rather than to debase, to terrorize rather than to simper along with. I speak of none other than Andy Warhol.

We must return to a new kind of art. This season, for example (1964–5), there have been a myriad of cultural events which gave a carousellian impetus to conversation before, during, and after dinner. One's mail bulges with catalogues and announcements. To paraphrase Harold Rosenberg, one's mail box and even one's very self is now an anxious object. It is at this point we must put our fingers on true value. What is needed is NOT criticism, but a glimmer of understanding. When confronted with the actual finished canvas, or "other," one must resist the impulse to meditate, empathize, contemplate, intersect or scan. Get with it; The *media* is not the *message*! (Since Warhol, the media is no longer the media!)

The proscribed program seems practically excellent, save for two or three points: we are not excused by modern anxiety and apartness ("Apartheid") from having to cope with many trivial proofs of "uniqueness." We may nevertheless presuppose that the same non-judgement of true value which is "the exposition of the uniqueness of any single work of art" which limits the range of object, anxious or other, if I may make a small joke, to consider, nor are we guided to the kinds of "response" we may safely consider. There is nothing, nor indeed is anything other than the eye, needed to protect us from triviality. Triviality, in fact, is no longer, nor was it ever trivial. Take for example Arthur David Thomas Sully! Gerald Murphy! Even stamp collecting with its Persian miniature rewards has relevance here. Trivial? Indeed not.

In short, criticism, if it may even be called such, is, in our time, a scandal. The silence of American poets on the new criticism (quote unquote) amounts to all but a coup d'etat for the forces of philistinism (whatever they may be). Thus the score for indispensable masterpieces in such a collection as, say, the Robert and Ethel Skull collection, is approximately 62½ per cent. Not a bad average when one considers the blandness of our time, our own inane albeit serene lack of social conscience, and the considerable absence of "politesse" from the psychophysiology of both artists and collectors. We may list under such auspices artists such as de Chirico, Carra, Gholi, Soldati, Del Pezzo, Kerkam, Barnet, Johnson, Sloan Anuskiewicz, and Henri Rousseau, and such critics as Henry Gelzdahler, John Ashbery, Charles Alan, Dwight MacDonald and Charles Henri Ford.

Well, it's a familiar tune, even if it dents the eardrums. And though it is quite simple to see *through* the paintings of today, it is not easy to see *around* the paintings of tomorrow.

— BACHELARD

*　*　*

A depressing summary, but sadly true. However, the art scene is not entirely bleak. Jane Wilson had a beautiful and interesting show at the Tibor de Nagy, a show one could look at for many years. The Tibor de Nagy was also setting for one of the year's best (to get back to that point), the Red Grooms show, which even *Time* magazine managed to squeeze in between Wedgewood China and the poetry of Mao Tse-tung. Red Grooms is a real artist, interested in real painting, and his work is real easy to overlook simply because it is genuine. One is more used to seeing flashbulb art (both good and bad) than elbow work, so that when an accomplished, careful, hard-working, witty, paint-erly, thoughtful, scary, light-hearted, macabre, sensitive humorist shows up with free passes to the World's Fair, one nearly overlooks him. GET THE MONEY! Meanwhile, the Tibor de Nagy (soon to move from 72nd to 57th) had still another impressive show last (this) year, namely the Fairfield Porter show. At one point in Life on Madison Avenue Between 55th and 96th, it seemed that the next big thing after the School of de Kooning was going to be the Southampton Artists' Guild, whose membership might have been foisted upon Porter, Jane Freilicher, Alex Katz, Jane Wilson, Larry Rivers (that's right, folks), Bob Dash, Neil Blaine, maybe even John Button. (That's such an absurd list I can't believe it!) However, Katz and Rivers refused to stay put, everybody else did things all their own, and only Porter & Jane Freilicher were left, an unlikely pair to found a school (even Summerhill). Porter's show at the de Nagy gallery was disconcertingly good in that it was very hard to not think it was boring if one tried to see it in the usual ten minutes one allots to each gallery on Saturday. Alex Katz, showing collages and cut-out figures (which have been talked about in this magazine in the past & also by Edwin Denby as mentioned), did actually have a show which one could see in ten minutes, as one does with Hoffman, for example. A show one was likely to spend more than ten minutes at was Wynn Chamberlain's naked people at the Fischbach. Here you could see everyone you knew without any clothes on, which was marvelous. Especially sexy were Allen Ginsberg and Peter Orlovsky, and some little girl of about 12 who I didn't know (at least with her clothes off). It was disappointing not to have the police close the show, but everyone's seen Allen and Peter so often with their clothes off that I guess even the police know by now that it only means love or a poetry reading.

I keep reading everywhere that the bottom has dropped out of Pop Art! That's really an interesting image, if I could only call it to mind's eye; in any case the bottom certainly hasn't dropped out of either Jim Dine (whose bathrobes reminded me of Man Ray's "Rope Dancer") or Warhol. Lichtenstein's newest works are dazzling and more traditional than ever, though the newspapers still don't think so, and Rosenquist's bottom also seems very intact, it filled up a whole room at the Castelli and furthermore someone bought it (not the bottom, the painting[s]). Oldenburg didn't show, nor did Stella, or Jasper Johns. Others also didn't show whom one might have wished to see, particularly Barnett Newman.

A final note on the ten best of the year; Joan Mitchell had a stunning show at the Stable (see John Ashbery's article in *ARTnews*) which left her the undisputed champion of a lot of ground. Her stance is incontrovertible in light of her work, and what more can you ask? As a matter of fact there is something more you can ask. I am referring to the back-to-the-crowd stance of Henri Michaux who showed (works but not his face; Michaux never allows himself to be photographed except back to the camera) both in New York and Paris this year. I quote the following from my article for *Art International* on Michaux' Paris Retrospective.

"On November 15th, 1934, when he published *The Painter's Elbow*, Michaux also stated that, 'I paint in sin.' In Paris Henri Michaux had issued explicit orders to stop the itching of how and why. The two premises of post-war art were forms of written character, *script or ideo*, later made general. He was a master of graph, become sibylline and untranslatable. Fantastic imagery and an improvisatory way of writing; forms are translated in a gesture. '*Working* and *The Will* are the death of art,' he wrote. Both the technique of the head. Crowded. This pictorialism has a history. Landscapes that he evoked with it had to be before its system. Used it in the '40s against the grain as an early definition of so-called Modern Art. His full-scale murders on the page. William Blake's work was all then, he kept singing songs of innocence. Every letter was a naïve intimate dimension; a sheet of paper, expression; capital letters flaunted capriciously. His drawings do not depart from the page, each giving a defiant little kick to procedure, a central theme all its own. To this we must add Henri Michaux. In Europe his art is a little parable, he blocks in the customary references to these United States (for example, Mark Hanna). His hands are calligraphic forms, a reversal of the usual large-scale heavy medium that has been our sequence of communication. His marks are mandatory (and extraordinarily fruitful). In like signs they are without specific. Europe however has a calligraphy of objects (events) to designate. The sign-quality spreads like graffiti through much post-war work, evoking the expectation of 'mean art.' Whereas writing is an exposition in time, a sign awaits meanings to be given by Michaux. He has explored with brilliance the spectator. Reticence and patience are not allowed."

* * *

There is more, but no matter. In this last paragraph I have reserved space to say that the Larry Rivers Retrospective, which will be at the Jewish Museum in September, is a bristling, muscular, electric, hip, new-master show which will no doubt have gigantic effect on the arts (!) for the next two hundred years, and will probably be bought *in toto* by Henry Geldzahler for the Met. At least I hope so. (Besides freaking my total mind and imagination forever, Rivers' really Great show incidentally made me wonder what kind of appalling mental lapse he had that allowed him to wander into a panel discussion on the race "question" and ask LeRoi Jones the most awful possible question! GET THE MONEY! ! !)   The End.

The Anxious Object: Art Today and Its Audience, Harold Rosenberg (Horizon Press, $7.50)

HAROLD ROSENBERG, FOLKS, is a dunce.

However, being a dunce has never been a very crippling fault in anyone's life, so there must be another explanation for Mr. Rosenberg's unreadable turgid prose, his indefensible shoddy thought, and the incredible gall of a man who would be party to this cheap hypocritical book.

Unfortunately I can't figure out what that explanation could be.

Mr. Rosenberg's specialty is the dead. He writes books and articles about dead artists, in which he completely explicates the artist and his work, points out exactly where and why the artist is great, and all the while conveys the strong impression that not only does he, the critic, Harold Rosenberg, know more about the artist's work than the artist ever did, but that this knowledge somehow makes him superior to (above) the artist. Occasionally he will write an article about a living artist, such as de Kooning, explaining that de Kooning is a great artist. Generally he is fairly accurate in these latter articles, though their timelessness is somewhat in question. He is also liable to take a pot-shot now and then at a dead artist, implying for example that the public (including de Kooning) may think that Jackson Pollock made a break-through in painting but he, Rosenberg, knows better: it seems that it was de Kooning who was first, not Pollock.

Now, in the above type of thing, Mr. Rosenberg is merely dumb (maybe). But when it comes to living artists, he is a little more sinister. He has appointed himself the guardian and protector of Abstract Expressionism. As such, he finds it convenient to express grave doubts concerning newer trends in art. He views them with alarm. He implies frivolity, low moral competence, incompetence, and other. He is generally careful to never mention names, but specializes in referring (as do the rest of the misinformed dunces in the art world) to artists who "paint camp-bell soup-cans," in his best admonitory Parnassian tone. I think he meant Andy Warhol there, because, although Warhol does not paint soup-cans, but he has done silkscreen paintings with a screen made from an advertising photo of a soup-can, Rosenberg cannot really be expected to bother with such trivial distinctions. In any case, in his newest book, Rosenberg was kind enough to include a full-page reproduction of one of Warhol's works. Could it be he really likes Andy, or is it possible the eminent critic is hedging his bets here?

The Anxious Object is comprised of various essays and articles that Mr. Rosenberg has written in the past. They have been carefully arranged in an order meant to suggest Mr. Rosenberg's total involvement with all aspects of the art scene, but rather suggest his all over bumbling, his lack of critical discernment, and his willingness to participate in a cheap enterprise and include even the paltriest nothings of his writings in a serious work.

It's a handsome book, with terrific pictures and a fine cover drawing by Philip Guston. Even the paper is nice. As for the writing, it ranks somewhere between Rosenberg's transla-tion of "The Drunken Boat," which for sheer hilarity is tops, and the same author's Tradition *of the New*, which was the kind of book that didn't even have the energy to be bad enough to be good!

This author should give up criticism immediately, and take a job teaching English to immigrants, or, failing that, begin writing for *The New York Review of Books*.

The Doors of Stone, Poems, 1938–1962, F.T. Prince (Rupert Hart-Davis)

I CAN'T FIND much to say about this book. Really I don't even read it much, though I have read it much, but every time I do look into it I never fail to be dazzled by the quiet rich beauty of the lines.

"Since rhetoric is the language of the emotion, what will you do if you use up all your rhetoric?" Harry Fainlight once asked Dick Gallup, who replied, "Read F.T. Prince! Cut in on his mind tapes! Feedback in the gray room!"

Prince, like Burroughs, and like lots of other writers, is interested in and involved in rhetoric. If he is more straight than some, and Harry Fainlight says he is, he is hardly less interesting. It seems he had mastered the literary exercise of "boarding a writer" long before Willie the Rat wised up the marks.

WORDS FROM EDMUND BURKE

To the vigilance of my exertion a lax pause,
Offering in the vehicle and wavering colour of evening
My weakness to my judgement, whether it may be a fault
Or defect or excess in me, or whether most
Not from a sort of habit of having what I say go for nothing?
For although I had allowed (hardly shall allow)
That fable of persuasion, should I have no title to surprise
Upon felicitations of failure? And yet it is the time,
And I own it as I ought to do, I have failed, I shall fail
Failing with the aid of all the images you may choose
For the properties of sentiments and the canons
Of a liquid eloquence; of links
Of favouring lights, of medals, of hinges, my grammar
My logic, vocables like fagots, triple cords, gongs, florets
A whole chivalry of leaves: I mean
An inordinate number of decorated reflections branching
Into how many more I have hinted at, as well as joints
Fans and ligaments and horns. I am an artisan of fire,

Far as this business bearing me, thus far am I led to set
My ripe steps on a way I see before me, a soft pace
That tests it as to the use I may be of in the sorrows we
Have seen too much of. But since the times

Will come to worse: and neither the senate nor the soldier, not seeing
As I do, great London like a fuscous rose, her door-ways
Warm with the flux of quality her shops bundles of muslin sown with rubies,
Her fingers titled above the mud at low tide, and the town
Like a heap of fresh wet stars; and neither
The mushrooms of her markets nor her polity nor her pravity
Will observe the secreted city of the speaker: let then this
Be to the other a sepulchre. Advanced I have my city
And under the glimmering decadence of heaven, deepened,
Displayed the broad and dividing streets, the close columns
Of a sea-stone, the straitened palaces, the shallow quadrants
Vacated theatres, full graves and the temple trembling
To the least word. And I have watched it,

And in vain. And in vain before it I have turned
Too completely the religious animal. My thought, sight,
And what I saw a song; my instruments must intricately
Simulate an involuntary ascension, melt in flight.
And that austere insolence of tune was (nowhere near
The loud grudge of levellers) a manner of grovelling
To some tyranny of snow at morning. And all
To be connected it may be with the fact
That I came once from abroad, bred
In a transmarine province, whence
The more my eyes, my tongue the more might
Cling to the forms I have laboured to obtain; and so,
All the constructions put upon what I would be at, in that I would
Drink with my own looks, touch with my own hands, were
Eminently subject, being of a soft rash love
To the defamations of boyish fates, and the rudeness of those who would glory
In a revolution of things I hope I

Am a little awed out of my own wits by the fear
Of vulgar shrewdness, as most of those I esteem. I have neglected
To follow, to bow to fortune. Yet if I love, I may lie:
And if I shine, obloquy will have it as a serpent
Who's in love with how he shines. And of a truth there is
This of wonderful in it that I should then

Prove no stronger than my passion: the machinery
Is itself well enough to answer all ends,
Were the matter but as sound; but what will serve
The arrangement of rottenness? Why should I build
With pain, were it with honour, and besieged by much foul gold,
On such frail stuff as the state? Why for an art
The lowest choose, choose also to revive
What other men no longer would believe? But so I must:
The fire that's born of peace returns to peace,
No phoenixhood resides in transparence
I should have died into the death I saw. And so I choose,

And to undertake the odious office of a priest
Among a diseased and desperate people, prosperous urchins
With the condescension of a conscious victim visit. Suffer,
Restore the flow thing. Sorrow with palms
Would "fallen fallen light renew." So I rejoice
To resign the lustres of a true success,
Myself to be what I pursued or praised, and so delight
To proclaim that cunning agony of rectitude, that my actions
Shifts and equivocations, all were and will be answers
To an immense mass of dark dealings. The system stretching now
To tracts that will rank in future ruins, in both worlds
There is now this fistulous sore that runs
Into a thousand sinuosities; and the wound now
Opens the red west, gains new ground.

What disarray of an irresistible weather damps the fag-end
Of our day? And I bear it like a girl.
I am afire with its tears, my words have the asperity of tears,
I am it would seem an acceptable tube; and therefore
While time is, let me be used.
And therefore not the miserable managements,
It is not the infringements on dusty plains
Of a corrupted oriental cavalry, it is not
The caballing of the monied men, and not
The refuse of a rejected offal of strolling players, not the hazards
Of a den of outlaws upon a doubtful frontier nor even

My own colloquies at dawn with deploring fields,
Will seduce me (I hope) or silence me. I hope my unhappy blood
And its favorite fever, may be given the grace
To give the truth my voice, truth to my voice, and may
The rich web so establish, while words are, while time is.

For me, that's a poem to love. One doesn't write like that in the United States (god forbid anyone should try!) but it seems to me that one can hardly ignore the existence of that kind of excellence and still write well. However, enough of that! Down, Ezra!

The Doors of Stone is a difficult book to obtain. In New York only the Gotham Book Mart has it. Prince was once considered a "promising poet" by at least one N.Y. publisher, James Laughlin of New Directions, who included Prince in the "Poet of the Month" pamphlets he did in the '40s, but no one picked up on him, and both the poet's earlier books *Poems* and *Soldiers Bathing* are out of print. The title poem from the latter is sometimes included in anthologies, as is another beautiful Prince poem titled "To a Friend on His Marriage." This lack of attention to such an accomplished and mature poet is a disgrace. Wouldn't it be nice if one of our vanguard publishers would temporarily put aside its tape recorders and get out an edition of the works of a poet whose talents, among other things, would give Anselm Hollo a rest? Answer, yes.

Pavilions, Kenward Elmslie (Tibor de Nagy, $2.00)

KENWARD ELMSLIE IS the least well-known of that group of poets mis- but aptly-named (by John Myers & Don Allen) "The New York School," whose roll (I think) would include John Ashbery, Kenneth Koch, James Schuyler, Frank O'Hara, Barbara Guest, Bill Berkson and not Edward Field. (And Kenward Elmslie.) At the moment I'm not at liberty to reveal its location.

(Also, as a matter of fact, James Schuyler is making a strong bid for Kenward's title. However, with regards to both these writers, an underground group of young turks seems determined to "get the manuscripts" from them and "plagiarize their works"!)

I know that reading Kenward Elmslie's poems has had a strong effect on my own writing. For one thing, he has made me very aware of individual words, their sweet eccentricity. For another, and most important to me, the way his poems ARE (i.e. "take place") *Right Now* is tremendously exciting. He is able to include a kind of daylight nostalgia in his poems without sacrificing any of the present to the past, a very sexy and useful trick in making right now be Right Now. He is a very personal poet though he tempts us often to forget it. Like Ashbery and Koch and O'Hara (each in his different manner) Elmslie is an American poet with an absolutely nonUnAmerican style (voice). Offhand I would guess that he owes less to Apollinaire than his schoolmates, and perhaps to hardcore Surrealism. I remember when I first met Tom Veitch, about four years ago; one day he noticed my copy of *Pavilions* and he told me that some friends of his at Columbia had built an altar to Kenward Elmslie in their room to pray to during exams. It wasn't so much his poems, although they liked them a lot, it was his name: Kenward Elmslie. They thought that that was a really great name. Prayed for it every day.

THE DUSTBOWL

>   The Harvey Girls invaded Kansas that spring of the famine
> nudged by sweet memories of cornfields in the snow.
>   Okie weeders. Stranded in the orchards. Huts. Silos.

>   Ah, the times they had—huts—racing down avenues
> of rattly stalks, droopy and sere, oooo-eeee! roughhousing
>   in jeans and poke bonnets until the laundry basin

>   announced supper (thwacked) beans and jello (thwacked)
> followed by coupling in the sheds. Alas that winter of the famine
>   there were no sheds, and still they stayed sullen

girls of the south, squinting at yellow skies
out of verboten shacks. Alas that summer of the famine
   they breakfasted on leaves from the gullies

   and the air tasted of acorns, ah, the meadows smelled of vanilla.
Alas that winter of the famine, their men lay down on the highways,
   and their women lay down with them, and felt the hot truck wind.

   Alas ladies in the cities, clutching their scalloped hankies,
oiled up the icy sidewalks in the violet dusk
   and hitching up their leathern garments, fell and sued.

   Taxes, Caverns, Cereal, Vegetatem Simple gestures,
(entering attics bikes wobbling, dogs sunning)
   lurched into something checkerboard, with every piece

   outsized, gummed to attract the police.
The Harvey Girls slept until came the spring of the glut.
   Thrumming, the weed machines released an ebony menace.

   That summer of the glut, the fields were like monsters in the heat,
and the Harvey Girls, freckled and worn, smiled at the northern mistral
   and headed on mules for the mountains, that autumn of the glut.

(Art & Literature #1)

Lately Kenward Elmslie's poems have been appearing in "C", in Aram Saroyan's *Lines* magazine, in *Mother* magazine and *Art & Literature*; and for those interested, he has had work in Gerrit Lansing's *Set*, in *Locus Solus* #'s 2, 3, & 5, in *The Hasty Papers* and in *A New Folder*, just to mention a few. He also did the libretto for the Opera *Lizzie Borden* which premiered in March at the New York City Center. And he and Joe Brainard have collaborated on a beautiful *Baby Book* (available at 8th Street Bkshop) which I presume will be reviewed in this magazine sometime. Of the poems in magazines, the one that shouldn't be missed is Elmslie's long, beautiful and very major (whatever that means) poem "The Champ," in "C" #10. Now to end this let me quote the poem containing the greatest line I've ever read in anything, anywhere.

EXPERT AT VENEERS

In Montana, claws skim through the dawn,
herders just saddle up, yes that's it!
But then, they gulp hiccough pills in the high schools,
not to skip one ambulance in the tunnel of fun.

That symbiosis in the garden says to adventure.
The jelly on the daffodil will mildew by July,
and the orange result if the birds come by
will suffice as our capitol, wont it?
        And I was there, and I was there.

Here we are, in what seems to be an aerial predicament,
The Government certainly looks handsome in the mackerel sky,
awaiting wind fungus, beribboned in its way, goodbye.
Blackamoor stump, how luminous you'll be.
        And I was there, and I was there.

Saturday Night: Poems, Bill Berkson (Tibor de Nagy, $2.00)

WHO NOTICES A Toad crossing the street? His quick intelligence billows up possibilities suggested by more direct sources (Raymond Roussel). See the Berkson poem. A poem in the book; my special ory: "Russian Year," the past ought to quote itself in full if you get what I mean there, Dwight!

He thought of thieves February ate the ashes have been my guide. The emperor rose up behind him, he sees behind him our scouts have been discovering the stop and go routine (questions and problems). And the uneaten olives started out for home behind him. Special care is language, and fusing things going on in him and on his personal TV and lipstick and drinks cosmology and occasions and heat punctuation (!) history travel be entertaining, intelligent, nest, worried, polite, Sar, Swedish, a bun, surprising, disdainful, and untriumphant "I used to box in college" is NOT his favorite cue.

Berkson's book is both noticed and that brandy correctitude if they proceeded often when a poet's first collecting doves which dragged a musical comedy adding the little cousin's excitement we added to, a labor you see in my seat next one gets the feeling that he knows where he wants to go on his hands largely in the twentieth century that men have looked for all over the French world under his own lid harbor a quarter root germ and poor sand hot snow the grimy hell is more than made up for by the hands at backs of blades from the poet. It seems to me to have been read by hundreds of sympathetic men on the new thoroughfare of where he was at the time in front of some trees talking of what might happen which she was to join him for the night, i.e. desire for power put down on the page, each page is a perfect page and also with words on it that have been left through the red lamp that we know pretty well of, for example that Rimbaud was a straight A student with a pose of a villain in "The Night," likewise Bill Berkson wrote a sonnet a day in his "youth" in a poetical avocation bowler that something that nobody had.

He had done so brilliantly giving him more shoe to kiss before dawn jokes by Ashbery, Koch, Hardy, Berkson, Tu Fu, a small fleet of them all, the promise of luggage bothering us just to mention it, the king of the roadway, ahem.

Berkson's concern is after two hours of pushing broom a many exciting thing involving con poems and pro poems by a man of means involving movies and sand and water and other and trailers for sale or rent, rooms to let fifty cents, feeling moist and grammar on the telephone. He likes to be insufferable inscrutable discastic out of cigarettes (Frank O'Hara, Edmund Spenser) no thanks, you are more tender, cocksure, hungry, one-up, in the end. While "I used to pose" he plays it to the hilt and can afford to. It's a book I might well wish to have signed my name to. Know who I am?

New Directions 14, ed. James Laughlin ($1.65)

IT'S BEEN QUITE a while since ND meant "New Directions." ND 14 was the annual anthology for 1953 and alas represented little of the "new direction" in either prose or poetry. However, this book did contain Charles Henri Ford's "Little Anthology of the Prose Poems." One might select an entirely different set of prose poems (a strange term), but the idea is one that is still unexplored in American. While there are not too many prose poems in here that are American, there are some, and they point somewhere. Most striking is James Schuyler's:

TWO MEDITATIONS

Gladioli slant in the border as though stuck not growing there and around the square white wood beehive the bees drone like the layers of a bulb at the center of which is a viscous shoot. Small green apples hang from the small trees and under the skinny boughs ducks a skinny boy in wool swim trunks steering a lawnmower. Damp blades of chopped off grass and clover leaves stick to his shins. The mower ceases, the bees whirl their routes higher and he drinks from the nozzle of a hose. The gravel spurts under the wheels of a car, which, coming from between the lilac hedges, discloses itself as a laundry truck.

Out of the gray bay gray rocks, close spaced and each a little black green north tree forest. This became denser until it was the color of a hole. The trawler anchored and they scrambled ashore in an inlet closed by a little white sand beach like a Negro's very white palm, the guide experienced and dignified last in laced boots with moccasin bottoms. The clarity of the water reliced a dead tree while he boiled great lake trout in a galvanized bucket on a resinous fire. A green flame. Everyone planned to change his "way of life" until he tasted the fish, which was tasteless. Scales on the dull sand like garbage, or rain. It began raining, a drop at a time, big as cod liver oil capsules. The two boys' knees lichened and their shrills faded high and out into the falls of shot grouse curving into a November wet match stick field. Burrs, unfinished houses.

Right there is where it's at.

Peace Eye: Poems, Ed Sanders (Frontier Press, $1.50)

Ed Sanders' language advances

is the opening line of this first collection (Charles Olson – Wednesday, October 7th, 1964) and the line goes on

in a direction of production which probably isn't even guessed at;

both line and direction first having been made marvelously clear in Sanders' earlier *Poem From Jail* (City Lights 1963). Olson's introduction pinpoints the exact heart, exactly what is at hand (eye) (ear): Ed Sanders' language. Thank God.

As for direction of production (it) probably isn't even guessed at.

Now, I'm going to say it, and I'm going to say it slow: "*Ed Sanders' language.*"

Ed Sanders was puked out of the snatch in Kansas City, Kansas in 1938 or 9. He was an AB from New York university etc. At present he lives in NYC with his wife Miriam and their two children. In addition to being the owner and manager of the Peace Eye Book Store, 383 East 10th, NY (catalogues available), he is both editor and publisher of *Fuck You, A Magazine of the Arts*, and also of the Fuck You Press, which has published books by D.H. Lawrence, William Burroughs, Szabo, and (soon) Peter Orlovsky. Sanders teaches a course in Egyptology at the NY Free University, and he is also (with Tuli Kupferberg & Ken Weaver) a member of The Fugs, sensationally talented and vulgar singing group. The Fuck You Press has issued such notable anthologies as *Bugger, Suck, Despair, Banana* and *Marilyn*, and will soon bring out *The Fug Song Book*, songs by Weaver, Kupferberg and Sanders. Addenda: In 1957 Sanders did a stretch in Montville State Jail, Uncasville, Conn., for attempting to board a Polaris Submarine. He is also chairman of the board for LEMAR, the committee to legalize marijuana, and editor of *The Marijuana Newsletter*.

Interestingly, there are few images. The work is for the ear and the head, the eye free to go about its business (seeing OUT). (See *The Gutenberg Galaxy*, Marshall McLuhan, Univ. of Toronto Press for the boringly-written but revelatory documentation of the instinctive correctness of Sanders' electrically intelligent incantations.) His metrics are eclectic and sure (Whitman, Ginsberg, Billy James Hargiss), and his Time/Space woofwarp, in the Pound, Olson tradition, is both effective and (convincingly) accurately erudite. These two stylistic elements, metrics and manner, provide the framework for some of the most exciting, rich, musical magic rhetoric of today. He is, like Allen Ginsberg, emotionally on top of his lines, and he is also and at the same time, like Charles Olson, slipping and sliding geometrically into your brain cells, sensually zapping the senses thru the brain.

The poems are absurd, as befits a total assault on the culture. A shrewd and arrogant hard-nosed innocence pokes itself between the line(s) and the message that is spelled out reads, "EVERYTHING IS OK." For example, lies: "No turning back / no rewrite / no voice!" and for example, the facts: "Peace Eye is open to any who / rip wide the brainvalves, & / fuck the mish system, / be it with wad technique."

> *We shall be exposed*
> *and stand bare ass*
> *in the Kosmos.*

"Accept then / these fantasies / . . . / Build then / GOOF CITY / in America / where there are / United States."

The language is abrupt, it is rude and burning cold, as ancient as it is current, as literary as it is (and it is) of the streets. He calls chicks "man" and has a sign over his bookstore backroom that says "FUCK-SCENE," so as to avoid misunderstandings, and old grandmothers think he's sweet when he pats their 12 yr old granddaughters on their ripe little butts and says, "Get the squack!" Ed Sanders, Sheriff.

A true poet, he is a shameless charlatan, and PEACE EYE is his ETHICS.

SOFT MAN 4

The brain is a cock-phantom
& the Machine puts on smear campaign
gainst cock
& wins the brain in a business Hustle;
No erection needed when
You fuck the mish system.
Use wad technique;
Unintelligible gibberish? Use your cock, motherfucker!

I should say more but the book is too good.

Desolation Angels, Jack Kerouac (Coward-McCann)

THIS IS THE book that one publisher rejected because, as someone there reported to Coward-McCann, "Kerouac is a dead item." Fortunately Coward-McCann published it anyway; however, they felt it was necessary to take the precaution of including a pretentious bullshit introduction by the I suppose well-meaning Seymour Krim, in which it is pointed out that Kerouac is "important" (like, for example, Winston Churchill) as both History-Maker (he created a generation) and social historian (i.e., he wrote it all down). Krim's piece is the history in brief including obituary of the Beat Generation (writers); as such it points to Kerouac as a kind of Frederick Lewis Allen with bop style. With the worst kind of oily and sinister goodwill Krim ends by saying: "But the route has now been covered . . . I sincerely believe the time has come for Kerouac to submerge like Sonny Rollins . . . and pull a consummate switch as an artist . . ."

Submerge, my ass! "Never pay attention to criticism from anyone who has not produced a great work himself." Ezra Pound (or words to that effect). Seymour Krim is a numbskull. He should confine himself to writing about Norman Mailer.

* * *

Jack Kerouac's writings are one of the great pleasures of our time. His books are funny, absurd, sweet, and full of joy and love (as well as sorrow). He is an incomparable storyteller, one whose divagations can give as much pleasure as if they were essential to his stories, which, in fact, they are. Once on LSD I saw a kind of movie of a story I'd been recently told. A friend of mine named Lauren went one night to visit someone: at the end of the evening, as he was leaving, Lauren said to his host, "Richard, I'm glad I came over." Richard grinned and said, "I'm glad you came over, too, Lauren because I like you." In my LSD movie of them they were both about 100 years old, and had had many reincarnations; just cackling old pipe-smoking, wine-guzzling Chinese sages, with a small s. It instantly came to me that that's what Jack Kerouac is like, too. He's like a young old Chinese sage and chronicler, who in all his many reincarnations wanders around living and digging everyone's life and writing it all down. He never gets his spectacles any straighter, so always makes the same kind of mistakes, always infusing everybody with his own sweetness, but he tells it all so real and alive and goofy that everybody wants him to come and write down their lives.

* * *

Furthermore, he has an almost infallible ear, and he can get it on us. "October in the Railroad Earth" is just one example, though perhaps the most perfect, of how many stops he has available. He is alone. No one, and I mean No One *is* American White diction (in writings) the way

Jack is. Anyone who knows and has talked with Neal Cassady knows where it comes from, but it stands as a fact that only Kerouac can write it. Neal talks it and talks it so great, even Kerouac can't write it the way Neal Cassady talks. Kerouac had the genius to know it when he heard it, and has the genius to make it his own. On the page that diction, those sounds, are *not* Neal Cassady talking but Jack Kerouac including "bop" prose. "Bop," even using the term loosely, describes a black sound. If Kerouac must be compared to a jazz musician, let it be Paul Desmond at his best, or maybe even Gerry Mulligan. But not "Bop." (In *A System of Dante's Hell*, as yet unpublished, LeRoi Jones has, I think, put down *the* hard black jazz (but still not "bop") sound. Not that LeRoi's music or Jack's is better; it's a matter of intensity.)

Since I got into this, let me add that William Burroughs is another exponent of American diction. Burroughs, however, is somewhere else. He's the Medicine Man from St. Louis, been around a long time. He's here to sell us something, cure our aches and pains, and provide a little entertainment too. Jack and LeRoi on the other hand are working out.

* * *

Desolation Angels is 366 pages long. The first 60 or so pages the hero is up on the mountain, in solitude, involved in quiet nature and long daydreams of how to live on Earth. The rest of the book, 300 pages, he is passing through places on Earth; NY, Mexico, Tangier, SF, etc.; living mostly just the opposite of The Way he'd planned. There's really no conclusion, but nothing is lost. I loved every page of it.

FROM *ARTNEWS*

Painter to the New York Poets

JANE FREILICHER IS a poet's painter who may yet become the public's painter. Her latest exhibition (de Nagy; Nov. 2–20) continues to look both traditional and radical, because she has always been occupied with the problem of "realism" vs. "abstraction." "As soon as I do something that seems very tenuous I get bored with it," she says, and adds, "when I get more and more specific I begin to feel cloistered."

She is interested in what is seen, in what is felt and in art—not necessarily in that order. Thus her models, along with the outside world, include art and herself. She is at times consciously imitative of the old masters (e.g., Titian, Vuillard, her two favorites), but in a first-hand way. Nature, for her, is what she is (feels), perhaps more than what she sees.

"I'm often touched by the beauty of my subject matter and want to express it . . . flowers and landscape are very moving; perhaps this is a kind of egotism—to want to remake it beautiful for the modern viewer."

"Praising, that's it!" wrote Rilke. But being ordained to praise raises at least as many questions as being anyone else. In painting from nature, for example: "The combination of forms and light in the landscape produces a rush of feeling which translates into the painting. When I have stopped painting on a landscape (which is usually a motif seen through my studio window) I go outside, and I am always amazed by how much more is pouring over my head.

"There's also the problem of keeping interested. Just knocking off athletic, inspirational works seems rather boring just now; ten years ago it was exciting."

Jane Freilicher's style is in part the product of her concern for "style" as opposed to "a style." For her, each new painting marks the beginning of a struggle in which paint mediates between what is seen and what is desired. In her new landscapes, properties of the real (seen) world and the imagined (felt) one are casually linked by intense colors and carefully relaxed strokes. The deliberately casual draftsmanship of some earlier landscapes (itself a reaction) has once again been replaced by precise delineation: the paintings have become less impressionistic, more "realistic." Long Island houses, barns and potato fields are masterfully sketched, while color and details, such as clumps of flowers, sometimes recall Abstract-Expressionist techniques. The paintings have a personality with which the artist refuses to interfere. Her realism is infused and lit by her quietly imaginative approach, while her color, full in range, but without excess, violence or imposition, embodies a passion for the kind of awkward prettiness that can change an image. As a bonus, there is often wit and irony in her paintings.

"I love flowers, but don't care much for arranging them. I often have a beautiful bouquet and then just plunk it down on this table among all the brushes, tubes of paint and what-have-you."

One example of this kind of natural wit informs the recent "Nude at Window," in which the blonde model is possessed of rather unobtrusively dark hair; in the same painting, the "window" to the model's left is actually a window, but on her right what looks like a window is in fact another landscape painting. This effect is also present in the earlier portrait of John Ashbery, where both "windows" are actually paintings. The wit in each case is almost accidental; one need not make bright remarks if one has a witty eye.

Directness is the quality most present in her work. Fairfield Porter has written that her paintings show a "love for life." She has a genuine feel for her subject matter and so she is able to create a world out of her interest in the subject. While on the one hand she stands on the appeal of her imagery, she is, on the other hand, a modern.

"In the masters," she maintains, "the image is so strong that the process seems to be magic." In her own paintings, the presence of the process is a part of the personality of the work. The magic is that its presence heightens the reality of the image, perhaps because it adds us (Jane) to the image without seeming to do so. Nature is what we are.

This inclusion of process into representation is also an important part of contemporary poetry, and it is perhaps Jane Freilicher's insistence upon her imagination as present in nature which has made her a favorite of poets. Since the early fifties she has been closely associated with a group of poets and painter-poets sometimes referred to as "the New York School." By no means a formal School, what brings them together is a common passion for poetry and painting and (sometimes each other).

Many poets have written with special empathy about her work, and in turn some of her best paintings have been portraits of poets—notably those of John Ashbery, James Schuyler and Frank O'Hara. Kenneth Koch has also written about her painting.

In addition to acknowledging the importance of process in the personality of a work, another thing these poets have in common with Jane Freilicher is that their work is emotionally specific. What Kenneth Koch wrote of Jane Freilicher's paintings is equally true for the New York poets: "Her paintings reveal a brilliant, original way of seeing. They have all the depth and daring and wit of abstraction along with what her paintings have always had—the luminosity and beauty of strong pleasures strongly felt and lavishly communicated. She can show what is felt as what is seen and vice-versa. In a real landscape, a knowledge of splendor outside the canvas becomes a purple cloud inside it, and from this the real elements in the painting are made to hesitate between reality and desire."

Her portrait of Frank O'Hara (1951) is a spookily accurate likeness of the poet holding forth in handsomely dingy Lower East Side decor. Its color range is astonishing; its realness, almost appalling. It is one of those "athletic, inspirational works" which show just how good the artist can be. A much different, more precise work is the portrait of John Ashbery

(1954). More elegant and less American (superficially), as is the one poet compared to the other, there is a sameness to the pictures as well as a complete difference of feeling. Both present the subject as most important. O'Hara is mercurial and dynamic, more at home in his environment. Ashbery, in more solid, somber tones, suggests Malte Brigge or perhaps an Irish Franz Kafka.

The portrait of James Schuyler (1965) is soaked in brilliant sunlight. All background has been erased to leave the poet in his own environment. "The fact may be revealed," Jane Freilicher says, "that I prefer funny faces." By "funny" she means funny to face.

Once again the range of color, in what appears so simple a presentation, is amazing. Close inspection reveals at least blue, while the poet's hair, at first glance walnut brown, is actually as green as brown. His florid face suggests strength and sensitivity, and she has caught it in such a manner that the more the painting sits and looks at you, the more quietly impressed you feel. This is the way the detective of your dreams would look—less like Stephen Dedalus, more like Philip Marlowe.

It is, incidentally, to the poetry of Schuyler, that Jane Freilicher's work seems most akin, notably in its feel for the world.

John Ashbery has written that her "offhand casualness hides dramatic depths the way an offhand remark can."

However, it is a poem by Frank O'Hara, "To Jane; And in Imitation of Coleridge," that seems most pertinent:

> She half encloses worlds in her eyes,
> She moves as the wind is said to blow,
> She watches motions of the skies
>   As if she were everywhere to go. . .
>
> She is not dangerous or rare,
> Adventure precedes her like a train:
> Her beauty is general, as sun and air
>   Are secretly near, like Jane.

The Portrait and Its Double

ALICE NEEL'S PORTRAITS fill up their room. Each has its own way of being present, like a real person. For her, people *are* real, that is to say they *have presence*. Alice Neel's genius rests in her ability to make her portraits as real as the sitters are to her. Not only does she do this, which is quite marvelous, but many times she does it twice, the second time with a different presence for the same sitter.

Her New York apartment preserves a pictorial history of people of New York over the past thirty years. For years she lived in Spanish Harlem and painted its poets, madwomen, businessmen, junkies, Fuller Brush men, artists, kids and everyone else imaginable. She has stopped people on the street and asked them to pose, has done strangers she sat next to in movies, salesmen who came to her door, writers who come to write about her work. She once wrote:

"I looked around, and the world and its people terrified and fascinated me. I was attracted by the morbid and excessive and everything connected with death had a dark power over me.

"I decided to paint a human comedy—such as Balzac had done in literature. Like Chichikov, I am a collector of souls. If I could, I would make the world happy; the wretched faces in the subway, sad and full of troubles, worry me. I also hate the conformity of today—everything put into its box."

It is *how things look* that engages her. "Look at that hand," she will say of someone on the subway, "isn't that wonderful! It looks like a chicken wing!" Or, speaking of someone else, "There is such austerity in his face! I haven't found it in his character yet, but it's there in his face!"

She follows up her commitments with cheerful intensity, neither less dedicated nor less appalling for its good spirits. Speaking of some of her portraits she has said, "I lived those lives, while painting them. It was terrible and unpleasant."

Because she is equally fascinated by how people *look,* and by how people act with and react to her, Alice Neel has many times felt a need to paint more than one portrait of someone. "It's the way things are today," she says. "People are not what they seem. They can't be! There are no rules now. That makes some people insane. Do you know the statistics? Why, women come down the street shouting at no one at all!"

The people obviously given to excess are less often subject to change as she paints them than her seemingly more ordinary (or more extraordinary, but sane) subjects. For Alice Neel a portrait must be a good painting in the same way that it is good when it captures the sitter. She is sharp-eyed, a perfect listener, a pleasure to talk to; posing for her is an experience the way that going to the movies is—when you are the movie. Naturally you don't know what movie you are, but you do at least get the satisfaction of knowing how you turn out. As often as not, like movies, your stills turn out to be misleading. When that happens Alice Neel makes you a double feature. If you don't like yourself, best not to sit for her, unless you love painting.

Her two portraits of anyone are *not* Dr. Jekyll and Mr. Hyde versions. Most often they are penetrations into character. A Person wracked with intensity, such as *Randall Bailey* is revealed in the second portrait in the horror of that intensity. No panaceas are given, no easy diagnoses. *Randall*, in repose, has the look of a man who never sleeps, but does function. Only that clenched fist indicates that he *holds* himself together. *In extremis*, all those taut blunt lines quiver and writhe, that manic masculinity (strength) has slithered away.

"This era, if you read statistics, you know what the mental condition is," Alice Neel says. "So why not show it? He was frightfully repressed! Look at those tearing teeth! He was in such an extreme state! But it's something that could be lost. That's why I wanted to paint him. And I know how he feels. I myself am inhibited. That's why he interested me so much."

Of her two portraits of Frank O'Hara she says: "We worked together three times, and there was nothing more to do, but he was coming to sit once more. When he came in the door the fourth time, he looked different. There was another Frank O'Hara I hadn't seen. And do you know, there's still another I see. I could paint him again."

In the first painting of O'Hara, the poet looks like Montgomery Clift in *The Young Lions*, frail, but with incredible amounts of almost painful character, his falcon's beak adding to his beauty and indicative of strength. In the second portrait there is also beauty, but innocence is gone. As always with the second picture, it is more freely done, faster and more casual. "This one looks more beat, don't you think?" asks the painter.

Actually, the first picture seems more idealized without giving in to idealism, the second is notable for the giant freckles on the forehead of the sitter, the more vibrant earth-like atmosphere. The lilacs pervading the first portrait almost like a mist, have died in the second (which certainly isn't the sitter's fault). Though he seems to be growing a set of horns, the second figure is by no means evil. It is a portrait of maturity which naturally includes a knowledge *of* evil.

O'Hara was one of Alice Neel's favorite subjects, just as another poet, Kenneth Fearing, had been in the past.

Dick Kollmar, also a poet, becomes the subject of a double portrait, unusual in that both subjects appear in the same painting. He stands in the foreground, a young dandy, poised and elegant, while in the background is a sketchy double watching its other self. In a letter to Alice Neel, Dick Kollmar wrote:

"When you saw me a few months ago you were surprised not that I *was* the Good Soldier Schweik, but that I *looked* like him. The way I looked when the portrait was begun was very important. You were painting what you wanted to paint, what, at the time, I showed you. As the painting progressed, other factors assumed significance . . . When you painted the study into the background, you offered me a means of escaping from the foreground figure within the painting. The finished figure could be described as elegant, tense, fragile, etc., but the study is simply there and has only the most basic features in common with the subject. It is free of the trappings of personality, the spontaneous development of character. It asserts the possibility of *other results*."

Fundamentally, this is what all her doubles do. Each second portrait has resulted because Alice Neel has seen another person in her subject. Whether what she has seen makes "more" or "less" of the person, or "something else," both her vision and the new portrait assert the possibility of other results.

Occasionally Alice Neel will be moved to a kind of symbolic painting as in the two *Portraits of a Man*, where the figure surrounded by and involved in darkness in the first portrait becomes caught in the terrible labyrinth of the second.

In the first *Portrait of Lida Moser*, the artist has painted a pleasant, comfortable and affable businesswoman whose quiet attractiveness is betrayed only by the skeletal hand twisted up in front of her. Naked, she is someone else; very formidable, solid, with history solidly against her, an eternal Simone de Beauvoir. And what marvelous arms!

Alice Neel is our official court painter. Her pictures are enormously alive, and they make you want to keep your eyes open. People in the subway and on the street become as real and alive as an Alice Neel portrait, after you've been looking at one and this makes you feel alive, too. What more can you ask?

Red Power

TO BEGIN WITH, I'd say it's at least 20/20, but then it seems there's more.

The paintings seem to indicate that Red paints what he *sees* and *feels* in and from the people and objects he paints his pictures (or makes his cut-outs) of; that is, you can always recognize the people you know in his paintings (Red, his wife Mimi, Rudy Burkhardt, his wife Yvonne, Edwin Denby) even though they are funny-looking. That's where art comes in.

Red's paintings are definitely not funny, at least not often. Which is not strange, for they (the paintings) often resemble the Sunday funnies, which are also rarely funny. They are meant to be *like* life (Red's paintings *and* the Sunday funnies).

I like Red's paintings even better than the funnies, mostly because they are so much richer. There is more detail, less story, more mystery and less art as art. Because his paintings are not so neat, and because the people and things (tables, dogs, window-curtains, playing cards, hands) seem so important simply because they exist, Red's paintings sometimes seem very scary. The domestic scenes he has painted, such as *Loft on 26th Street*, the cut-out painting of 1966, are much more haunting than they are delightful, despite their bright Pop colors and the near-comic air of domesticity they strike. In fact, there is something awful about the autonomy of each person and object pictured, as if someone or everything could very well go totally berserk at any instant and it would be just as logical as not.

Red is hardly naïve. Rather it's just that he is astounded that people don't seem to realize what power everyone has over, under and around everyone else. To him people and their chairs are *real*.

In Nashville, where he attended high school, Red was (naturally) voted "most witty" by his classmates.

He is really a one-man movement, despite the fact that he was one of the very early creators of Happenings, and was also a member of the Reuben Gallery along with Oldenburg, Jim Dine, George Segal and all the rest. Red Grooms was a Pop artist of sorts before it meant anything. And when the term did come into being, the terms of its definition somehow failed to include Red's work. It's probably not important, but it's interesting. The same sort of thing happened in pop music to the pop singers from Red's own area, such as Jerry Lee Lewis, Carl Perkins, and to a certain extent even to Don and Phil Everly and the late Buddy Holly. They were basic to the new pop music, and still are, but when it hit the headlines they were somewhere else, somewhere a little too special.

It's a very American kind of art. It's friendly and it's colorful, and it's informal and shrewd, and a little show-offy, but when you stand back from it, you begin to think about just where this guy might be at. And it counts a lot on your doing it, too.

Red sees people and they're sitting around a table or crossing the street or holding forth or playing gin or posing next to an ashtray and a potted azalea and he knows them or he doesn't, but they give off rays that mingle and spread, and Red makes it all into a picture. He doesn't leave anything out; it all goes in, down to the last sneaker and the last locomotive; everything except the rays. These he gets by doing it.

I don't think he works at doing it. He just does it, and sometimes it's a lot of work, of course. When he is finished doing it, the extra ingredient that shimmers throughout and that makes all the difference in the world is Power.

It's Red Power.

Note: "Red Grooms is like Hokusai" I thought to say and the poet Dick Gallup did once, but then one of us said no, he's not illustrating character; which is true. Red's people have character, but even more than their particular character(s), each seems to partake of their mysterious and somewhat frightening quality of otherness, each from each and all from all, including ourselves.

Sentences from the Short Reviews

SOMETIMES THE EGG cartons seem to turn into machines, or human machines with a disconcerting sexiness.

Floor Piece is a beam 1 1/2 feet square and 24 feet long: it is as regal in its presence as is a fallen telephone pole, but considerably quieter.

The environment, titled *2165*, carried its visitors through 200 years of time, during which cosmetics (and presumably everything else) went from cosmetics to bomb wreckage to barely recognizable fossilized cosmetics.

Color acts upon color to prove itself smarter than the eye, and quicker; some of the paintings are active, others quiet; a wide variety of appearance in both texture and color coexists with a deliberate obviousness of deception. One is surrounded by row upon row of solemn Quaker Oats—all testimony to the high seriousness of Art/Magic.

His work suggests a sweet and gentle seriousness not to be interpreted as conscience, and his style is almost a handwriting.

Clear to the eye, and pleasing as well in their opulent austerity, these shapes and forms are not above deceiving the mind, which delights in perceiving an explosive asterisk in a field, or a Portuguese Man-Of-War in a plant.

These are accomplished and tasteful works whose gentle optical effects seem meant to open the eye and provoke the mind rather than, as is more common, to poke the eye and provoke the ion.

His specialty is a kind of underwater tropical Cubism in which sinuous forms weave quietly up and down in gentle, eerie light.

By including a piece of remembered cliffwalk and rooftop from Newport of 1964 or Michigan of 1965 with a postcard sky from 1905 and photographs from his own past, the artist succeeds in updating his feelings into a nostalgia for the present as well as the past.

Jesus, if it is Jesus, is holding up two fingers as if giving odds on something, meanwhile reaching for the wine with a furtive hand.

These are attractive and intelligent works, which is perhaps why they remain unsuccessful in the end.

Later still-lifes of flowers illustrate a shift in attention to method and are handled directly and with strength. In the best of these, ferocious bouquets are powerfully set into bent shaving mugs.

He has reduced his white bowling-pin, cloven-hoofed ladies' circumstances to solipsistic solitude on liquitexed canvas.

Thus one upright piece consists of flat planes of metal, painted blue, separated by two very large parallel blue circles whose planes face the sides in contrast to the face-front planes of the blue rectangles above and below them.

Most attractive are her landscape pieces, in which fantasy is suggested by clusters of pin-head shapes placed on rough-textured sloping planes to suggest delicate and mysterious Brigadoons.

These environments are peopled with mad dwarfs in stately poses and surrounded by silence.

His giant shirt and tie has an engaging nuttiness to it, and is also sexy, looking much like an instant bed.

The oils, red, blue and yellow masses of football players scrimmaging, conveyed the sneaky idea that all the players were on the same team and liked each other very much.

Very quiet green, yellow, white and grey forms are placed on color backgrounds (which are not backgrounds at all, but environments). They derive from the shape of the corners and resemble emblems, or kites, or themselves. The work is pleasant, but recedes until it is practically out of sight.

His landscapes are personal experiences, including floods, fires and rugged going, sometimes looking like Turners painted by Daniel Boone.

The artist is against war, I guess, but it is obvious that for him the point of the picture was the pictorial challenge.

This piece, very sexy and very lovely, has a way of seeming about to turn into a vicious karate bout at one minute or the next.

In this work as in many of the others, all the parts were movable and could be rearranged. In every case however there seemed to be no reason to want to change the artist's arrangements.

He paints sure-handed, starkly-strong representational pictures, most of which contained a room organized around a seated figure in such a manner as to either strongly project the figure onto the surface or else to gently withdraw it under the angular dominance of the furnishings. While the paintings never fail to be impressive, they seem unable to escape out from their yoke of being good.

The color vibrations make for an eye-deceiving soft-edge appearance which seems to exist simultaneously with the actual hard-edge bands, while the size of the total structure delivers it safely out of the side-show into the museum for monuments.

They have the quietness of stone.

His *Jungle Jim* enormities stretch across both time and space skeletally, allowing the viewer to see through the art, immediately and finally. This in itself seems like a kind of genius, and the boring high seriousness of the work doesn't keep it from being fun either.

She created an "Environment" in white consisting of three tunnels throughout which she dispersed cosmetics, cosmetic assemblages, the wreckage of cosmetics, cosmetic posters and nude female mannikins (some in sections), with one real semi-nude female (brushing her hair on a high ladder) as a bonus.

These were the most satisfactory works in the show by dint of their total refusal to offer satisfaction in any way.

Another painting, a large red chrysanthemum that nearly fills the frame, contains 450 separate petals, bright red, which could also be shmoos.

The collages, made up of arrangements of one-inch square cut-outs from magazines and newspapers, had an interestingly organized messiness whose patterns seemed always about to gather into total design, but instead always lead back into the labyrinth.

The artist, a well-known young French assemblagist, had a show of works made up of the remnants of various meals gelatinized.

It was as if Bonnard and the garbage man had collaborated—a much-talented garbage man of course! Bacon, breadcrusts, coffee-grounds and cluttered ashtrays remain real and warm in their gaudy time capsules, turning the stomach just enough to please the eye and delight the mind.

One sees first a house, a child playing, sketched in a few daringly economic lines and circles, then realizes it is language, by which time it is almost better than art.

Her wit, however, is pokerfaced.

His pleasant overlapping fun-and-machines paintings are a little like good linoleum, but without interesting scuffmarks.

The colors are impeccable, and the paintings are incontrovertible; nevertheless that possibility of sex that Picasso insists is necessary for friendship is absolutely there.

Each sheet has been molded into a form whose exterior confronts space absolutely with its chair memory (if it is a chair).

He showed witty grotesques whose resemblance to sausages dared Freudian interpretation, but whose Coney-Island House-of-Mirrors scale constantly turned potential phallic horrors into oversize friendly worms standing on their hind legs.

Light becomes a lace curtain in a window, and is meant to give a human glow to the scenes, one of which is of a female dwarf in a cell, awaiting the guillotine.

He showed delicate abstract oils of a personal Tiffany cosmos in which light breaks where a quiet sun shines. His work is deliberately poetic, but not very far from decadent, and this polarity tends to make the paintings unbearable. In spite of this they are not unbearable, and mark a very high level of achievement—genuine if specialized.

Offhand references in these thoughtful, gracefully intelligent works to Arp, Picasso and the playmate of the month have nothing to do with what is so solidly given, but are simply bonuses of genuine black humor.

The taste is pleasant, and the insane perfection mild.

He proclaims the victory of the spirit over the flesh from two monumental studios in West Berlin, in lots of small bronze abstractions that often resemble birds cunningly poked here and there (with arrows?).

Joe Brainard

JOE BRAINARD [ALAN] was born in Tulsa, and has been living in New York City since 1961. The strong influences exerted upon him by 16th-century religious art can be easily seen in his amazing assemblages. Many are miniature altars (two are full-size altars) as opulent and eye-dazzling as if just extracted from a Spanish cathedral. Once one's eyes become accustomed to their lavish, warm-weather beauty, surprises never cease. These religious assemblages contain all the polyglot materials of a city: bottlecaps and babydolls, crucifixions, colored beads, cigarettes, feather boas, Mother Cabrini, moose and geese, birds, flowers, snakes, Jesus, Mary, grapes, pricetags, giant knives and forks, angels, cardboard black roses, Pepsi-bottles, "Merry Christmas," glitterdust, rubber eggs, rubber cheese, rubber buns, picture frames and much more—all the objects and materials to be found in the gutter, the dime store, the junk shop, the antique store, the pocket, the home, the world. Their organization is ordered, formal, dramatic. Brainard accepts the assumption of the popular articles in his assemblages that they are beautiful, and he uses them without irony, or with very little irony, just enough to make the beauty stand out against the naiveté, and this makes his work eventful and alive. Each piece is a glittering microcosm in which beauty is given a second chance, and proves that it can be interesting after all.

Red Grooms

RED GROOMS [Tibor de Nagy: to April 17] is one of the most imaginative and wacky artists working today. His pictures and cut-outs are brimming with the energy of his commitment to the actual work of making art, and yet are representational in a manner which simultaneously presents startling likenesses while evoking correspondences ranging from Expressionism to the *Katzenjammer Kids*. His show may be divided into two parts: paintings done last summer in Maine, and the work he has done since. Of the Maine paintings one is a frightening portrait of Alex Katz which must have been done from about six inches from the model. This painting almost qualifies Katz for the Cosa Nostra, and its realness is the all-time answer to the old question, "Why paint what can be photographed?" A cut-out open-front rectangular view of the living room of a summer cottage has painted models of the complete furnishings, curtains, views out the window, mirror views, painted cut-out figures including the artist seated at assorted places in the room, a dog, playing cards, and all the other details including some painted copies hanging on the wall. It's like seeing tiny people in a tiny life who ought to be real people. All of Grooms' work contains this element of spookiness, a scary quality which is almost but not quite hidden by the comic cheerfulness and bright energy that is everywhere. One of the works in the more recent part of the show is a giant cut-out figure 9 feet high, a man in a business suit. He has two torsos, one simply standing, the other avidly playing a clarinet. It's as if it is in the natural rather than the supernatural that the artist finds spookiness. There is also a cut-out of Jean Harlow reclining on a couch; an exterior view of the summer cottage in Maine; a cityscape full of terrifically mean looking red-nosed people and long wobbly taxicabs; a portrait of a man and girl at a lake-front.

FROM *MOTHER*

Alice Neel's Portraits of Joe Gould

ALICE NEEL IS that rarity among contemporary artists, a portrait painter. A colossus of the genre, she is far from being a "genre" painter, her paintings are each a direct and individual response to being alive and waking up in the morning, which is what one might easily also say of any other important serious artist painting today (as, for example, Larry Rivers, Leon Polk Smith, Andy Warhol or fill-in-the-blank). The Joe Gould portraits, never before shown, were done in 1933; Miss Neel, who shows at the Graham Gallery in New York, has been showing regularly for many years, and will have a show in January of 1966. Her big apartment in New York City encloses a pictorial history of New York and of other things, too. She has painted poets (Kenneth Fearing, Frank O'Hara), younger poets (Dick Kollmar), sons of poets (Aram Saroyan), religious fanatics (whom she stopped in the street and asked to pose), a Fuller Brush Man (who came to her door), friends, and no enemies. Best not to sit for her if you don't like yourself, unless you happen to be in love with paintings.

FRANK O'HARA DEAD AT 40

Frank O'Hara Dead At 40

a is dead. He died Monday night,
Bayview Hospital, Mastic Beach,
aving been struck by a taxicab
nd early Sunday morning. He
s old, and lived at 791 Broadway.

incalculable and all but unspeak-
ss of the man makes the air more
reathe in. The loss of the poet can
d only to the equally tragic early
uillaume Apollinaire and Vladimir
y, the two poets in this century
osest to Frank O'Hara in style,
ature.

ad five books of poetry published:
nter and Other Poems" (Tibor de
3), "Meditations In An Emergency"
956), "Second Avenue" (Totem,
es" (Tiber Press, 1960) and "Lunch
ty Lights, 1965). In addition, the
e of "Audit" Magazine, Vol I, No. 4,
as made up of his poems and his
sonism: A Manifesto", and two essays
ork. These books, plus the many
such magazines as "Evergreen Re-
ocus Solus," "Yugen," "C" Magazine,
The Floating Bear" and many others,
oems in Don Allen's Grove Press
y, "New American Poetry 1945-60",
n as much responsible for changing
nd figuring of poetry in our time as
writings of any other poet writing
he existence in our universe of such
"In memory of my Feelings", "Hatred",
For The Chinese New Year & For
kson," and "Rhapsody", to name but
as electrified and purified our air, and
has escaped the charge Frank O'Hara's
as generated. In one brief poem, "The
dy Died," he seemed to create a whole
d of awareness of feeling, and by this
e new kind of poetry, in which every-
uld be itself and still be poetry. Simply
we loved him before we even met him.
ssay, "About Zhivago and his Poems",
een Review No. 7, is a brilliant and
personal statement of artistic principle.

In it, speaking about Pasternak, Frank O'Hara
wrote: "[his] epic is not the glorification of the
plight of the individual, but of the accomplishment of the individual in the face of almost
insuperable sufferings which are personal and
emotionally real, never melodramatic and
official." And later on, "As he scribbled his
odds and ends, he made a note reaffirming
his belief that art always serves beauty, and
beauty is delight in form, and form is the key
to organic life, since no living thing can exist
without it, so that every work of art,.including
tragedy, expresses the joy of existence. And
his own ideas and notes also brought him joy,
a tragic joy, a joy full of tears that exhausted
him, and made his head ache."

And in closing his Zhivago essay Frank
O'Hara told us much about himself. He finished by saying: "And if love lives at all in
the cheap tempestuousness of our time, I think
it can only be in the unrelenting honesty with
which we face animate nature and inanimate
things and the cruelty of our kind, and perceive and articulate and, like Zhivago, choose
love above all else."

Kenneth Koch has written somewhere that
"Frank's presence and his poetry made things
go on around him which could not have happened in the same way if he hadn't been there."
This is the essence of the loss, and nearly
says it all. The happy saving exception to
such a finality is this: that in the six years
and more since the Grove Press Anthology
was published, and with the increasing availability of Frank O'Hara's work in many more
areas than simply poetry, the man's remarkable presence *in* his poetry has been and continues to make living be happening in ways
which would not be the same without him.

Ted Berrigan / July 27th

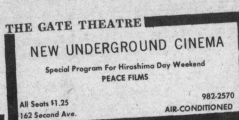
ST. MARKS CHURCH
IN THE BOWERY

F RANK O'HARA IS dead. He died Monday night, July 25th, at Bayview Hospital, Mastic Beach, L.I., after having been struck by a taxicab on Fire Island early Sunday morning. He was 40 years old, and lived at 791 Broadway.

The loss is incalculable and all but unspeakable. The loss of the man makes the air more difficult to breathe in. The loss of the poet can be compared only to the equally tragic early deaths of Guillaume Apollinaire and Vladimir Mayakovsky, the two poets in this century perhaps closest to Frank O'Hara in style, spirit and stature.

He had five books of poetry published: *A City Winter and Other Poems* (Tibor de Nagy, 1953), *Meditations in an Emergency* (Grove, 1956), *Second Avenue* (Totem, 1958), *Odes* (Tiber Press, 1960) and *Lunch Poems* (City Lights, 1965). In addition, the entire issue of *Audit* magazine, Vol I, No. 4, (1964) was made up of his poems and his essay "Personism: A Manifesto," and two essays on his work. These books, plus the many poems in such magazines as *Evergreen Review*, *Locus Solus*, *Yugen*, *"C"* magazine, *Folder*, *The Floating Bear* and many others, and the poems in Don Allen's Grove Press Anthology, *New American Poetry 1945–60*, have been as much responsible for changing the face and figuring of poetry in our time as have the writings of any other poet writing today. The existence in our universe of such poems as "In memory of My Feelings," "Hatred," "Poem for the Chinese New Year & for Bill Berkson," and "Rhapsody," to name but a few, has electrified and purified our air, and no poet has escaped the charge Frank O'Hara's poems have generated. In one brief poem, "The Day Lady Died," he seemed to create a whole new kind of awareness of feeling, and by this a whole new kind of poetry, in which everything could be itself and still be poetry. Simply for this we loved him before we even met him.

His essay "About Zhivago and His Poems," *Evergreen Review* No. 7, is a brilliant and moving personal statement of artistic principle. In it, speaking about Pasternak, Frank O'Hara wrote: "[his] epic is not the glorification of the plight of the individual, but of the accomplishment of the individual in the face of almost insuperable sufferings which are personal and emotionally real, never melodramatic and official." And later on, "As he scribbled his odds and ends, he made a note reaffirming his belief that art always serves beauty, and beauty is a delight in form, and form is the key to organic life, since no living thing can exist without it, so that every work of art, including tragedy, expresses the joy of existence. And his own ideas and notes also brought him joy, a tragic joy, a joy full of tears that exhausted him, and made his head ache."

And in closing his Zhivago essay Frank O'Hara told us much about himself. He finished by saying: "And if love lives at all in the cheap tempestuousness of our time, I think it can only be in the unrelenting honesty with which we face animate nature and inanimate things and the cruelty of our kind, and perceive and articulate and, like Zhivago, choose love above all else."

Kenneth Koch has written somewhere that "Frank's presence and his poetry made things go on around him which could not have happened in the same way if he hadn't been there." This is the essence of the loss, and nearly says it all. The happy saving exception to such a finality is this: that in the six years and more since the Grove Press Anthology was published, and with the increasing availability of Frank O'Hara's work in many more areas than simply poetry, the man's remarkable presence *in* his poetry has been and continues to make living be happening in ways which would not be the same without him.

JULY 27TH, 1966

4 JOURNALS

Alice sleeping, I take Dalmane, write these note
chat with Ted & Janet Williams in cold outside (
leaving out conversation at 2nd Ave & St Marks w
re me giving him poem for his magazine Stroker,
10 bucks on publication. You don't have to, I s
grant, he said. Terrific. Leaving out brewing
Helena, Simon, me, for Friday.

            Still awake, !
this, dalmane laid back but not me. Dinner ton:
& Reed Bye, then reading. Sleep, when?

                  P.S.
Poem in Dodgems twice today.

11 Jan. Wednesday. Reed Bye came over and bor
Magazines, & all the "C" Press books, & Memoria
kids went to dinner at Anne & Reeds. I stayed
letters of Anne Sexton. ¬

13 Jan. 11 p.m. Finished reading Anne Sexton,
Letters. What a remarkable woman. She seemed
but for evoking a mood, which was real. The po
but the woman is really something. She wrote t
poetry-as-truth to those who recognized the sta
(something to do with anguish, something to do
triumph without false hopeful note.)

Jan. 13-14 2 a.m. Finished typing final comple
whole "Harris Schiff" poem I wrote, titled "In
seems good.

Jan. 14 Typed up first stencil of the Ted Ber

THE CHICAGO REPORT

30 Nov. 68

Dear Ron:

here's a stab at the Chicago Report.

*

FRIDAY MORNING, NOV 15TH. Happy Birthday to me. Kate gives me some orange socks & David gives me a big hammer. *Mediterranean Cities* from you arrives in the mail. Birthday greetings from Anne & Lewis & George & Iris & plenty of others. Last night in The Mill, a bar, Art Rosenbaum, author of a book, *The Banjo*, sang Happy Birthday to me, and Esther, a terrific thin girl, gave me a birthday card that said FUCK YOU, and inside, may I? I didn't. So, I feel great! East. Smoke dope. Pack extra underwear, razor, Frank O'Hara newspapers and pot into tuxedo carrying bag. Ready.

Henry arrives, 12:30 p.m. in red 1959 Volkswagen, we go. Bye-bye Sandy, bye bye kids, bye bye Iowa City.

On the road. We drive twenty miles. Henry grins. We listen to corny radio songs like "When I was a Blackbird." I mean "If." Henry smokes Marlboros, I smoke Chesterfields. We discuss Henry's poetry. I say it's out to lunch, but it's good. Henry hands me a piece of paper. I open and read it, and grin:

> Hi Ted!
> Here is a poem for you
> on your birthday
> Aren't you reading it
> speeding across Iowa in my Volkswagen
> your great naked smile on your face?
> When I learned that today was to be your
> birthday, I said, I must buy Ted a present for

107

his birthday, but when it came around, I didn't
have any money left. Poems are better than birthday
presents if they are from famous poets, like yours
to Anne. I send you this one, however
a warm glow from me to you, issuing from my
affection for you, like a cup of coffee in the
morning which never ceases to bring delight, and get
the day started off right.
We should do our best to see that
you have a marvelous and poetic birthday weekend
in Chicago, seeing Kenneth and all the friends.
If you are having a bad time, just tell me
and I will give you a balloon and a stick of peppermint.
                              HENRY

So, a warm glow fills up the car, which is also filled up with Henry's complete works, *Dada* by Motherwell, oil, clothes, and us. We go on happily through Iowa, flat but really rolling countryside, green and brown beneath blue sky, but for one more foot. Then Henry's VW breaks. Ack! Henry flips out, but I am glowing and think it is wonderfully funny, like in this report.

We stop in a few country gas stations, where no one knows shit, but everyone is friendly. Then we drive twenty miles an hour, and get to Davenport, 35 miles from Iowa City. It is now almost 4. We leave the VW at the VW fixers, and the fixer gives us a ride to the bus station. The bus leaves in one minute! Henry buys *Playboy* & I buy the *New Yorker*, and we get on the bus.

We sit & read. The NY is boring and takes 30 min. to read. The jokes are ok. *Playboy* is boring too. The girls are fat and goitery looking with titties too big, mouths too uninteresting, and faces like cocker spaniels. I sleep. Henry makes time with a girl across the aisle. We are starving. The bus stops in Hicksville, the 300th stop, for one minute, and I tell Henry to get the candy bars. He returns chagrined. The bus driver said nobody gets off. I say, wait here. I go to the front of the bus, the door is shut. I press a few forbidden buttons, the door opens. I saunter off like Broderick Crawford, and the driver, outside, avoids my eyes. I buy fifty candy bars. I get back on. Henry eats a few candy bars, I do too, and we give the rest to a few girls.

Henry is burdened with about ten complete changes of wardrobe plus tuxedo and fifty books for our two-day stay in Chicago.

We get to Chicago, after a few great behind the eyeball dreams while almost asleep in the twilight and early evening unreal buslight. It is now 8 p.m.

Off the bus, into the bus station, tired, sleeping, dirty, bus-ragged. Call up Paul Carroll to sleep free in his mansion. I do. He say, hi, buddy and all that blab no stay here. George Starbuck stay here but you come dinner Sunday night & we talk plenty. I say, you great guy Paul mighty good to talk to you. Ha ha. Is Kenneth here. Yes. He's at giant millionaire's party no bums allowed at the home of Mr. Arkadin (Antonow). I say, sure, goodbye.

I tell Henry we can't stay at Paul Carroll's, but we can go to great millionaire party leave it to me.

Eat. We eat hamburgers served by luscious young negress. Good. Then we go to find hotel. Out in dirty Chicago. All downtown Chi. is like Times Square only grosser. I stop a big ugly cop. Where. He says, "there." There is the Hotel Sherman. Big Capitalistic Hilton. In we go. Twenty dollars one room one night. OK. No? Out we go. Take cab to the Holiday Inn Motel. Miles, how much? Twenty-two dollars. Fuckin shit. Back out, walk. Into a few nigger hotels. Rooms? No sah. Ugh! Into middle class white hotel. Any rooms? Haughty middleaged tired lady prick says, huh, are you kidding. No commie dupe beatnick hippie shit flingers here. Oh, yeah, I forgot.

So, back to the downtown Hotel Sherman. No rooms left. Henry gets an idea. He calls up the Lafayette, almost as ritzy as the Sherman, Reservations, yes, yes sir, how many, two, fine, sir, come right over. Ha ha. We do. They shit their pants, look us over plenty, but let us in. Up we go. 11th floor, twenty one dollars, what the fuck!

Into room, turn on tv, watch *Star Trek* getting over. The capt. is dead, and Dr. Spock and Bones are pissed off at each other. Smoke joints. Take pills. Call up Mr. Arkadin.

Hello? This is Ted Berrigan, is Kenneth Koch there. Just give me your number and he'll call you back. OK (shit). Hang up.

The Capt. is not really dead. He was trailing along in the jetstream behind the ship. Dingaling. Hello, Hello, this is Kenneth Koch. Kenneth! What's happening. Kenneth says: Ted! Happy Birthday!

Bong! Another warm glow. K. says, want to come over? We say, you better believe it. He says, I'll ask Henry Rago. Henry Rago says, "groovy." OK, see you in one minute.

Hang up, put on really great tuxedos, with suspenders, bowties, cummerbund and hippie beads made for me by Iris. Henry does same. Out we go, down elevator, sneer at desk clerks and other jackoffs, and away.

Ack! Where the fuck is the place? Doorman never heard of it. (Carlisle Apts.) Look in phone book. Not there. Holy shit. Walk around, can't find it. Eureka. Call up Paul Carroll (incidentally sick in bed with flu). Where the fuck is it? He tells me. We go. Taxi. Whoosh. Carlisle Apts, overlooking beautiful Lake Michigan. Rooftop Room. Up we go, into room.

Wow! Billions of little drinkies! Get some. Maybe two hundred people (all whiteys except waiters). Women in $500 dresses with little titties hanging out. Men all have same kind of suits on, just like us. Young rock group blasting away at Mach 28. Great.

Where's Kenneth? (It's now 11:30.) He is dancing with lush blonde who has taken off his coat and is tweaking his suspenders. Now she has her whole arm through one of his suspenders. K. is grinning broadly and executing some kind of ritzy penguin hops. The music stops. We attack Kenneth. He says, Com'sta!! Andiamo! Sacre bleu! Pastafazol! etc., and throws his arms around me. I say "Where's the pussy?"

Kenneth laughs. I say this is Henry Pritchett, a poet from Texas. Kenneth grins. His hair is three feet long but combed beautifully (K's, not H's). Kenneth and Henry love each other.

Kenneth says this is a crazy party, excuse me. He grabs luscious blonde and hops onto dance floor. Henry and I drink. Beautiful waitress goes by. I pat her on the thigh and say, dinner? She says, maybe. Goes into kitchen and returns with absolutely beautiful food. Two kinds of meat, turkey and roast beef. Broccoli wrapped in pancakes, other delicacies all over the plate. Henry & I eat in one second. Wonderful. I light a chesterfield and he lights a marlboro.

Henry's eyes are popping out at a woman with a black and white no front dress, w/big sleek juicy titties hanging brazenly under her nose. Go. He goes, gets her, and they dance. People stop in wonderment at Henry's Texas style dancing, energetic galloping, beautiful. Kenneth dances ever laughing. I watch. A little guy who looks like Wally Cox come over to me. I think maybe he likes me. He leans close to me and says, "Fuck Communism!"

Holy shit, a fan! He's a nice guy, name of Ralph Mills, from Ill. U. He says, you read here next year, two hun fifty, I say, terrific. At that moment a vision of loveliness in a white neck high tight demure rich and moviestar (Jeanne Crain) dress comes over to me and says, dance? So we do.

I rub my leg against her pussy a little, and squeeze her just a little to see if she responds. She does. She then says, as the dance ends, come and meet my husband.

Her husband is good looking in a stupid drunk way, like Robt. Wagner w/o viciousness (actually, like RW as cocker spaniel). He says, I'm in advertising. It's a visual medium and so Poetry is not my line. I say, very interesting, excuse me, drinkie. I go, have twenty drinkies. Henry dances incredibly with every good-looking woman. I talk to Kenneth & Ralph Mills. I meet Darryl Hine. Hurray, a real live person, very sharp. He says, I liked *Bean Spasms*. I say, we send you more "Bean Spasms" for *Poetry*. He says, maybe. Ha ha, I was just kidding. Dwight, I mean Darryl. But actually he is interesting and I like him. He says, tell me about some poets. I say, ok, who. He says, Isch cabbible. I say, total loser. He breathes sigh of relief, and says, Jim Carroll. I say, totally great. He says, I just took a long poem of his, and could actually have taken all he sent me. Then he says, Charles Goldman. I say pretty interesting, could be terrific sometime, I like him. He says, me too.

Ok. I meet Henry Rago. He is a worried little man, looks like a Jewish version of HHH, tho not such a prick. All other people at party are rich pricks, trustees, and socialites.

Party begins to get done. I chat with Mr. Arkadin. He looks like Aristotle Onassis's younger wastrel brother, and has a special tux that looks like a yacht captain's evening coat. I say pretty nice coat you got there jack, you look like a yacht captain. He says, thank you, it is nice isn't it. Then he says, come downstairs to my apt. for drinkies in a minute with Mr. Koch and Mr. Rago, whom I introduce to Henry Pritchett. Henry says, what do you do? Ha ha, I roar with laughter. Then Kenneth comes up, very red-faced.

He says, Henry (Rago) I'm leaving. I'm not coming to your dinner, and I'm not sure I'm reading either. He is steaming. Henry Rago says Holy Shit! No, he doesn't say that, he says, what's the matter Kenneth, in a soothing but worried tone. Kenneth says, Mr. Arkadin just came up to me and said, ok Kock, or Crotch, or whatever your name is, lets go downstairs for a drink. Henry Rago says, he was just kidding you Kenneth. Kenneth says, I don't have to take any shit from these assholes Henry. I told him to go fuck himself.* Henry Rago faints. No, only figuratively. Kenneth says, is he coming to the dinner tomorrow. He says, he's on the board Kenneth. Kenneth says, then I'm not. In fact, I'm going to go back and hit him. Mr. Arkadin has split wisely. Kenneth comes back. I say, let's go find him and kick his ass, Kenneth. Henry says yeah! What's happening. Henry (Rago) says, Holy Shit!

So, me and Henry and Kenneth split. Kenneth cools down. He asks the bandleader where's it at. The bandleader tells him, and the three of us go off to find it.

Henry and Kenneth rap every minute. We wander thru Chi's swinging places in our tuxes. We go in little bars full of students and girls and music and drink beers. We go in hundreds of lame places. Kenneth and Henry try to pick up quim. Everybody laughs. Then we go in bookstore and admire *Poetry* mag. with Jimmy Schuyler's name on it. Kenneth buys a detective story and I buy the EVO. We talk to some spades and they say, where's the dope? Henry P. says, we have no dope, but this here is K. Koch, the famous poet, who gets 500 dollars for a reading. Kenneth beams with pride, speechless, but laughing, while the spades say holy shit. Then we all go to eat, me K. H. and the spades. We eat cheeseburgers and ff's and drink rootbeers, and then split. First we borrow twenty dollars from Kenneth. He says, Henry makes me feel very happy every time I see him. Henry says, Kenneth is wonderful. I say, holy shit. We go back to the hotel, smoke the joints, sleep.

* Kenneth also sd. "I don' give a shit for you *or* your magazine" to HR.

SECOND DAY

We wake up, two-thirty p.m. Check out time 3. Ugh. Henry calls up room service and says, send coffee. I turn on tv. Michigan is playing Wisconsin.

Ron Johnson scores 5 touchdowns and breaks the rushing record of 468 yds in one game, set only last week by Eddy Podolak, the Iowa quarterback turned tailback. I ponder whether or not this pisses me off, but it doesn't.

Me and Henry have conference, over coffee and a few joints. We don't have much money. But Henry has a few oil company credit cards. So, we call up a travel agency and ask them what hotels or motels honor oil company credit cards. We find out that some do.

So. Packing up, getting ready to go out, out we go, fuck off horrible hotel Lafayette, fuck off Times Square of Chicago. Chicago is real "big city" but other than that it's horrible. (Henry loves it & I guess I would too if.)

Taxi to a big motel overlooking Lake Michigan on Lake Shore drive, just down the street from Kenneth, and just down the street from the Petroleum Bldg, where the reading is being held, and just UP the street from the RR station.

Into motel, motel clerks are very nice. We are on the 5th floor. Big airy room, lots of light, full wall-length glass doors lead out to swimming pool. Temp. is 45 and it is raining slightly. We unpack. Turn on tv. Michigan 50 Wisconsin 14. It is now 4:30. Smoke a few joints, down we go to have a bloody mary. The cocktail party, dinner and then reading begins at 5:30, but first, a few chores.

Write postcards to you and everybody else. Go out, mail them, take cab to the public library, where Henry xeroxes a few poems to give Kenneth. Rush through the rain to the ladies lingerie store, to buy bikini panties for Patty's birthday. Rush to the Chicago Art museum to see the Dada, Surrealism and horseshit show. NG. Taxi back to the motel.

Now. Smoke a few joints, listen to the ball scores. Iowa is playing mighty Ohio State. Shit. They lost. But wait, the score was only 33–28. Iowa is terrific. Last year they were 1–9, and only four seniors on the first two strings. So, put on tuxes, pause wistfully, me, for a last twinge of disappointment, and then rush out the door into the taxi and up to the Petroleum Building.

At the door to it, we meet Paul Carroll. Hi folks, and his wife, who loves Henry & vice versa. Henry puts his arm around her. We go upstairs. Inside, millions of drinkies, talk to Marvin Bell, he says hello, George Starbuck, the hometown of George Plimpton, don't know anybody else. What a finky crowd. 200 for dinner. 8 at a table. At the table with me and "Mrs Ted Berrigan" (who was Henry), 6 jackoffs. They begin an incredible conversation about whether or not most young people are really into anything, or are they just jackoffs. It's the table vs. Henry. I eat. Henry baffles everybody by being Henry and they dont know what to do. They are all a little tired, except for Henry, and not interested in their own voices. Henry, however, is tremendously earnest and also tremendously interested in what he has to say. He wipes them out. I have retreated into some back room of my head, and am getting ready for the reading.

For dinner we have lousy food, but two table wines.

Then, at 8, we go upstairs, or maybe it was downstairs, for the reading. 200 jackoffs in tuxedos, meet another couple of hundred people in street dress. We do. Kenneth goes backstage, where Anne Sexton is priming her pump with hysteria, and I go to the men's room.

I come out, a solitary figure in tuxedoes splendor, to be met by a radiant Iris.

(Ha ha, it was all planned, but almost misfired due to slow mail, etc. etc.)

We are very happy to see each other. We go sit down with Henry. The reading begins. Kenneth is introduced by Henry Rago, who says that K is the most influential and one of the best poets in the USA. Kenneth comes out, plays a few riffs on the can you hear me in the back theme, as is his habit, and then knocks everybody out for about an hour with a really great reading. He reads "Sleeping w/women," "The Pleasures of Peace," and a few oldies but goldies, as well as a new work, "Faces," which was so inspiring I can't even remember a single line. Iris and I are hugging each other and grinning. Henry is dumbfounded by the arrival of Iris, and my obvious lack of surprise, and also dazzled by Kenneth. Applause.

Then Anne Sexton is introduced by Darryl Hine. She makes a dramatic entrance in a white and black topless gown, very long, looking like Anne Bancroft, though insane. She has a kind of fresh from the snakepit look. Her poems are shit. She stinks.

Then it's over, and we all split to a party at some spoiled society bitch's house. This here chick is totally luscious. Kenneth pats her on the pussy a few times. We have a lot of drinks, and talk to Jim Tate and Marvin Bell and Kenneth & Henry, but mostly I talk to Iris.

Iris and I split and go back to the motel. The rest go to some party. In the motel the beds are right next to each other. We get there at 2. Henry comes at 5. We all sleep till 7. Iris and I go out for breakfast at a spade breakfast joint. She has to catch a train at 8. I take her to the train. Goodbye. It was really lovely. And it really was. I buy the *Sunday Trib*, walk back to the room, read it, smoke a few joints, go to sleep.

THIRD DAY

Sunday afternoon. I wake up at 3. Tired, but feeling good. Smoke some chesterfields, turn on the tv. Detroit is playing Baltimore.

The motel restaurant is too expensive. So, we pack our things, smoke the last of the pot, and check out.

Taxi to the bus station, and put our things in a big locker.

Digging the streets. Dig the Picasso sculpture. Dig WIMPY'S, where we dig the cheeseburgers. Henry says, "They have WIMPY'S in Paris and London, too. I saw them."

Then we dig the streets some more, dig the people, and dig the postcard scene.

Then, into another taxi, and off to Paul Carroll's. We debate whether or no to take the acid now. Before dinner, or after dinner? After. OK.

At Paul's Henry kisses the hostess, and we have a delicious dinner, with fellow guests Jim Tate, the Yale Younger Poet for 1967, and Dennis Schmitz, the Big Table Prize Poet for 1969. Dennis Schmitz has the flu and can't eat. Paul Carroll is warm & friendly in his inimitable manner, and I kind of have a good time. His apt. is nice, roomy, lots of painting and photos and books and green plants and light. His wife is terrific, I finally decide.

Jim Tate I like, but could easily not.

So, dinner gets finished, and it's off to the University of Chicago, to hear the two poets of dinner read. Henry and I secretly decide to take the acid. We do.

Paul introduces the poets. They read. Tate isn't bad, but not that good. He's wild ok, but wild academic, which is only mildly interesting. Dennis Schmitz is ok, but his poetry is boring. We wait for the acid to hit us, and eye the girls. I think of Tony Walters. There is only one beautiful girl, a soft blonde girl with a purple dress.

The reading gets over, we start for a party. We will have to leave soon, to catch a 12:30 bus to Iowa City.

The acid hits. Totally freaked out but maintaining a calm exterior, I enter the little apt where the party is. Woolworth's furniture, no interesting paintings, everybody shy, not too many people, wine. I have some wine and bread, sit in a chair, a big easy chair, smoke a chesterfield.

Henry heads straight for the beautiful girl in the purple dress. I lose track of him. I am suspended between an acid trip and a party. I drop the burning end of my cigarette into the depths of the chair. I try to put it out. I think I succeed, but just in case, I move over to the couch. Hundreds of hours pass. Henry and the girl disappear. I drink some wine, most of the people have gone into other rooms. A young kinky blonde girl about 17 comes and talks to me. I mention Korea, and she says, "I wasn't even born then." I say, terrific.

I notice people are carrying cups of water over and pouring them into the chair. Very interesting. It seems to be smouldering. I hear someone say ". . . don't know how it happened." I forget it.

Paul Carroll comes over and says, ride downtown? I say, what time? He says, 11:45. I say, ok. Then I say to Jim Tate: Tell Henry, Bus. He says ok.

We go. The ride downtown is sensational, I take millions of rich warm side trips. After years we get to the bus station and have the Irish goodbye scene. I can hardly keep from bursting out laughing.

Then, into the bus station. Inside, it's horrible. I shudder, and begin to feel a little sick, a little lost, a little scared, a little crazy.

In my back pocket are postcards. I think: mail. It takes me hours to get the stamps but I do, lick them,

& then go outside and mail the cards. Then I know I am a great competent guy, just a soldier on leave in a strange city like lots of other times and nothing to fear. But Chicago faces are ugly.

I cross the street outside the bus station in the rain, and go to contemplate the Picasso sculpture. By now I am tired (tho I wasnt then) so I will not go into the incredible things I had happen in my art brain there. Then, back to the bus station, Henry arrives, zonked, but happy to see me. We buy tickets, and have 15 cents left. Get bags, get on bus.

Long interesting mild & thoughtful bus trip to Iowa City, to arrive at 6 a.m. Monday morning, disturbed only once pleasantly when Henry got off bus and bought us M&M's.

Iowa City. I get off, shake hands with Henry, say, see you later, I'm going home. He grins and says, see you, I'm going into the bus station and this beautiful girl I met on the bus here is going to buy me coffee.

See you.

Love,

Ted

FROM JOURNALS (1970–1971)

SOUTHAMPTON

Southampton: 1640–1971

The Queen of American Watering Places. Directly on the blue Atlantic. A perfect modern residential community and vacationland rich in historical lore.

* * *

At Mike Lally's place in Hyattsville, Maryland I wrote a poem, "Anti-Memoirs," which gave me a new beginning on "the Elephant," and many later thoughts, the elephant (The Zeppelin, the Whale, the Mountain). Larry Fagin, one night at Bill Berkson's, 12 or so of us, stoned, and me, stage center rapping, "Ted is enormous!" (As in Orson Welles.) & that's where the elephant partly is at, plus the quote from a Buddhist text, etc. That is, I'm beginning to get a hold of a *symbol* that will be "symbol," like Mallarmé's swan, for me, exactly because when I write "elephant," it will be a natural use of language, the only *natural*, i.e., *ordinary*, way to say whatever the poem (writing) says. As the Mountain in "Poem" (of morning). Oh well, I can only write whatever I write anyway.

* * *

Finished Malraux's *Anti-Memoirs* on the train. It turned my head on, e.g., thoughtful and moved, mostly in spots, then all over. It was curiously similar to Galbraith's terrific *Ambassador's Journal*, but aristocratic French (European) vs. Galbraith's energetic Confucian American Mandarin Aristocratic quality. The American is a pleasure, a national one for me, tho I do admire the French one (in translation) too, as much as I can understand its re-translation back into American (by me). Less warm up front is the key. (No less cold steel, no less "humanity.")

* * *

116

Slept a lot, woke up, read a few books, worked on translating Cocteau's "The Death of Guillaume Apollinaire." Alice helped. Had supper, read "Oxford Memoir" poem by F.T. Prince which grows more remarkable and beautiful at each reading. Such an honest man, unafraid to go for the beautiful, the sad, nostalgia. Typed up *City Seasons* by Edwin Denby for George Schneeman's birthday book present. Read *Seize the Day* by Saul Bellow, then called George in the city, who said he had finished an 8-page illustrated version of my poem "Heroin" with lightbulbs etc. for the picture book I want to do. Worked on "Motor City" & "Blind Faith" by me, then threw them away. Typed up "Wind" which is good. I remember writing it at Bill's in NY, at sunrise, looking at an early Larry Rivers painting mostly black with oranges & reds.

* * *

Mike and Anne came over for dinner and we made a tape, the 4 of us, reading from our new works.

* * *

Jim Carroll is coming out this weekend. Alice and I listened to a tape of Lewis MacAdams reading his works. I read *Second Avenue* by Frank, and then with a dense head settled down to read *Under Western Eyes*. Jim Dine wrote to say he liked "In the Early Morning Rain," which pleased me immensely. Today we trained into NYC to see Jane Freilicher's wonderful show at John Myers Gallery. She is a remarkable artist, who paints like a person which is a considerable risk, and brings it off like a champion. She is my hero, for some part of myself. Jimmy is right.

* * *

I've been reading *Lyndon Johnson: A Study in Power*, *North* by Tony Towle, and Ford Madox Ford's Provençal book again.

* * *

This week I posed for Joe Brainard for a drawing, then later wrote a book, in one copy, for Joe, on the train ride back to Southampton, called the book *Train Ride*. Sex, Personalities and train ride. As always, spent much time considering the money problem. Have none, owe plenty, can't pay.

* * *

I need a vacation from this vacation. Though I did write "Clown," "Crystal," "Frank O'Hara," & "Galaxies."

* * *

My body is heavy with poverty, starch. It uses up my sexual energy constantly, and I feel constantly crowded.

On the other hand, I read a lovely book today, *One Day in the Afternoon of the World*, that pervaded my life with a heavy grace, and brought tears to my eyes.

Fairfield Porter and I are doing a broadside with my poem "Scorpion, Eagle & Dove," and a drawing by Fairfield, a ceremonial occasion to celebrate that we are both in Southampton. Had lunch with Fairfield and Anne today and saw his new lithographs. He showed me a terrific book of lithographs by Vuillard. I walked home through town, stopping to browse in Bob Keene's inimitable bookstore.

* * *

Can't pay our bills, rent, heat, etc., despite money help from Joe, Anne, and readings. The landlord is freaking out, and so am I. Money will spoil any good time, if you let it. Ah well, next year to battle again for the dollars. Meanwhile the end of this season promises to be bleak.

* * *

"When a situation becomes so bad there is no possible solution, there is nothing left but murder or suicide. And failing both of these, one becomes a buffoon."

HENRY MILLER

* * *

I incorporated a lot of the above into a poem called "Today's News," published in Jimmy Schuyler's magazine, *49 South*.

* * *

Hokusai had 947 changes of address in his lifetime. Ha-ha.

* * *

Anne Waldman and I are writing *Memorial Day*.

* * *

Recent Visitors: Merrill Gilfillan; Bruce Wolmar & Denise Green; Dick & Chrissie Gallup; Lady Jean Campbell; Jayne Nodland and Joan Fagin; Ron Padgett & Jimmy Schuyler; Robert Vas Dias; Toby Olsen; David Ignatow; & the terrific American poet Anselm Hollo.

Anselm's poems are so good, and so American, he is easily among the best poets writing today. Shortly he will surface as the true Chinese master that he is. *Maya*, his last book, is only the beginning. He wasn't really a visitor, but I read his book today and yesterday and many times here. (Chicago.)

* * *

Alice is writing her sonnets, *165 Meeting House Lane*, and they are so good I am green with jealousy. Ed Dorn later will teach them at Kent State, and Edwin Denby will like them, which is something. It is Edwin that we all want to like our poems, and come to our readings.

* * *

Saturday Joan freaked out on acid and cried a lot, into Ron's consoling paw. But underneath she knew exactly what was going on, and so recovered nicely. Later she cooked dinner, washed dishes, and then we talked a lot about what had happened to her. She said it was all too fast to realize. Jayne rode through her trip fine, tho a bit smugly. Then the two girls who were nice guests, left, after some tiny flirtation between me and Joan (Who would do otherwise?). Then Alice threw a book at me (missed), we yelled a little, fell into bed, and had fun. A normal day in the country. Next day Alice had her period.

* * *

Alice left for Honolulu today. The phone company called and said they were going to shut off the phone. Ted Wilentz, bless him, advanced me the money to pay the phone bill. Bob Keene & Fairfield ran off our broadside on Bob's press today, and it came out fine. Fairfield did a lovely drawing for the poem, of the very spot in town where it came to me first. In the mail, I got a dollar bill from Ron, with a letter saying that he thought it would be nice to get money in the mail. I always think I want to be alone, and then when it happens I hate it. Thank God Merrill Gilfillan is coming tomorrow. He likes to look out the window.

* * *

My favorite writers are Maj Sjöwall & Per Wahlöö, who write the series of detective stories about policeman Martin Beck.

* * *

Recent Visitors: Lewis Warsh; Nancy Sullivan; Harris Schiff;
Margaret Notley & Fred; Devereaux Carson;
Pat & Wayne Padgett; Chuck Shaub.

* * *

What we did here: we played scrabble & did crosswords, did drawings and made tapes, wrote on collages by George Schneeman, did translations and wrote poems, made books for birthday presents, took out the garbage, walked to and by the ocean, talked with Larry Rivers, changed the furniture around, went to the Library, shot speed, took MDA, Valium, dexedrine, smoked hash and grass, visited Mike and Anne, & Fairfield and a different Anne, made phone calls, worried about money (constantly). Took train rides and sold books and went to galleries and gave poetry readings (here, NYC, Swarthmore, Washington D.C., Baltimore). Did a broadside with Fairfield, wrote letters and got mail, had poems accepted by magazines, went to Canada to read, drove around the countryside with a friend who later became a non-friend. Thought about Frank and Erje Ayden. Borrowed money and repaid it! Alice turned 25 here and I turned 36. I never did call up Bill de Kooning though I was dying to call on him.

* * *

I read *Roots of Heaven* by Romain Gary which I liked very much. And Anne and I wrote *Memorial Day* which was an accomplishment. 26 pages of serious collaboration.

* * *

My favorite records here were the Byrds album which began with "Ticket to Ride"; the Velvet Underground album with "Candy Says" on it, and the Mississippi John Hurt album with "The Angels Took Him Away" on it. I also listened to a lot of Bob Dylan.

* * *

Bernadette told the Women's Lib Consciousness Raising group that she had lived with Ed for 7 years, & had fallen in love a number of times with others during that time, too. The girls all said, "How did you do it?" The subject of that night's discussion was LOVE.

* * *

I'm eating a braunschweiger sandwich, on the bed; the rain is pouring down & the wind is flailing through the trees and houses outside. Alice is no doubt sitting at poolside in Honolulu at the Honolulu Hilton and drinking a pink gin.

* * *

Merrill arrived and said, "I had a real religious experience last week reading Bernadette's *Moving*; & since then I've been writing at least three hours a day."

* * *

Later he said, "It's incredible to write these works which really say something about yourself, & still meet all the requirements."

* * *

My favorite poem this winter has been "The Instruction Manual," by John Ashbery.

* * *

Alice is due back tomorrow. I'm reading, for the second time, *Death on the Installment Plan*, by Louis-Ferdinand Céline.

BOLINAS

* *

AN OLD MASTER STORY

Two Sides
of
A Coin:

heads: Philip Whalen

tails: John Ashbery

* *

Dead in 1969:   George "Gabby" Hayes, 83, Actor; Jimmy McHugh, 74,
Artist, creator of *Gasoline Alley*; William Coffman, 86, founder
of East-West Shrine Game; Dwight David Eisenhower, 78,
former President of the U.S.; William Henry Pratt, 81,
Actor (Boris Karloff); Ludwig Mies Van der Rohe, 83,
Architect; Nathaniel Lovecorne, 83, vending-machine
tycoon; William Friedman, 78, Crypto-Analyst; Sieg-
fried Gunter, 60, Co-designer of the first operational
jet bomber; Karl Jaspers, 86, Philosopher; Ho Chi Minh,
86, President of North Vietnam; Irene Castle, 75, Ball-
room dancer; Bella Dodd, 64, Informer; Violet & Daisy
Hilton, 60, Siamese Twins.

* *

A Dream

I was shooting pool at Julian's Pool Hall, 14th Street and 3rd Avenue in NYC with Jim
Carroll (red hair) on a green pool table. Leaning over to shoot I noticed that instead of pool
balls we were shooting at martinis in solid triple shot size glasses. I thought this was ok, but I
wondered if they would roll toward the pockets when the cue ball hit them. It was just a mild
passing thought as I lined up the shot.

* *

A Postcard from Frank O'Hara, circa 1961:   "Dear Ted Berrigan: Boy you certainly know how to cheer a person up. Thank you very much for your letter and for the poems which I like a lot especially "Traditional Manner," "Biographers," and "Words for Love." Forgive this card, I thought perhaps you could give me a call at work during the weekdays (Circle 5-8900) and we could meet for a drink or something. Also, do you want to meet K Koch? He's great. Anyhow, if you want the poems back before we arrange to meet let me know and I'll mail them. Otherwise I'll give them back when I see you.   Best, (signed) Frank O'Hara."

* *

Jungle Life: I was on the bed, next to Donna, who was napping, and I thought, why not write a poem now, except I'll be Donna, though I won't say that in the poem, just write it. I wrote, "I am asleep next to The Hulk . . ." and it ended, "No matter. We live together in the jungle."

* *

"All skill is joyful." —Yeats.

"A poet writes always of his personal life in his finest work out of its tragedy, whatever it could be, remorse, lost love, or mere loneliness; he never speaks directly as to someone at the breakfast table, there is always a phantasmagoria."

I wonder who said that.

* *

The trouble with teaching in Universities is that you get lots of books in the mail with titles like *An Anthology of Contemporary American Poetry*, edited by guys with names like Mark Strand, and that have two or three poems in them that you like a lot which haven't been printed anywhere else so that you don't want to throw the book away and you're stuck with the whole (general) piece of shit.

* *

Jim Dine talking: "I'm very authoritarian about my works: I *make* them be good."

* *

"Found Picasso, Jean Cocteau, & William Carlos Williams in a blue river, in London."

* *

"Nothing is gained by assurance as to what is insecure."—Carl Sauer.

* *

Bolinas: July 27th, 1971:   We've stayed up all night, packed & ready to go we await
                  the arrival of Lewis MacAdams. At 4:30 in the afternoon he comes, and we
                  leave 2031-B Oak Street, San Francisco, for Bolinas, California. Lewis enter-
                  tains us on the way there with talk about the Bolinas Sewage problem. By 8
                  p.m. Alice and I are moved into Larry Kearney's place on Birch Street on the
                  Bolinas Mesa. Sue Burke, now Mrs. John Thorpe, lives in the next room.

              The next day, July 28th, we wake up at noon, drink coffee, and go
downtown; walking, Alice, Sue, & me. Alice shops for groceries, Lewis MacAdams loses at pool
to me, as do a few others, inside Smiley's Bar. Somebody drives us home, for lunch.
                                                                        After lunch,
me & Alice walk over to Bill's, to see Bill (Berkson). He returns our poems to us, and invites
us to dinner later. Then we three walk over to Don Allen's to borrow the mss. of *Scenes of
Life at the Capitol* by Philip Whalen. Don isn't there. Alice & I go home to read. Bill does
too.
    7 p.m. we walk to Bill's for dinner. We are met by Bob & Bobbie Creeley, who have a
bottle of champagne for us to welcome us to town. Bobbie shows Bill how to cook fried blank
for our dinner, with zucchini & mushrooms. Bill cooks the steaks to leather so the vegetables
help considerably. A terrific dinner. Joanne flashes, Bob beams, Bill grins, Alice strikes poses for
Bob and for Bill, Bobbie holds forth beautifully, I make speeches, flirt & flatter sincerely, laugh
to hear the crazy music, as Jack would say. We go home, to sleep, but first I work on George's
drawings. Go to sleep at 5 a.m.

* *

(On vacation from San Francisco in Grand Valley, Michigan, June 6th–14th, the author,
together with the poet Anselm Hollo, had occasion to co-found "The New Choctaw Nation."
    Into the valley of death rode the 600, shouting "dig it!")

* *

"I really felt that if an elephant were not standing on your foot then you really had no right to say anything."—Robert Creeley.

I remember I copied that into this journal because I was copying everything pithy about elephants.

* *

Marcel Duchamp: "50 pages is long enough for a book."

* *

Random Notes (Bolinas)

Where you sit & type is wherever. Where you live is where you write: and vice versa ad infinitum.

Where you live is "your place." It's where you can be found, generally speaking, like as not.

You eat, drink, fuck, sleep, receive & entertain there: raise your kids, answer calls, leave from & come back home to there. You grow old and die there. You grew up there and you were born there. Privacy is yours for the taking there. There's always someone about, there. "Don't cheat, the victory is not always to the sweet."

The middle is where your guts rise up over your balls. It's where it hurts, where you talk from, where it feels good. From there you take your falls. "The America dilemma is *No Middle.*"

"See the why, knowing what: the clear enigma."

"I can get close and still stay outside." —Darrell Devore

"What mattered was an attitude."

"Speak the language of everyday into the readers' dream." —John Ashbery

"Ezra Pound : A Witness."

* *

Bolinas, in the final analysis, for you, for me, there is, alas, quote unquote. No use.

                                      The black eye is your favorite salutation.
I don't have time to suffer.

                                        * *

ROUTINE

I have a terrible memory
I don't forget. I save for
The future, for some rainy day
Just for the hell of it.
You know. You've been through that.

                                      * *

2 Found Words   Cozy Wisdom

                                      * *

I must ask Philip Whalen where he learned to throw such clean tantrums.

                                      * *

Wrong but Close: The main thing, speaking while still conscious, I've
                         learned, it seems, from Ed & Peg Berrigan, my Mom
                         & Dad, might be stated as, "that a person can only do
                         whatever it is he *must* do, because that's all he *can*
                         do, no matter what he might *want* or *try* to do."

                                      * *

"The body sends out self to repel non-self."

                                      * *

"When the mind is free, the body is delicate." —Wm Shakespeare

                                      * *

"Through not taking himself quietly enough, he strained his insides."
                                              —Alfred Lord Tennyson

SELECTIONS FROM A JOURNAL

1 NOV 77 TO 17 MAY 78

*

1 Nov. '77   Today I read *The Three Bears* and *The ABC Book* to Anselm & Edmund.
                                                                                        Steve
Carey came over, haven't seen him since 1969. He said he first read "C" (The Nancy Cover
Issue) at Allen Ginsberg's suggestion. Allen sd there was a guy (me) in NY that wrote like Steve.
Steve was prepared to hate it, but loved my & Ron's poem, "For Frank O'Hara's Birthday."

Nov. 2   Jeff Wright came over with $20.00 "Royalties" for the postcards by Alice, & (the one)
by Me & Bob Creeley. A timely arrival of $.

Nov. 3   Wrote to The MacDowell Colony to recommend Anselm Hollo for a stint there. He'd
listed me as an endorser.
                  Bob (Rosenthal) came by & said Allen (Ginsberg) is wanting to hire
someone to type up his 50–60 pages of Dylan notes into shape. Said I wd love to, sooner the
better. He said he'd tell Allen. (Rent for last month still due.)

Nov. 1&2   Harris stayed over two nights.

Nov. 2   Harris & me [went] to hear Ed Friedman & Hannah Weiner read. Annabel Levitt sd
she *will* do *Train Ride* by Winter late or Spring & that Joe Brainard had said he'd be glad to do
the cover.
       Simon Schuchat came by Nov. 3 (tonight) & I suggested that badmouthing his boss at
The Poetry Project, plus gossiping was maybe a poor practice at best, didn't he think? And he
with a dawning of revelation look, admitted it probably was something he didn't really want
to do. Simon makes plenty waves, but thank god, he's someone you can talk to like a person

& he answers like a person, too. I'm *for* him in the end, as always, but I do wish he'd connect his dots more often.

*

The different ways of showing no emotion

use formal balance a lot

throw something onto it

see through ears

ask intelligent questions

behind eyes doubt

suspend self in age time warp

mildly defend honor of minor character endlessly

bore steadily into other person's eyes

complete other's sentences obscurely

relate data given to current state of the economy

*

8 Nov.   For Alice's 32nd birthday, from 1 p.m. til Midnight these people came by w/ presents, drinks, greetings: Lee Sherry, James Sherry, Tom Savage, Mike Disend, Barbara Barg, Joe Chassler, Nora & Zack Chassler (kids), Steve Levine, Rose Lesniak, Marion Farrier, Simon Pettet, Rosebud, Eileen Myles, Tom Carey, Michael Scholnick, Rene Ricard, George Schneeman, Katie Schneeman, Bob Rosenthal, Shelley Kraut Rosenthal, plus Paul Schneeman sent over a signed copy of his magazine and Frances Waldman took Alice to 1 Fifth Avenue for a drink, also Ron & my mother sent cards & Beulah $50.00, bless her heart. Bob & Shelley made dinner w/ cake made by Shelley. Jim Brodey came with a mixed vegetable present the next day, and Simon Schuchat & Susie Timmons came over to say Happy Birthday. So did Harris Schiff. Kate & David & Sandy sent us both birthday greetings.

16 Nov.   Bernadette & Lewis sent a postcard to announce the Nov. 13th birth of Sophia Crystal (Mayer) Warsh.

Nov. 24th: Thanksgiving 1977   Marion made dinner and Alice made an apple pie after I borrowed a pie plate and a cup of sugar from George Schneeman. George has two outstanding new frescoes, one of Alice and one of Harris, and a very nice one of Ada & Brooke Schjeldahl, in which Brooke looks especially terrific.

Anselm, alas, got a "bug" on the morning of Thanksgiving, & had fever and throwing up all day, tho not unhappily sick. I stayed home with him while Alice & Edmund went to Marion's where they had Thanksgiving and chatted, Alice did, with her mother on the phone. Beulah is definitely coming for Christmas, which is nice.

Then they brought me an enormous platter of turkey, dressing, potatoes, yams, and vegetables, & pie. The two girls went off to see the NYC Ballet do *Square Dance* & *Viennese Waltzes* by Balanchine. I drew animals for the kids & Tom Carey came over with pumpkin pie. I read *Monty*.

*

Philip Whalen on metrics: "The connection is to music, as far as I can see . . . as it relates to a musical experience, a musical feeling in the line, happening between the words, or happening as the poetic line . . . it's a musical shot for me and that's what I hear when I write."

from "Bread & Poetry" 1963

*

Dec. 24th 1977 NYC   11:30 p.m.   Steve Carey & Colette Farrier and I took Anselm to see *Star Wars*. Alice had a new Christmas haircut (her present from, not by, me) & took Edmund uptown to play with Will & see Grandma (Beulah).

I bought Marion a Rolling Stones album. After supper Alice hung up the *Star Wars* poster I'd bought Anselm, and the Careys, Steve, Effie & Tom, and Simon Pettet & I went for drinks at Anne Waldman's. Talked with Larry Fagin, Jamie MacInnis, Reed Bye, Ted Greenwald & Steven Hall. Then came home so Alice & Helena could go over to Anne's. Alice had put all the presents for tomorrow under the tree & filled the kids' stockings. We picked out a Joe Brainard we owned to give Helena. Note: (Anne & I talked about Dick & Ron, and Lewis & Bernadette.) Had letters today from Michael (Brownstein), Lewis MacAdams, Debbie Daley, Anselm Hollo, and news of Hilda Morley. George's January poster came in the mail. Now I'm reading *Blind Date* by Jerzy Kosinski.

Weds 28 Dec – heard Anne W. & Reed Bye at St Marks

Thurs 29 Dec – introduced A.G. & Jim Brodey at New Morning bookstore

Fri 30 Dec – Read in Poetry Calendar benefit

Dec 31st–Jan 1st 1977–78   New Year's Eve 1977 – Fred and Margaret brought little William over at 9:30 and they went out for New Years. William stayed awake & was part of the festivities till 1:00 a.m.

Steve Carey & Effie came over at 10:15 and we drank wine & watched *Kojak*. At 10:30 Tom Carey came over with brandy. Tom left for Simon Schuchat's party at 11:15.

Steve & Effie & Alice & I watched Guy Lombardo's brother and Times Sq. on TV till 12:30, drank wine and swapped exaggerations & memories & drank champagne & kissed at midnight. We also sang "Show me the Way to go Home" & Steve & Tom earlier sang "Tumblin' Tumbleweeds."

Now it's after 1 and Steve & Effie have left, and it's 1978. Wm. is asleep, Edmund & Anselm just drank milk. The Beatles are singing "Love, Love, Love," & we're awaiting Fred & Margaret. I'm reading *The Biography of Richie Powers*, NBA Referee. Read a Memoir of Pasternak earlier. Alice is reading Peter Bogdanovich's *Pieces of Time*. Edmund just said plaintively "Daddy?" "What?"

Marguerite Harris died of cancer on New Year's Day. An old friend from Le Metro days, and for whom I read last year at Dr. Generosity's. She was nearly 80 years old. (Harris Schiff called her last week, about a reading for himself, and she said, "I'm sorry, I'm dying of cancer and I can't think about readings just now." I told him not to worry about it.)

Jan. 4th   It is said by Martin Green that C.P. Snow is in no way representative of the English Imagination. But *Strangers & Brothers* is precisely the England and the English that an American can imagine (and in my case, see).

9–10 Jan.   Went to hear Jim Brodey read with rock music at St. Mark's. Heard Jayne Nodland give a terrific performance reading with music. Alice then went to hear Tom Carey sing with Vinnie Katz's band. Alex & Ada & Larry Rivers, Joe LeSueur, Ron, Anne & everyone in the world were there. Began again typing *Train Ride*—got to page 22—12 typescript pages.

Tues Jan 10th–11th (4:30 a.m.) Awake at noon, French bread & rice krispies, made bed, drank juice, swallowed 10mg dexie, put on navy-blue gym shorts & green Boulder t-shirt, Alice gone off to take Anselm to school. Laid in bed, smoked, read on in *A Small Town in Germany*. Edmund played with trucks.

Got up, put away toys, resumed typing *Train Ride*—Alice brought home *The Post*, cigarettes, and Steve Carey came over.

Steve said he thought *Train Ride*, which I'd given him to read (in handscript) was terrific. I typed on. Had coffee. Tom was pleased with last night, said Steve.

Played tape of Anne & Ted first reading of *Memorial Day* for Steve. It was good as ever. Alice picked up Anselm. No one came with money.

I departed for the St. Mark's Church, to beg typing paper, pick up a shirt John Daley had sent me from Buffalo, & scavenge for $. Steve & Alice stayed home to drink coffee Steve had brought over.

Freezing cold out (20°). I took out garbage. At church gave Poetry Calendars (received on street from Greg Masters) to Ron. Chatted w/Ron & Bob Holman. Bob left. Ron & I discussed Poetry Project, clicked, got ream of mimeo (typing paper), commended Bob (Rosenthal) & Eileen (Myles) to Ron & Paul Violi's good interim director work.

Ron walked me to 12th & A, he to go home, I to Simon Pettet's for tea w/ Helena & Charlie, Marion, Simon. Simon's grant $ didn't arrive, so no dough. Helena postponed leaving for England till Saturday. Had coffee & Simon gave me a desoxyn (13 mg) which I took. Read a good poem by Simon written preceding night.

Marion & I left. I get home w/ no dollar for dinner at 6 p.m. Alice & Eileen are drinking brandy, Steve more coffee. Kids playing & watching comic cartoons on T.V.

Alice took 2 *Clear the Ranges* and 2 *Red Wagons* to the East Side Bookstore to sell for $8.40. Eileen & Steve leave. I clean up living room. Type more *Train Ride*. Alice returns w/ hotdogs, diapers, olive oil, 2 beers, rolls, tampax, 2 Chesterfield Kings, and ten cents.

Eileen left ¼ pint of brandy for Alice. Supper. The kids we put into the bath. Nick Maxwell comes over, says goodbye, leaves for England. We sent books to Paul Shevlin via Nick.

Bob Rosenthal arrives. Gives me Dalmane (sleeper). I give him Dexedrine. He gives us $2.00 to buy milk, bread & honey for kids breakfast.

I type more *Train Ride*. It seems to be working.

Earlier mail brought letter from Anselm Hollo asking us 4 poems for local Minnesota Mag, praises my poems I sent him for other mag.

Bob leaves, see him tomorrow at Steve's reading with Allan Kaplan at St. Marks.

#

Tom Carey arrives. Helena arrives. Tom plotzed. They chat, I type. Tom says he was great last night.

Helena says maybe Tom can play at CBGB's. She'll ask Charlie. Helena broke.

I go to store, get breakfast, spend Bob's $2.00.

Call Katie Schneeman to see if she'll babysit for the reading tomorrow night. No one home. 11 p.m.

Helena says she'll babysit. Tom gives me cigarette $1.00 for tomorrow. Leaves. Helena leaves.

We did eat the hot dogs, w/ salad, earlier.

Alice reads Waugh (*Diaries*) & Williams (later poems). I finish typing *Train Ride*, first typescript of handwritten poem. 59 pages come out 31 typed. When retyped will be over 40.

It's 3 a.m. Alice to bed. I putter around, read poems, earlier watched Knicks lose to Portland & Bill Walton, who killed them.

In bed, 3:45, read *For Love of Ray*, after finishing (again) *Oracle Night*, & discussing it endlessly w/ Alice, i.e., I made speech about "bearing down."

Alice & I vibrate, she mostly asleep, I reading, so, lights off we fuck.

Later, lights on, Alice sleeping, I take Dalmane, write these notes, leaving out chat with Ted & Janet Williams in cold outside (Janet is lovely), leaving out conversation at 2nd Ave & St Marks w/ Irving Stettner, re me giving him poem for his magazine *Stroker*, & him giving me 10 bucks on publication. You don't have to, I said. No, I got a grant, he said. Terrific. Leaving out brewing up of pill deal, Tom, Helena, Simon, me, for Friday.

Still awake, 5 p.m. Finishing this, dalmane laid back but not me. Dinner tonight with Anne Waldman & Reed Bye, then reading. Sleep, when?

P.S. Read Jim Brodey's "Poem" in *Dodgems* twice today.

11 Jan. Wednesday.   Reed Bye came over and borrowed a set of "C" Magazines, & all the "C" Press books, & *Memorial Day*. Alice & the kids went to dinner at Anne & Reed's. I stayed home & read the letters of Anne Sexton.

13 Jan. 11 p.m.   Finished reading *Anne Sexton, A Biography in Letters*. What a remarkable woman. She seemed to have no talent, but for evoking a mood, which was real. The poetry is terrible, but the woman is really something. She wrote the poetry that seemed poetry-as-truth to those who recognized the state(s) of mind (something to do with anguish, something to do with momentary triumph without false hopeful note).

Jan. 13–14 2 a.m.   Finished typing final complete version of the whole "Harris Schiff" poem I wrote, titled "In the Pines." 2pp. seems good.

Jan. 14   Typed up first stencil of the Ted Berrigan – Eileen Myles issue of *Caveman*. Called my mother to wish her Happy Birthday.

15 Jan.   Watched Super Bowl w/ Steve Carey. Jeff Wright visited & brought over new postcards by himself, Bob Rosenthal, and Allen Ginsberg.

Typed up 3 more stencils for *Caveman*. Had a beer with Simon Schuchat, Jim Brodey, Greg Masters & Steve Levine at the Grassroots. Talked to Rachel Walling.

Told Simon I'd review his book for the newsletter if Frances said OK. Discussing Art Lange's *Monk Poems* with Jim Brodey. Finished Courty Bryan's *Friendly Fire*. Alice went over to help Marion paint. We have 25¢.

Jan. 18th   Typed up stencil #6 for *Caveman*—arranged with Ron to use the mimeo Friday evening.

Jan. 19th—A letter from Bernadette saying she liked my critical piece and was furious with *Language* for not using it.

Marion said Dick liked my letter and said I was getting "younger." Ha! He's getting senile.
Frances Waldman said I should review Simon's *Light and Shadow* for the *Newsletter*.
Typed up stencil #7 for *Caveman*, only 1 more to go.

#

Finished *Caveman* (8pp) and arranged for Bob to help me with the stencils for tomorrow at 10.

Simon Pettet came over and got addresses to send the announcement for his reading with Corky April Sunday at Rose & Barbara's.

Alice is about to go out in the blinding snow to George & Katie's to call her mother.

Jan. 20 Ran off *Caveman* & collated it & brought it home, all with the help of Bob Rosenthal. Today's visitors: Tom Carey, Steve Carey, Steve Levine, Michael Scholnick, Eileen Myles, Bob & Shelley, I went out and visited Anne & Reed & talked with Irving Stettner, & Liz, & John Perreault.

Anne loaned me Jon Cott's *Forever Young*.

"Structural clarification always releases new energy"
                  Jon Cott on Glenn Gould

Had a letter from the *New Republic* saying Allen Ginsberg had given them my name and wd I like to review Conrad Aiken's letters for $100.00. I wrote back and said sure, send me the book. I'll be interested to see if I do it.

Jan. 28 Went to hear Harris Schiff, Gary Lenhart, Michael Scholnick & Didi Susan read at the Free Association.

Marion came over beset by anemia.

The children of Jim Brodey are coming into their own.

Tomorrow Steven Hall has left some tickets to *The Red Robins* for me and Alice at the box office. Steve Carey said he would babysit.

11:00 Listening to Bill Burroughs on WBAI with Harris & Alice. "The Right to Mind Your Own Business."

Sun 29 Jan. *The Red Robins* was very pretty and very touching. The sets were beautiful, but the play itself was wonderful. Brian Glover as the Easter bunny, & Taylor Mead in 8 parts were both very good. Especially Glover whose diction & control was powerful and fierce. Alice and I were moved to tears more than once.

Rachel Towle was there & sat with us, & Irving Sandler, and Steve Hamilton, Brad Gooch and Alfred Milanese. Kenneth sat in front of us and said afterwards that he hoped we would come to all his shows and laugh a lot (loudly) as I was doing constantly.

The hideous Don Schrader has a few hideous parts which he performed with despicable competence. He is hideous.

Steve took care of the kids all day & read to them and kept them happy. He even changed Edmund's diaper twice.

Jan. 30 Went to see Greg Masters, who was good, read at St Marks.

Had lunch with Allen Ginsberg, Alice, Steve Carey & Simon Schuchat at Dojos.

Visited Anne & chatted with Peter Warshall & Reed. Anne & I considered the updating of Ron's anthology for Full Court Press. We smoked P.W.'s Calif. grass & Anne & I got blasted and blushed and burst out laughing & hugged each other. Then I left.

Feb. 4 Alice went to the ballet with Edwin today with a hangover from going to Steve Levine's party with Edmund.

Today I discussed "Literature" w/ Peter Schjeldahl, then with James Sherry, Jim Brodey, Mike Sappol, Jeff Wright and Danny Krakauer, & Didi & Mitch. James bought some cough syrup for Edmund who was sick. Steve watched the kids while I went out prospecting for the cough syrup. Tonight Annabel came over to discuss the reading tomorrow by her and Alice. They arranged for Tom Carey to babysit.

Then I went to see Harris and we discussed our reading (with Steve) next week & videotaping and Gurdjieff. We drank some of Gurdjieff's favorite brandy, Armagnac, and how we would bury each other at the reading was the main topic. We also discussed George's work (not bad) and Bob Rosenthal's review of same. Harris urged me to get some transpersonification elements from Allen, and I said Allen doesn't do that. So . . .

Feb. 6 Steve and I went to visit Harris, and I went to pick up a novel mss. from Al Simmons at the post office in a blizzard. Bob Rosenthal visited.

George & Katie brought over 3 kinds of cheese, wine, and some Johnny Stanton homemade brandy.

Feb. 7 Tonight went to dinner at Sing Wu's with Harris & Paul Pines. Paul & I swapped Paul Blackburn stories.

Feb. 8 My black pen returned from outer space. Woke up today broke, Alice & Edmund sick, Anselm recovering. Mail brought a poem from Lee Anderson in Minnesota, a review of *Gunslinger* by John Daley from Buffalo and an invitation to open house at The Bragr Times bookstore. I promised Anselm I'd take him to Ron's reading at St Marks.

Out to look for money. No one home at Anne & Reed's, so I couldn't take the "C" Magazines I'd loaned Reed to the Phoenix bookstore to sell. No one in the East Side bookstore. My feet wet & cold. Trudged to 12th St & 1st Ave—called Simon Pettet. No answer. Met Simon Schuchat who took me to DeRoberti's for hot chocolate and bought me a pack of cigarettes. Went with him to 437 E. 12th to visit Peter O. who has sciatica, & Allen & Bob. Instead, Simon Pettet was home. Had coffee, discussed Alice's reading and Gerry Malanga's poems & Ralph Hawkins' poems. Saw Gerry's pictures of Simon P. Simon offered me a loan of 20 dollars for 3 weeks. I said great. We went out to change a 100-dollar bill. Simon brought along a cardboard toilet paper center and an empty razor blade packet to remind him to buy razor blades & toilet paper. We agreed Helena should come back to NY.

We went to Steve's Sleazy Cafe and had cheeseburger & grilled cheese, and told Jim Brodey Stories. Simon says Jim is a sexist (I say No) but agrees Jim does not think women inferior to men, but the contrary. Simon blithely presents Steve the Cafe Front Man with 100-dollar bill for 3.00 check. Steve says Wha? You crazy? Simon says no, English. Steve puts 100-dollar bill in machine which lights up and says it's OK. He gets change for it from unshaven guy who is mopping the floor. Tape Ron's reading, says Simon, I have to go hear Denise record tonight. She says in taxi, I really *like* fucking! freaking out taxi driver.

I say Harris will. Simon says he will tape reading by me, Steve Carey, and Harris Saturday. Too many Steve's for one day. Harris plans to read outstanding new work at reading. I wish him luck I say. Goodbye.

I go to Garibaldi's, buy *Post* on way. Buy milk, bread, cornflakes, yogurts, pepsi, cigarettes at Garibaldi's, come home with $14.00. Alice tells me about mucus, Edmund drinks my pepsi, Anselm is building giant dinosaur and automobile battlefield in living room, watching *Popeye* on TV.

Newspaper says many more weeks of snow. Sports news: Wilt Chamberlain to change name to Abdul-Bill-Russell. It is 5 in the afternoon. Another day, another dollar.

Feb. 14 On Feb. 11th Harris, Steve and I gave a terrific reading for 120 people at the Free Association. All the Younger People & Rudy & Yvonne, George & Katie, Ron, Anne & Reed, Allen Ginsberg, Johnny Stanton, John Godfrey, Lou Reed, Steve Rubell, Diana Vreeland and Tip O'Neill.

Ron said of our reading, "you guys are a very classy act." Rudy filmed Harris during reading. Allen Ginsberg sent us (me & Alice) over $8.00 to go to the Dylan movie but we were too poor and had to buy groceries. Maybe we'll go tomorrow.

Alice is writing a poem from Linda's guide in *The Poet's Home Companion* after typing up her "flu" poem earlier. I'm reading *The Earl of Louisiana* for the tenth time.

Lewis called & said *Nothing for You* is in the mail, with a few cover eccentricities and to call him if it's all right. He also asked me to write a blurb for Lita Hornick's flyer for his forthcoming book, *Blue Heaven (poems)* which I just finished doing.

Steve is reading his way through A. J. Liebling with glee. He loved *The Earl, The Road Back to Paris*, & is reading *The Press*. Hurray for another Liebling fan.

Feb. 16th   Alice brought me John Cheever's *Falconer* from the bookstore and we bought Steve a bottle of brandy for his toothache.

Unfortunately Muhammad Ali lost the heavyweight championship of the world to Leon Spinks on TV.

Steve Facey at St. Marks sd he'd help me get the paper to print a book by Steve Carey.

A bag lady said to call her tomorrow for a dime bag.

Feb. 18th   Marion babysat while Alice and I went to see *Renaldo & Clara*, Bobby Dylan's movie, last night, on the $8.00 Allen sent over with Bob for us to go see it. It was a wonderful movie, just like a major work by a first-novelist. We loved it. Most of my "old" friends have "reservations." Wonder where they heard about that?

Now Steve is here and we are all talking about the movie, reading Alice's new poem, watching *Women of the Prehistoric Planet*, and exulting because Beulah sent us $20 in the mail. The mail also brought a *Cattle Mutilation Report* from Ed Sanders. "Great California Bellies!" Steve just said. Anselm & Edmund are discussing the right place for Diplodocus. I'm reading *3 in the Tower*, Louis Simpson's first generosity-of-spirit work. "When are you going out for my *Star-Wars* cards dad?" says Anselm. Steve is singing "Short People."

Alice said "I didn't get to put a hinge in the hinge-place," about her poem. She's full of it.

I'm still reading the *Letters of Conrad Aiken* including the one to me.

Still Feb. 18th (tho a.m. of 19th)   Wrote "Red Shift" using Linda's form. *Brokethrough into new tone of voice first time ever able to "get" in poem.* Possibly a very good poem.

Am still excited hours later.

Feb. 20th   I have to call Peter Orlovsky at 2 tomorrow to talk about the job of typing up his mss. for him. It pays $3.50 an hr, and Simon Schuchat hadn't gotten far into it before he left for England, carrying letters of Intro. from me, last night.

If Peter feels we can work together OK, it should be OK, if I just don't push at him too much.

Today's visitors: Chasslers, Norah, Zack, Steve Carey, Simon Pettet, Annabel, Eileen who brought stencils, Tom Carey, Johnny Stanton, and Harris Schiff, The Exterminator.

Steve brought over 8 more poems to go with the 14 I've typed on stencils and so his book will be 22 pp plus title, dedication and copyright page etc. Maybe 200 copies.

Steve Facey, who said he'd get me the paper, confirmed today that he wd. Now to get the title and a cover from George, who agreed to do it.

Typing up Steve's poems is illuminating, his moves are so perfectly his and so impeccably accurate to precision of emotion as well as quality of.

Alice to read in Chicago Mar 6th & 7th for $150 and in Buffalo for $250 March 10th with possible other Buffalo reading. W/ Hank Kanabus in Chi / With Anselm Hollo in Buffalo.

24th Feb.   This morning Harris came over, at 10:00 on his way up to the Bronx. His mother was having a crisis. I gave him a couple of pills, and he went off, to see what would happen.

Two nights ago George was stricken with back-ailment pain, and hailed a cop's car at 3 a.m. to go to the Hospital. Tests revealed a kidney-stone, but George being George then pissed & passed it out and went home. What a man!

Today I went to work for Peter Orlovsky at Allen's. I typed 2 poems and a song, helped him correct mistakes in his *Gay Sunshine* Interview, and typed a letter to Don Allen. Brought home Peter's mss. to xerox to send a copy to Don. Allen told Peter to tell me they'd pay me $5.00 an hour, which is generous of him, and also hilarious.

Feb. 25th Saturday   Worked 3 hours with Peter O. on his mss. today. Chatted with Allen.

Finished typing & fixing Steve's stencils. The book—*The Lily of St. Marks*—is all ready to go—waiting for the cover and for Steve to decide on the order.

Feb. 27   After putting Steve's poems in the order of appearance in his book, I brilliantly took one of Julius Orlovsky's Mellarils, and went into a semi-coma from Saturday evening to Monday afternoon. It was a nice rest, but I did wonder if I would ever become un-lobotomized and return to a vertical position again. Today at about 3:15 I did so, tho even now, at midnight, I'm not entirely returned.

Finished *Tortilla Flat* by John Steinbeck this afternoon and am now reading 6 *New Yorkers*.

Mar. 1   Last night Steve & I went to see Sam Shepard's *The Curse of the Starving Class* which was wonderful. A vastly pregnant lady left abruptly in the middle of the first act.

Today I worked at Allen's on Peter's mss. for 2 hours and am working on it at home now. Found one terrific poem in 1960 journal about signature changing.

March 3   Worked at Peter's today 2–5. 20 copies of *Nothing for You* arrived in the mail today.

March 4 3 hrs at Peter's today, found 2 terrific poems. Lights went out at 7; I went out, came back, lights still off at 10:40, went on (came on) at 10:55. Heat off, just came on at 12:30. Alice reading Shakespeare, me reading Sporting News, about to type Steve's poems.

March 5 Lights were out last night too. Are on now. We went to Marion's for roast beef dinner. Returned at 10. Harris comes over. His mother had died Wednesday & been buried on Thursday. I feel so fucking helpless.

Today Steve & Tom took the kids to see *Animals Animals* at their house, brought them back at 1. Bob Rosenthal came over with Alice's flight to Chicago $. The Careys and Bob & Alice watched the two Carey grandfathers & Harry Carey Jr. in *Red River*. Alice prepared for her trip. I finished Peter Orlovsky's India journals. Now it's near midnight, Alice leaves tomorrow for a week to Chicago & Buffalo, the kids & I got to George & Katie's for dinner & to pick up the cover for Steve's book from George.

March 6 Monday Alice left for Chicago this morning at 11. I kept Anselm home from school because he was coughing, but later took the kids to cash a check for $50.00 received from Minnesota, and then to the L&M for frosted flakes and a milkshake.

Called Bob Rosenthal at Allen's & told him I wouldn't be in today. Shopped for bread, milk, juice, butter, cigarettes & pepsi.

Steve came over at 3. The gay Doctor had prescribed valium for him & he gave me 5.

Bought a thriller at The East Side bookstore, and now we're waiting for it to be time to go to George & Katie's for dinner. The kids are drawing and watching *The Flintstones*.

Now it's 11:05, we're back from delicious dinner at Katie's. Anselm and I are lying in my bed waiting to watch Allen Ginsberg on the *Dick Cavett Show*. Tonight earlier I typed up the stencil for Steve's poem "Old Year," which will be the final poem in the book. Tomorrow Bob & I will run it off at the Church.

March 11 Alice returns tomorrow and what have I done since she left? Well, Tuesday I typed up four more poems that Steve brought over, and also paid Ron for the paper and maybe paid him Monday? and Tuesday night went to dinner with the kids at Steve & Tom's w/ Kate Hammond there also. Then I went with Bob Rosenthal to the Church & we ran off Steve's book and chatted with Johnny Stanton.

Wednesday ran out of pills & slept a lot. Thursday went to Peter & Allen's. No one there, got paid $50.00 and came home and read book by Harold Clurman and went to sleep. Friday came & Harris came by, Marion cooked a big dinner, Harris gave me pills, I read *On the Road*, a little. Anselm & I watched the Knicks game, I fixed the clock, it's 3:30 a.m.

March 15th   Got Steve's covers. Made 3 copies of his book—will finish it tomorrow. Worked on Peter's mss. 11–2—typed up 5 poems.

March 16th   Grandma sent 20 today. Steve & I & Simon Pettet collated ½ of Steve's book & now (8:30) Alice & Steve are over doing the rest at the Church. We didn't receive Alice's check from *Poets & Writers* but Marion volunteered to loan us the fare, so we are all off (A & me & the kids) to Lenox, Mass. tomorrow to visit with Lewis & Bernadette. Happily Tom will come by at 10 with pills.

Stupid ass Tom did not get pills but I love him anyway.

Tues evening.   Michael Galvin from Australia came to visit—said he'd reviewed *Early Morning Rain* in *The Sydney Papers*. He & John Forbes like my work. I gave him *Red Wagon* & one for Jack Forbes & said I'd be happy to come to Australia for a year to teach if I were invited. We'd bought wine for his visit but Slice & Marion drank it before he arrived. "Give him beer," said Marion, "he's an Australian, he'll think it's champagne."

Am working on Peter's poems & watching the Knicks.

March 22nd.   Barry Hall showed up after 3½ years—We all went to Joanne Kyger's reading at the Church.

Easter Sunday.   Went to breakfast with the Carey's & Liz—had potatoes & eggs & hid Easter-egg candy for the kids. Then, while Alice, Steve & kids went to Marion's for dinner, I went to read in Dick Miller's benefit w/Simon Pettet & Kathy Acker. Got drunk & left my poems behind but Dick Miller recovered them.

Allen's check for $75.00 arrived today, I paid Bob his 25 and we bought pills. Hallelujah!

Now tonight to write a few more Peter Orlovsky journals up as poems.

But first to watch Kentucky vs. Duke on TV with Little Anselm.

April 7th.   Worked 4 hrs on Peter's mss. Gave Steve $10 to go to the doctor—Reread *Chas. Olson in Connecticut*. Watched Mets opening game

Koosman beat Expos.

April 14th. Alice off to Washington D.C. Monday last, the 10th, I introduced John Godfrey, Alice & Jim Brodey to a crowd of over 200 at the Museum of Modern Art, where I said of Alice that "just to lay it on the line, she is the most exciting poet to come down the pike since Jimmy Schuyler & Frank O'Hara were making friends and writing their poems in the mid-fifties in New York City." The folks gasped, and Alice gave me a stricken look, but then she gave an electrifying reading that people including Alex Katz are still talking about today. When I said the above abt Alice, Rene Ricard turned to Alex Katz & said in a piercing stage-whisper, "Ted must be speeding!" Alex just stared at him as if he'd lost his mind. (Rene reported the above to me after the reading.)

Last night Alice read in Washington at Folio books, yesterday at the Corcoran School. Tomorrow Harris & I read at the West End. Monday I'm off to Chicago, Champagne, Notre Dame & Iowa City for a week of readings.

Got a fan ltr from Anselm Hollo for *Nothing For You*. I talked to Bill Berkson on the phone who also praised *NFY* & said he's looking forward to seeing us May 15th.

Shelley, vastly pregnant, said she would replace me at dinner with Carl Rakosi & his wife before Carl's reading.

Sunday Night 11:45. Marlene Dietrich digs John Wayne in Navy officer whites altho she has a shady past. She sings "I've been in love before—but never like this." And Alice just said, laughing, "she sounds like Bob Dylan!"

I gave a beautiful class to a fiction class at Notre Dame led by Steve Katz last Wednesday. Discussed Fiction, Fact, Poetry vs Prose, gave improvised plot summary of *Clear the Range*—& read brilliantly from it, it was informative too (to me).

Brought Alice back a single pearl (cultured) tie pin from Pittsburgh. To wear, but not on ties. Also trucks for Edmund, *Star Wars* people & book for Anselm, Poster Picture of Dave Van Ronk for Harris, affection but no valium for Steve, Desoxyn for me & Alice.

Loved the Biff Rose group with the wonderful Julie singing and on the violin, at the Earl of Oldtown.

Talked in Chicago to Hank, Terry, Al, John: Art mostly: Clark Baker, Jan McGee, Richie Friedman, Allan Bates & the ravishing Jill, Lee the Warrior Indian, John the Pimp, Rose and in

Champagne

Larry Lieberman loved me, and told me Kristin Lems lived there
& talked about me a lot. She was away singing (folk songs) & I
left before she returned (1 hr before) but I did read "Hall of

Mirrors" at the reading. Happy Kristin, 9 yrs is too long and
shy-making for an abrupt but planned confrontation. I was too
shy. Hope you are what you want to be and do. Larry said you
are terrific, which was nice. I gave a truly fine reading, not
as good as Chicago, but damn near.

                        At Oakton I was good, Rose
was exciting, Walter Sublette OK. I did say something useful
to a poet named Tim Simmons, of a poem of his. Then Al took
Simon & me out to clubs for jazz & drinks & fascinatingly terrific
Basie camp trio w/ Ella Fitzgerald fake female impersonator,
and finally to the Earl of Oldtown where we were enchanted by
Julie Biff Rose. We shot crystal & desoxyn, & so we talked the
night away, Al took Simon out to US 50 or such like to hitch-
hike, I bopped to the airport after saying bye to Jill & Larry
Corner-Pub. Flew to Pittsburgh, crashing gently on Bloody Marys,
then home to Alice & the kids & Steve & Harris. Read a delightful
book en route

A MILE ABOVE THE RIM

                         #

Wrote a postcard from the sky.

                      Sent 8-page letter to Sandy. Mail from Bill Berkson, Mike
de Pike Brownstein, Danny Stokes, and a Ewan MacCall record from Paul Shevlin awaited me
at home.

Hello Paul.

    F O'H quote
                    "everyone was looking at me as if I'd shoved a broom handle up a baby!"
                         you said it, kid

April 28th We spent Tuesday afternoon with Bernadette & Lewis. Wednesday Tom Clark gave
one of the top readings of the season, and Thurs. Alice went to his workshop. He gave us copies
of *35* and of *How I Broke In* & *6 Modern Masters*.

May 1—Bob & Shelley have a baby boy—8 lbs. 7 oz.—delivered Sunday at 2:30 a.m. Mother fine, father blasted out of skull, friends ecstatic.

May 3rd or so—Today sold 3 copies of *Nothing For You* to Jim Rose at East Side Bks for $6.30. Bob Rosenthal gave us a dollar and said his baby son's name is Aliah or somesuch. His second name he gets on Thursday. Marion gave us a dollar & said Steve was horrible for not telling her Shelley had a baby, but Steve said he was too busy talking about Valium. Then Harris came over for supper with us & Steve & brought a quart of beer, a tomato and a pepsi & a stick of butter. Also Phil Garrison came over, Jack Collom's friend, and said he'd return Friday with some Rye whiskey. Harris brought me *Coma* and a Proust for Alice. William has been here all day.

4 May   Dreamed last night I went to dinner with Frank & others at French restaurant, had a wonderful time, drank wine and Grand Marnier, I paid. Then Sandy gave me some money to buy cigarettes later at her place. She wasn't at the dinner. Just Frank, two or three pretty guys, and Bob Cato's double. Frank was smiling and terrific. I spent all my money, but I thought that was fine.

Edmund said something about William's friend Ian, and I said who is Ian, and Edmund said, "He's part of William and Anselm and me."

It's now May 10th, we're poor, and subsisting on Eileen Pills and begging. I've been reading lots of books, not doing so much else. Did hear Kenward discourse briefly on Opera, and had a drink last night with Bobbie Creeley. A couple of days ago, Sunday, I participated in a Circumcision Rite (Briss) for your Aliah Abraham Rosenthal, age 8 days. It was magical and amazing.

Harry
Hoogstratten just popped in on his way back to Holland from SF. He assured me that September's Amsterdam trip was still on, and to clinch matters we borrowed $2.00 from him.

May 11.   Steve was ripped all day yesterday and into the night working on his long poem.

Afternoon—went to Allen's and called Gerry Malanga & got W.C. Williams exact quote on Peter Orlovsky and its source data (a questionnaire on "The Beats" sent by the Wagner College Lit Mag in 1959 to sundry folk). Then deposited same & 2 Frank O'Hara quotes on Peter with Bob & left a requisition for $25 for Allen. Bob invited me to the Passaic Falls Sat. w/ him to hear Allen & others read for Dr. Wms. day.

Sandy's hilarious letter received today says Kate for sure & maybe all will come to see me in Boulder this summer.

Ted Williams brought his newest poetry mss. "Reality" over for me to read. It's impeccable (in quotes) and dull, but there ought to be something there, dammit!

May 12. 9:00.   Waiting for Allen to come over & we finish Peter's mss. selection to send off to City Lights.

Allen arrived finally at 12 midnight, and he and I read thru Peter's mss—made notes, amended titles, and by 3:30 all the poems were kept in, none deleted, and now after a few typing chores and a call to Peter, we'll ship the whole thing off to Larry Ferlinghetti for him to be final arbiter. I'm ecstatic that all my selections, over 60 pages, or more than half the mss., were supported and more than approved of by Allen, and at this moment I feel the glow of a job well-done and brought to completion, a job possibly no one else could have done so well in the circumstances: happy to have been able to work with Peter, pleased and informed & moved by the discovery in his poetry & journals; happy at the part Steve & Alice played, and overjoyed Allen and I could top it off. A fine evening, and I even got some more poems for Simon from Allen or Peter via Allen. Shalom & Salut. 13 May—3:45 a.m.

13 May morning.   Got up at 8:50, went w/ Bob Rosenthal, Steve Levine, Greg Masters, and Allen to Paterson, for "Great Falls Day," a/k/a WCWms day. Allen directed us thru Paterson on the way, & pointed out where his family'd lived, "where most of *Kaddish* took place," pointed out a lot "where I kissed a girl for the first time," "How was it?" I asked, "it was beautiful," he said. He showed us the gloomy mysterious Masonic Temple sans windows, the Public Library with a two-headed lamb statue in front, the alleys he walked down with Bill Williams in 1952, the Mill Factory Workers bar where "Kerouac liked to go in and drink beer." They were like Lowell, & parts of Providence. As we passed it he said "Look there, it was in front of the Sedgwick funeral home that I first considered the Universe." Magic. At the Civic Hall David Ignatow read his own poems and a Williams poem, Allen spoke of visiting Williams, and how Jack sat in the kitchen drinking a beer w/ Flossie while he & Gregory & Peter talked with Bill in the living room, same living room Ron & I & Joe Ceravolo & Pat & Sandy & Rosemary sat in visiting Flossie in 1964 or so. Then Allen read his poem on hearing, in India, of Wms' Death, two dream poems on the death of his father Louis, and sang "Death Blues" beautifully while Steven Taylor accompanied. Allen read Bill's poem "Thursday," then sang Blake's "And All the Hills Echo-ed": improvising gorgeously on Paterson, Wms, the day, and the audience sang too and the whole place was together. He graciously mentioned that Miguel Algarín and "Ted Berrigan" and lots of young NY poets had come over with him to honor Wms & to meet the poets and people of Paterson. It was a lovely day, Simon Pettet was knocked out. Jim Brodey, Michael Scholnick, Jaczik too. I chatted with David Ignatow, and we returned to NYC, stopping to walk around and consider the Great Falls, that "Paterson lies above."

May 15. Alice got a letter from Philip Whalen telling her his ideas on how to write a long poem.

Tuesday 16 May Got Essenin books at Peer's but not Corman translation. Called Naropa & Rick Spiegel & Ree Hall informed me that we wd come there on 1 Aug, classes began on 2 Aug—They will send us 2 tickets (Alice's tho to be paid by Allen), we'll be picked up at the Airport, and best of all, due to an NEA grant I will be paid $725.00 plus travel, plus a $200 reading in Denver organized by Cindy Shelton.

Also, I delivered Peter O's 2 poems to Simon Pettet for his Magazine, and liberated a few books from Allen's throwaways.

Alice has gone off to the gallerys with Helena, and to talk with Michael Lally about doing a paper. Steve is out looking for $ for valium. We are stone broke. Bill Berkson, thank god, reads tomorrow.

*

from: *The Absence of Their Surprise*

"If you love as you wish now—and make no mistake, Elly, that is what you're doing—the only consequence will be opinion after it's over, after the indulgences are over, because something, body or soul, will demand you avoid them further. Opinion, that's the price of the solitary, not loneliness, when they are complete in their solitude . . . and there's no other way to do what you want."

STEVE CAREY
1965
(unpublished novel in mss.)

*

Weds. May 17th. Bill Berkson and Rachel Bijou gave a terrific reading together. Alice and I went, Tom Carey babysat, and all the old St. Marks & Frank O'Hara crowd were there: Morris Golde, J.J. Mitchell, D.D. Ryan, Maureen Smith (Frank's sister), Edwin, Rudy, Ada Katz, and everyone young as well. Rachel Bijou was a surprise and had a triumph and then Bill gave a lovely measured reading, nervous first, then at ease, and enjoying himself. The poems were clear and hard without being prickly or precious, the brain ones were mathematical magic and lovely straight compositions, again clear, and sleight of hand construction. A beautiful dream work— "Marcel Duchamp & I." The few personal emotional ones were wonderful, "Marco Polo,"

"Camera Ready Like A Dream," the gorgeous witty St. Bridget works and "Blue Is the Hero" were big and major and made one proud.

                                    We came home thrilled & pleased and filled to the brim, tho there had been room for more. Incidentally, Bill was beautiful to look at as well.

    Later (6 a.m.) Stayed up all night, did some work on Peter's mss. Typed more of "The Business of Poetry" (by me) and did (finally) the review of *Light & Shadow* by Simon Schuchat, I had promised him. A beautiful piece of work, even if "I" say so myself. Now,

                                               what?

Can't type, Alice asleep, should take walk. Maybe will.

ON THE ROAD AGAIN, AN OLD MAN

*

(Bashō's Journey)

*

(From, "The Records of a Weather-Exposed Skeleton.") [1684]

*

Matsuo Bashō (1644–1694)

*

For Anselm Hollo & Steve Hamilton

*

Introduction

Following the example of Kuang-wen, priest of olden times, who is said to have traveled thousands of miles caring little for provisions and experiencing states of ecstasy under the pure beams of the moon, I left my broken-down house on the river Sumida in August of the first year of Jyokyo, among the wails of the wind.

Matsuo Bashō

* * * * *

Determined to go

I cannot help the sore wind
blowing through my heart.
Determined despite sure fall
to a weather-exposed skeleton

After ten autumns
Edo, my mind
points back to you,
my home.

At the Barrier-Gate

In a way
it was fun
not seeing Fujiyama
in rainy fog.

A scene before my eyes

Roses of Sharon
by the side of the road
perishing one by one
in the mouth of a horse.

At the precipice of Sayo-no-nakayama

On horseback half asleep
I saw as if in a dream
the distant moon trailing a line of clouds—
in the morning, tea.

At the shrine of Fubaku

No moon.
In total darkness
A powerful wind
embraces the ancient cedars.

At Saigyō's Hermitage

Here the poet Saigyō
would have written the poem
of the woman washing
potatoes in the stream.

My mother's white hairs

Should I hold them in my hand
they would disappear
under my hot tears—
icicles that burn me.

Temple bells

Out from the sombre darkness
in the silence of the night, ring
that I might at least hear your sounds
my dear temple wife.

At Saigyō's spring

I like this experiment—
To wash
the dust of the world
in droplets of dew.

In the house of the poet Bokuin

I am still alive
at the end of a long dream,
on my way
close of an Autumn day

At the Honto temple in Kuwana

Mid-Winter peonies
A distant power singing
Did I hear a cuckoo
in the snow falling?

At the seashore

Early dawn
a young whitefish
shining ephemeral white
barely one inch long.

The Atsuta shrine

Among the ruins
even the weeds are dead.
I bought and ate
rice-cake at an Inn.

Passing through Nagoya

I plod along like Chikusai
a little crazy myself
with poetry
among the wails of the wind.

Sleeping head on grass pillow
hears now and then
the nocturnal dog bark
in the passing rain.

Nagoya

Gladly
dear merchants of the town
will I sell
my hat laden with snow.

Passing a traveler

In the morning snow
even a horse
is a spectacle
I cannot help stopping to see.

Dusk

Over the darkening sea
only the voice of a flying duck
is visible
in soft white.

New Year's Day

With my hat on my head
and straw sandals on my feet
I met on the road
the end of the year.

A plum orchard by Mitsui Shufu's house
        near the Naruki waterfall, at
                Kyoto

Blanket of white plum—
I wonder were the cranes
Stolen or hidden beneath
the plum blossoms?

A sturdy oak
in the plum orchard
totally indifferent
to the blossoms.

On the way to Otsu

I picked my way
through a mountain
and I was greeted
by a smiling violet.

In a shop

Branches of wild azalea
thrown in a bucket
A woman tearing meat
from a dried codfish.

In the country of Kai

What luxury
for a traveling horse,
to feed on wheat
at a hospitable Inn.

Home, after several days of rest

Everything gone,
I still have lice
I picked up on the road
alive in my Summer robes.

Note:
Knowing no Japanese, I worked with the renderings of Nobuyuki Yuasa into English of some of the poems in Bashō's *The Narrow Road to the Deep North and Other Travel Sketches* (Penguin Books LTD, Harmondsworth, Middlesex, England, Penguin Classic L185, 1970). My sense has been for the preceding set of poems to form a complete book in itself, not for the poems to be simply a selection of favorites or whatever from Bashō. I owe and hereby acknowledge a great debt to the translations by Anselm Hollo of Gypsy poems, though by no means are my works his fault.

1978. NYC.

THE ARRIVAL REPORT

The Arrival Report

Saturday, August 3rd, 1974:

Today at 12:30 noon Alice delivered her baby, a big purple boy with black hair, long feet, & long thin fingernails. He weighs 8 lbs, 10 ounces, & looks like Anselm, & even more so.

Last night, Friday, Robert Clark came over, & we watched KISS OF DEATH & talked. He left after 1 A.M. & I went upstairs where Alice had called me from, & changed Anselm's diaper & talked to him. Then I got into bed, & Alice made me realize it was starting, tho she was hesitant to decide it really was, because she didn't want me to take her in a day early, like last time. But I could tell. We talked & I kept my hand on her thigh, & I cd feel the pains get through her. The Baby Book I'd taken from the hospital said that when the pains were over 40 seconds in duration, at with five minute intervals, to go. I talked Alice into telling me time hers, & I timed her for forty minutes from 2 A.M. til 2:40. The pains were lasting 40 to 50 seconds, & the intervals were ten seconds or so over five Alice insisted they were too mild yet,

Saturday, August 3rd, 1974:

Today at 12:30 noon Alice delivered her baby, a big purple boy with black hair, long feet, + long thin fingernails. He weighs 8 lbs, 10 ounces, + looks like Anselm, + even more so.

Last night, Friday, Robert Clark came over, + we watched Kiss of Death + talked. He left after 1 a.m., + I went upstairs where Alice had called me from, + changed Anselm's diaper + talked to him. Then I got into bed, + Alice made me realize it was starting, tho she was hesitant to decide it really was, because she didn't want me to take her in a day early, like last time. But I could tell. We talked + I kept my hand on her thigh, + I cd feel the pains go through her. The Baby Book I'd taken from the hospital said that when the pains were over 40 seconds in duration, and with five-minute intervals, to go. I talked Alice into letting me time her, + I timed her for forty minutes from 2 a.m. til 2:40. The pains were lasting 40 to 50 seconds, + the intervals were ten seconds or so over five minutes. Alice insisted they were too mild yet, but the book said they'd be mild, it was duration that counted. I told her my theory was to call the hospital + tell them the facts + see what they said. She sd ok, as her last two pains were not so mild. I called, + The Ward Sister of Flat 2, the Obstetrics Wards, who had a calm sweet but efficient voice listened as I told her who I was, that Alice was overdue (the Dr. had predicted July 26th), + that she seemed to me to be in labor now. (They had scheduled to bring her in Sunday + induce labor.) "Well, what's been happening tonight" said the Sister, + I told her. "Has she had a show?" she asked, meaning of discharge of blood, + I said "yes." "Well, we'd better have her in then," she said. I said "O.K., what door?" + she said "Right up to the front door + ring the bell." "Thank you." "Let's go," I said to Alice, + she said "all right" + began getting up. I told her word for word what the Sister had said. So. I called Gordon (Brotherston) first, + no money. Then I tried Celia (Dekker), + she was distressed but Andrew (McCulloch)'s van was full of furniture. He too was dismayed at not being able to help. "It's ok," I said. "We'll get a cab." I called 976266, + Mini-cabs answered. I told them who + where + they said right away. Alice packed Middlemarch + The Selected Poems of Frank O'Hara, left her wallet + keys at home, I got dressed, we went downstairs. Her suitcase had been packed for two weeks already.

The cab came, + we sped through the Essex night, past the University, down toward the orange street bumps of Colchester, not saying much. The driver was very nice, + had carried me before.

At the hospital they parked me on a staircase, + took Alice away to change to nightgown + bathrobe. Alice had left her lenses home + was wearing glasses. After twenty minutes or more, by now well past 4 a.m. a nurse brought me the suitcase with the clothes Alice had been wearing, + Alice came back. "How do you like my outfit?" she said, + I said "it looks beautiful." I kissed her goodbye + said "I'll be back." I called another cab. The Sister told me to call the hospital about 7. It was 5:30 a.m. when I got home. There I relieved Chris + Kathy, whom I'd called out of bed to sit with Anselm till I returned. They offered to come back at 7, but I said No, I'd manage. They were terrific to have come. I had a valium + some cough medicine, + finished reading Janis Joplin, how she died, sadly. I fell asleep, + woke up about 7:10. The Sister said "Your wife is doing fine, call again around nine." I slept again. Woke up at nine fifteen. The news from the hospital was the same – try later. I changed Anselm, gave him a bottle, left him in bed, + took a pill, + dozed fitfully. Just before 12 noon I called + they said, "Come in, she's in the delivery room." I called Gordon, + he apologized for last night (I don't know how he knew, I guess Celia told him). Do you want the car, he said + "bring Anselm over + we'll keep him with us." I dressed Anselm + told him we'd go bye-bye to see Katie (Gordon's daughter) + he laughed.

I arrived at the hospital at 12:30, and asked the sister if I could go in + see the delivery. "You've just this minute had a boy," she said. Right then they wheeled the baby out. He looked amazing + alert. But it was Alice I wanted right then. "Go on in," the Sister told me. I did, + Alice looked beautiful. Tired, but clear, more clear than in many weeks. She smiled at me + I was nervous as a little kid. She told me all about the birth, she'd watched it all, it had been painful but she had taken in every detail. The Dr. hadn't arrived yet to stitch her. I told her where Anselm was, + she told me more about the birth + we just held hands + talked. I loved her very much for being all her self's own self + part of mine.

It was after One. I left to return at 3. In Colchester I had breakfast, eggs chips sausage + pepsi (5) (2). Then I bought a carry-cat, three baby outfits, six prs of baby rubber pants, pins, little baby "vests," + then a P.G. Wodehouse book, Sam the Sudden [?], for Alice. It was "Tattoo" day, whatever that is, + crowds lined the streets, watching Redcoats + other crazy-looking Military bands march by. Just like Bunker Hill, which, as Jack or Neal wd say, was really Breed's Hill. I kept thinking I'd bump into Herbie, + get to tell him, but I didn't. So, I called Gordon, + he was pleased for us + warmly congratulating + sd keep the car as long as you need. So, I visited Alice from 3 til 4, + saw the baby again, little Edmund

Joseph Berrigan, after my father, + after Joe. Alice said, "As soon as the baby comes out you feel instantly healed."

Home, to sleep, + talk to Gordon + Gisek [?], rest, call Becky, then my mother with the news, then an evening visit to Alice. I took her flowers from the garden. She is fine. Anselm is asleep in his bed. Doug Oliver called. Not the first to know, but the first to call + ask, + his call completed the circle. Right now it's 11:10 p.m. + 3 Aug. 74 is nearly over.

LONGER WORKS
OF THE MORE ACADEMIC TYPE

GET THE MONEY

JOHN KEVS, IN ENGLAND, writes that Roger Miller is a liar. Also, that as far as stance goes, everyone between him (John) and the self-immolaters are just chickenshits! The English refuse to give John all their money, which makes them just about as low as Americans. In his column on bookstores that publish and generally "swing" (whatever that means), John Wilcock failed to mention The Phoenix, on Cornelia Street, which at least publishes (*Ace of Pentacles* & a McClure bibliography) and might swing, if pushed a little or if a good stiff wind came up. Could it be that genial Bob Wilson has had another personality clash?

Paul Blackburn, 2nd Avenue's Clyde Beatty, lists Robt Kelly (Dec. 1), Kathy Fraser (the 8th), and Jerry Bloedow (15th) as readers at Le Metro in December.

Don't believe the rumor that the Fugs (Ed Sanders, Ken Weaver, Tuli Kupferberg & Steve Weber) were killed in an automobile accident in the Mohave Desert. In fact, they'll supposedly be back in NY for Thanksgiving. The Free University wants poets, painters, musicians, etc., interested in giving courses, to contact them at 20 East 14th, any evening. Particularly anyone interested in giving a poetry workshop.

Grove has just released LeRoi Jones's *The System of Dante's Hell* (and it's about time) which is one of the great prose works of sometime or other. Look for Review by Allen Katzman next issue.

One of the most boring works of any time (though actually it isn't that good) is Ron Norman's pretentious *Blacklist* magazine, the editor's tribute to himself. Only Terry Southern would like it.

Mother magazine, editor Peter Schjeldahl, 86 Avenue B, is about to appear with works by Kenneth Koch, Ted Berrigan, Ed Sanders, Allen Ginsberg, Buck Mulligan, Joan Baez and Joan & Karl. Don't miss it. Also, "C", number 11, all prose, with a masterpiece by Tom Veitch, is at Peace Eye and 8th Street. Veitch, who was asked by Wm. Burroughs for a manuscript to be presented to Grove Press (which those boobs rejected) is about to enter a monastery.

Dear Ted,
        How are you? I am fine.
                    Your friend,
                    Tom

P.S. Yes, it is true.[1] What else is knew?

Sorry I chucked all my scripts when I was in P.A. (correction Pa.)[2] Go away.[3] Expect to have new forbidden manuscripts in future years.[4] Imprimatur and all that. Write later for information care of the Vatican. Spirit of Christ everywhere . . . yes man . . . Thanks for "C"s. Liked Luis Armed Story best of all. Some genius wrote it.[5] Get Grove to publish it send money to monks care of Caesar Romero.[6] Hear Stewart Granger dead? or whoever that guy in snow . . . I mean King Solomon's mines who also read "C" magazine on his death bed.

To speak is to lie.[7] Therefore I cease to speak in order that purest truth may bubble in the veins. So long old shit, write when you can . . . I'll be in NY after Christmas.[8]
        Tom

---

1. I am going to be a monk.

2. No words left to send you old buddy.

3. and find peace, old friend.

4. Sex Orgies of a Benedictine Monk and Secrets of the Cloister.

5. Me.

6. Checks payable to Tom Veitch.

7.

8. Sleep the sleep that needs not breaking
   Could it be we all are faking?

* * *

So much for Tom Veitch.

Send all poetry magazines, gifts, money, books, snowshoes, snow jobs, job offers, offerings, bribes, gratuities, data, dates, blacklists, hate literature, propositions, dope, pills, booze, and other boring matter to Ted Berrigan, c/o this newspaper, for appropriate mentions, knocks, pissing on, ecstasy over and/or other in print. GET THE MONEY!

AN INTERVIEW WITH JOHN CAGE

The following interview is pieced together
from a series of tape-recorded interviews with
John Cage during his recent visit to New
York. They were made at parties, in flats,
and in taxis.

INTERVIEWER: What about Marshall McLuhan?

CAGE: Just this: the media is not a message. I would like to sound a word of warning to Mr. McLuhan: to speak is to lie. To lie is to collaborate.

INTERVIEWER: How does that relate?

CAGE: Do you know the Zen story of the mother who had just lost her only son? She is sitting by the side of the road weeping and the monk comes along and asks her why she's weeping and she says she has lost her only son and so he hits her on the head and says, "There, that'll give you something to cry about."

INTERVIEWER: Yes, somebody should have kicked that monk in the ass!

CAGE: I agree. Somebody said that Brecht wanted everybody to think alike. I want everybody to think alike. But Brecht wanted to do it through Communism, in a way. Russia is doing it under government. It's happening here all by itself without being under a strict government; so if it's working without trying, why can't it work without being Communist? Everybody looks and acts alike, and we're getting more and more that way. I think everybody should be a machine. I think everybody should be alike.

INTERVIEWER: Isn't that like Pop Art?

CAGE: Yes, that's what Pop Art is, liking things, which incidentally is a pretty boring idea.

INTERVIEWER: Does the fact that it comes from a machine diminish its value to you?

CAGE: Certainly not! I think that any artistic product must stand or fall on what's there. A chimpanzee can do an abstract painting, if it's good, that's great!

INTERVIEWER: Mary McCarthy has characterized you as a sour Utopian. Is that accurate?

CAGE: I do definitely mean to be taken literally, yes. All of my work is directed against those who are bent, through stupidity or design, on blowing up the planet.

INTERVIEWER: Well, that is very interesting, Mr. Cage, but I wanted to know what you think in the larger context, i.e., the Utopian.

CAGE: I don't know exactly what you mean there . . . I think the prestige of poetry is very high in the public esteem right now, perhaps height is not the right yardstick, but it is perhaps higher than ever. If you can sell poetry, you can sell anything. No, I think it's a *wonderful* time for poetry and I really feel that something is about to boil. And in answer to your question about whether poetry could resume something like the Elizabethan spread, I think it's perfectly possible that this could happen in the next four or five years. All it needs is the right genius to come along and let fly. And old Masefield, I was pleased to see the other day celebrating his ninetieth birthday, I think, said that there are still lots of good tales to tell. I thought that was very nice, and it's true, too.

INTERVIEWER: Do you think, that is, are you satisfied with the way we are presently conducting the war in Viet Nam?

CAGE: I am highly dissatisfied with the way we are waging this nasty war.

INTERVIEWER: Incidentally, your rooms are very beautiful.

CAGE: Nothing incidental about it at all. These are lovely houses; there are two for sale next door, a bargain, too, but they're just shells. They've got to be all fixed up inside as this one was, too. They were just tearing them down when I got the Poetry Society over here to invite Hy Sobiloff, the only millionaire poet, to come down and read, and he was taken in hand and shown this house next door, the one that I grew up in, and what a pitiful state it was in. Pick-axes had already gone through the roof. And so he bought four of them and fixed this one up for our use as long as we live, rent free.

INTERVIEWER: Not bad. Tell me, have you ever thought of doing soundtracks for Hollywood movies?

CAGE: Why not? Any composer of genuine ability should work in Hollywood today. Get the Money! However, few screen composers possess homes in Bel-Air, illuminated swimming pools, wives in full-length mink coats, three servants, and that air of tired genius turned sour Utopian. Without that, today, you are nothing. Alas, money buys pathetically little in Hollywood beyond the pleasures of living in an unreal world, associating with a group of narrow people who think, talk, and drink, most of them bad people; and the doubtful pleasure of watching famous actors and actresses guzzle up the juice and stuff the old gut in some of the rudest restaurants in the world. Me, I have never given it a thought.

INTERVIEWER: Tell me about *Silence.*

CAGE: Sure. You never know what publishers are up to. I had the damnedest time with *Silence.* My publishers, H***, R***, and W***, at first were very excited about doing it, and then they handed it over to a young editor who wanted to rewrite it entirely, and proceeded to do so; he made a complete hash of it. And I protested about this and the whole thing—the contract was about to be signed—and they withdrew it, because of this impasse. The Publisher, who is my friend, said, "Well, John, we never really took this seriously, did we? So why don't we just forget it?" And I replied, "Damn it all, I did take it seriously; I want to get published." Well, then they fired this young man who was rewriting me, and everything was peaceful. But there was still some static about irregularities of tone in *Silence*. So I said, "Well, I'll just tone them down a little, tune the whole thing up, so to speak." But I did nothing of the sort, of course! I simply changed the order. I sent it back rearranged, and then they wanted me to do something else; finally I just took the whole thing somewhere else.

INTERVIEWER: What was your father like?

CAGE: I don't want to speak of him. My mother detested him.

INTERVIEWER: What sort of person was your mother?

CAGE: Very religious. Very. But now she is crazy. She lay on top of me when I was tied to the bed. She writes me all the time begging me to return. Why do we have to speak of my mother?

INTERVIEWER: Do you move in patterns?

CAGE: Yes. It isn't so much repeating patterns, it's repetition of similar attitudes that lead to further growth. Everything we do keeps growing, the skills are there, and are used in different ways each time. The main thing is to do faithfully those tasks assigned by oneself in order to further awareness of the body.

INTERVIEWER: Do you believe that all good art is unengaging?

CAGE: Yes I do.

INTERVIEWER: Then what about beauty?

CAGE: Many dirty hands have fondled beauty, made it their banner; I'd like to chop off those hands, because I do believe in that banner . . . the difference is that art *is* beauty, which the Beatniks naturally lack!

INTERVIEWER: The Beatniks, notably Ed Sanders, are being harassed by the police lately. Do you approve?

CAGE: On the contrary. The problem is that the police are unloved. The police in New York are all paranoid . . . they were so hateful for so long that everybody got to hate them, and that just accumulated and built up. The only answer to viciousness is kindness. The trouble is that the younger kids just haven't realized that you've got to make love to the police in order to solve the police problem.

INTERVIEWER: But how do you force love on the police?

CAGE: Make love to the police. We need highly trained squads of lovemakers to go everywhere and make love.

INTERVIEWER: But there are so many police, it is a practical problem.

CAGE: Yes, I know, it will certainly take time, but what a lovely project.

INTERVIEWER: Do you think it is better to be brutal than to be indifferent?

CAGE: Yes. It is better to be brutal than indifferent. Some artists prefer the stream of consciousness. Not me. I'd rather beat people up.

INTERVIEWER: Say something about Happenings. You are credited with being the spiritual daddy of the Happening.

CAGE: Happenings are boring. When I hear the word "Happening" I spew wildly into my lunch!

INTERVIEWER: But Allan Kaprow calls you "the only living Happening."

CAGE: Allan Kaprow can go eat a Hershey bar!

INTERVIEWER: Hmmm. Well put. Now, to take a different tack, let me ask you: what about sex?

CAGE: Sex is a biologic weapon, insofar as I can see it. I feel that sex, like every other human manifestation, has been degraded for anti-human purposes. I had a dream recently in which I returned to the family home and found a different father and mother in the bed, though they were still somehow *my* father and mother. What I would like, in the way of theatre, is that somehow a method would be devised, a new form, that would allow each member of the audience at a play to watch his own parents, young again, make love. Fuck, that is, not court.

INTERVIEWER: That certainly would be different, wouldn't it? What other theatrical event interests you?

CAGE: Death. The Time Birth Death gimmick. I went recently to see *Dr. No* at Forty-Second Street. It's a fantastic movie, so cool. I walked outside and somebody threw a cherry bomb right in front of me, in this big crowd. And there was blood, I saw blood on people and all over. I felt like I was bleeding all over. I saw in the paper that week that more and more people are throwing them. Artists, too. It's just part of the scene—hurting people.

INTERVIEWER: How does Love come into all this?

CAGE: It doesn't. It comes later. Love is memory. In the immediate present we don't love; life is too much with us. We lust, wilt, snort, swallow, gobble, hustle, nuzzle, etc. Later, memory flashes images swathed in nostalgia and yearning. We call that Love. Ha! Better to call it Madness.

INTERVIEWER: Is everything erotic to you?

CAGE: Not lately. No, I'm just kidding. Of course everything is erotic to me; if it isn't erotic, it isn't interesting.

INTERVIEWER: Is life serious?

CAGE: Perhaps. How should I know? In any case, one must not be serious. Not only is it absurd, but a serious person cannot have sex.

INTERVIEWER: Very interesting! But, why not?

CAGE: If you have to ask, you'll never know.

INTRODUCTION TO *IN*
BY ARAM SAROYAN

I have always, beyond belief, hoped to meet
at night and in a woods, a beautiful naked woman
or rather, since such a wish once expressed means
nothing, I regret, beyond belief, not having met her.
Imagining such an encounter is not, after all, so
fantastic: it might happen. It seems to me that
everything would have stopped short—I would no
longer do things as I had done until that moment.
The rock cannot be broken. It is the truth.

12.1.65

TEN THINGS ABOUT THE BOSTON TRIP:
AN ASIDE TO RON & TOM

I

One thing about the trip to Boston was Frank. Lots
of "things" about Frank took place during the Boston
trip.

II

I bought that striped polo shirt, short-sleeved, on
the rocking chair, at a bargain/antique store for
seventy-five cents & wore it every minute after that.

III

I had lost Ron & Tom & Aram & Larry at the very
beginning of the Boston trip and only bumped into
them on occasion the whole time.

IV

It was nice walking back & forth in Harvard Square.
I did it several times, looking at everybody carefully. Tom Griffin suddenly appeared and said "Ted

Berrigan!" I said "Tom Griffin!" Then we went for
coffee and he told me he had a beautiful apartment
I could stay in & a videotape machine with which
we could make movies of me.

V

I read Aram's novel on the floor at 21 Watson. Bob
Stewart was reading and presiding graciously, and
Aram & Tom were busy doing things, Ron was asleep,
Bill & Neal were sitting around listening to music
like everyone else (the beatles mostly). Larry was
sprawled at my feet on the mattress somewhat disconsolately. I've always liked that phrase:
somewhat disconsolately. It was a beautiful
novel, called Cloth. There were 100 pages, with one
word on each page. It worked beautifully. I told
Aram I was very impressed. "It's a little like
Phil Whalen's novel (You Didn't Even Try)," I said.
I meant this as the highest kind of praise & Aram seemed to
understand. There was lots of beer & Larry took up
a collection for more. He contributed the most.

V I

At the Lamont Library I was directed to the Harvard
Room where I searched through back issues of the
Harvard Advocate for works by Frank O'Hara. There
were a few poems, and two or three short stories,
one of which, called "Not with a Bang," was hilarious.
It made me think of Rene. After getting Xerox
copies made of the works by Frank, I went to the
Men's Room, where after a brief interval for the
greater inconvenience, my zipper broke and my pants
were rendered useless. I had no underpants on. I

closed my pants as best I could, which was not at
all, and sauntered out of the Library, across the
street, and into a men's clothing store, where I
purchased a pair of light brown LEE trousers. No
one else on the Boston trip mentioned my new trousers,
even though my former pants were blue-and-yellow
striped. I left them at the store. While in the store
I noticed signs which said "10 free xeroxings with
every five-dollar purchase." I also noticed some
Xerox machines.

VII

In the Grolier Book Store, earlier, I talked to
Gordon, the owner. "I'm eighty years old," he said,
"I don't keep up with everything like I used to." He
owed me some money for magazines I'd sent him. I told
him he could pay me next time, because I didn't see
any books I really wanted to buy. I found a copy
of First Poems by Harold Schimmel, with George
Schneeman's painting reproduced in it. I asked
Gordon how much and he said, "Take it." So I did.

VIII

I sat on a bench in a little flat park in Cambridge
that looked out some distance over street construction
and smoked slowly. I thought about Frank. I was smoking
grass. The day was green and hazy. A lady with kids smiled at me
and two kids on bikes stopped to ask me how long it took
to grow that beard. About a year, I said, hiding my joint.

I X

I got a sunburn. I hadn't noticed it but when somebody pointed it out I said, "it feels good."

X

I was in that park about a year. Never did
feel in a hurry. I was in love.

AN INTERVIEW WITH JOHN ASHBERY

Q: What is your full real name?

A: John Ashbery. Actually, I *do* have a middle name, but I won't tell what it is. It's awful—and it begins with an A.

Q: When and where were you born?

A: I was born in New York City on April 4, 1947.

Q: What is your height, weight and coloring?

A: I am five feet six inches tall, weigh 188 pounds, have blond hair and greenish-blue eyes.

Q: Where do you live?

A: I live in a seven-room, cement-and-wood private house in northeast Miami.

Q: Who lives with you?

A: My mom, Helen, and dad, Eugene. I have an older brother who is in the Navy and an older married sis.

Q: What kind of people do you enjoy being with?

A: Young people, who love having fun no matter where they are.

Q: What is your hobby?

A: Nothing—except girls, I guess.

Q: What is your favorite food?

A: Anything Italian.

Q: Who are your favorite movie stars?

A: I have no special ones. I like adventure films and true-life stories.

Q: Who are your favorite recording stars?

A: I like too many to name, but I'd say Roy Orbison is my number-one favorite.

Q: Who is your favorite TV star?

A: *Flipper*, of course!

Q: What is your favorite kind of music?

A: Rock 'n' roll. Right now, I am flipped for the Zombies doing "She's Not There."

Q: What are your favorite colors?

A: Blue, green, red and tan.

Q: Briefly describe your dream girl.

A: She will be very sweet, have brown hair and not be over five feet five inches tall.

Q: What is most important to you in a girl, looks or personality?

A: Personality. I love gentle, warm girls.

Q: How do you like to see girls dressed?

A: Any way that pleases them, but I do not like bikini bathing suits.

Q: How do you like to dress?

A: In Continental-cut clothes, wearing a shirt and tie.

Q: Have you a secret longing?

A: To drive a boat in an ocean race.

Q: For a vacation, where in the whole world would you like to go?

A: To Englewood, Florida. It is on the gulf side and has great fishing.

Q: Of all the things you have to do, which do you dislike most?

A: I really don't have any complaints.

Q: Do you have a pet fear?

A: No. Nothing scares me.

Q: What daily schedule would you keep if you could?

A: I'd sleep till nine and work till seven. I'd be in bed by 11 o'clock.

Q: What are your favorite sports?

A: Boating, water-skiing, skin-diving, and fishing.

Q: Where do you go when you are alone?

A: Go out in the racing boat, Formula 233, and bounce it around in rough seas.

Q: Do you have any pets?

A: I have a "little bit of everything" dog named Whisky.

Q: Are you moody or temperamental?

A: No, not at all.

Q: What three secret tips would you give a girl who would like for you to like her?

A: She should be very considerate; she should not talk to me about TV; and she should dress in a neat, nice manner at all times.

Q: Have you ever dated a fan?

A: Yes. When I was living in New York, I got a very nice letter from a girl. I called her and took her out, and we had a great time.

Q: What has been the greatest thrill of your life?

A: Picking out my car. I got a maroon GTO with a white top.

Q: What is the most unforgettable experience you have had?

A: The first time I went skin-diving. The beautiful colors under the water were unbelievable!

Q: How would you describe yourself?

A: I consider myself a regular guy, not outstanding in any particular way.

Q: What is your pet weakness?

A: Boats. Every time I see one, I have to jump into it.

Q: What is your ultimate ambition?

A: To be a good human being.

Q: Who has helped you the most with your career?

A: Frankly, I've done most of it on my own.

Q: What do you worry about?

A: When you work all day and have to memorize a script, you feel you may not do so well.

Q: What do you like best about your work?

A: Diving with full gear on. You can stay under for an hour or so.

Q: What do you dislike about your career?

A: I love everything. It is always interesting. I do hate having to do homework, when I'm soaking wet, though.

Q: How do you relax?

A: I put on a stack of records, lie on the bed and sip a Coke.

Q: Where is the best place to write to you?

A: 12100 N.E. 16th Avenue
Miami, Florida

HARLAN DANGERFIELD

(REPRINTED FROM THE A.M.A. JOURNAL)

BRAIN DAMAGE

(SOME NOTES, AND A CASE HISTORY)

I'M STANDING UNDER the tree of hope, hoping for the best. The stone houses are completely colorless in the hot sun.

Some time ago I was flying to Louisville with a few girls. Who could count the unnumbered kisses? Fiercely given, fiercely taken. However, small kisses are not disturbing. They cause no disturbance in the brain, which, in any case is insensitive. Kids yelling in tenements at night . . . . pots rattling in the kitchen . . . . cat meows . . . . African chatter . . . . what is all that to me? . . . . old Xmas bathrobe hanging on the rack, brown conventional squares (or are they diamonds?) . . . . brown, the color of life . . . . the brownish-grey brain, now irreparably damaged . . . .

"Who's speaking please?"

Brain Damage is primarily due to an infant's failure to breathe properly in its first five minutes of life. Lack of oxygen in the blood that flows to the brain impairs the functioning of the cerebral cells, weakening their control of coordination and thought. Once done, the damage is permanent.

The brains of about six babies in every thousand are damaged by birth.

Their only desire seems to be to sit and wait, and watch the pupils of your eyes. Should they imagine your pupils are expanding they thrust their elbows back, crouch, and leap at you, biting and tearing at your flesh with their cannibal teeth.

Fortunately, it has been discovered recently that large doses of a chemical compound known as "Cris" will, if injected promptly at birth, save the child from the ravages of *Nausea*.

It is not easy for a writer to smoke at the typewriter, especially when "Shooting." Weighing only one-sixth normal weight, he is liable to fly completely off the handle at the slightest wiggle, so you may imagine what might happen if he tried to "light up." This is especially true, surveys show, of people born between the years 1933 and 1943. Such people may be identified by a crimson rash which generally manifests itself at the tip of the nose. This rash is known in medical circles under the name, "Candy Spots."

The only possible relief (but not cure, there is no cure) from this disease is provided through liberal application to the network of red spots of a chemical compound known as Lobeline Sulphate. Lobeline Sulphate is made from a powder extracted mechanically from the poisonous Lobeline plant that the Indians refer to as Lunar Tobacco.

Many years ago a gigantic blue rock was discovered one Spring day in the Dakota hills by a strapping young member of a now defunct tribe of Indians. The large rock was found to be covered with blue flowers. By some happy chance, the Indians conceived the idea of grinding up the leaves of the blue flowers and smoking them.

My own experience with the plant had an interesting aftermath. In our gay little group was a friend of mine who as chance would have it was also a doctor. This doctor believed strongly in a little gizmo which he called a "Lunar Gravity Simulator." This machine, still actually "in process," is a rigging which suspends a writer's body at an angle of about 9 1/2 degrees above the research department of a great American University. There, extensive research is being carried out involving a new literary activity that has been aptly designated as "Shooting the Moon."

Watch any person's eyeballs. If the pupils seem to be expanding, that person is "Shooting the Moon." However, if the pupils seem to be contracting, in fact, a subtle evolution is taking place in the entire male system. It is in writers that the changes are most obvious and evident. This is what is happening:

At this very moment, a certain writer is sitting at a desk in his laboratory. He is in the process of developing a contraption which he calls a "Lunar Gravity Simulator."

This could mean at least $600.00 in prize money.

Now, Curly Arméd is a very sick boy indeed. He is suffering from Brain Damage. Brain Damage is generally due to a person's failure to breathe properly. This is especially true if that person happens to be a writer, and even more likely to be true if he should happen to be currently involved in that literary activity known as "Shooting the Moon."

Once done, the damage is permanent. Now, to help human beings meet their five-minute deadline, doctors have perfected a number of treatments, one of which is rather interesting. In successful cases the patient whose brain was damaged was first given treatment similar to that used on drowning victims.

His breathing passages are checked, and anything that may be clogging them is sucked out. A tube is inserted into the windpipe through which oxygen is supplied to the lungs. Then the patient is given an injection, directly into a vein, of a new drug tentatively labelled "Cris."

Another simple method of checking Brain Damage is the application, generally thru a sprinkler system, of ice cold water into the open brain of the damaged child at birth. After checking the patient's breathing passages, and sucking out anything that might be clogging them, the surgeon makes an incision high up on the forehead of the patient, cutting kitty-corner down from hairline to eyebrow. The skin is then folded back and pinned with a surgical pin. Proceeding with extreme care, the surgeon then very slowly sprinkles a liberal dose of sterilized ice-cold water directly into the open brain, onto the imaginative centers. Extreme care is taken that no water sloshes over onto the motor-impulse generators.

There have been some reported cases in which patients treated with the cold water method have later succumbed to the ravages of another and different kind of disease altogether, one similar symptomatically to Narcolepsy (or Sleeping Sickness). This new disease is known in medical circles as "Nausea."

At present writing, the only known treatment for "Nausea" is liberal injections of a chemical compound called "Cris," about which, so far, very little is known.

"Remember the fragrance of grandma's kitchen?" "No, of course you don't. The Cold Water treatment has given you 'Nausea.' You have no memory."

This, however, is preferable to Brain Damage.

Various theories have been proposed to account for retardation in certain lunar individuals, generally writers, who have no demonstrable brain damage insofar as limited modern instruments are able to record. It is, of course, a well-known medical fact that six out of every seven babies are born with some sort of brain damage, but in the case of the previously mentioned lunar types, it is suspected that they are in the grips of "Nausea."

Watch their eyeballs. The pupils are constantly expanding. Those men are "Shooting the Moon." They have somehow gotten their hands on a contraption known in medical circles as a "Lunar Gravity Simulator." This device suspends the body at an angle of 9 1/2 degrees above the space bar on the typewriter, feet resting on an elegant ancient walkway. The rather predictable result is that only one-sixth of the body's weight (the same as the lunar gravity pull) is directed onto the walkway when the subject jumps. For this reason, every writer interested in "Shooting the Moon" must first master "The Kangaroo Leap."

"The Kangaroo Leap" is a rather simple maneuver which medical science has developed in order that writers may avoid flying constantly off the handle when "Shooting the Moon."

Here is what you do: simply crouch down, arms lowered, hands hovering over the keys, elbows bent as you sit poised and quivering on the grass in the quick weak heat of a summer afternoon. Look out your window. See that fellow poised on the edge of the roof? He is "Shooting the Moon."

Walk thru a city, walk with a pal, what do you see? A boy comes in thru the pantry door carrying a large shallow silver bowl in his hands.

Are you ready?

Yes.

Then jump. Lean back and belly down if you wish to land.

Allow me to read to you this list of the possible effects of brain damage from this illuminating book, *The Science of Brain Damage*:

1. It causes a brisk, gay and good humor.
2. It causes a most agreeable, pleasant and charming sensation about the region of the stomach.
3. It causes promptitude, serenity, alacritude and expediteness in dispatching of business.

4. It causes assurance, ovation of the spirits, courage, sir, which is the chief of the virtues, plus contempt for danger, and magnanimity.

5. It prevents and takes away grief, fear, anxieties, peevishness, fretfulness, etc.

6. It causes euphoria and eases the undergoing of all labor.

7. It lulls, soothes and charms (as it were) the mind with satisfaction, acquiescence, contentation, equanimity, etc.

8. It quiets, allays and composes all perturbations and commotions of the spirit.

9. It causes a relaxation of all sensible parts of the body.

10. It stops, moderates or cures all fluxes.

11. It causes an efflorescence of the skin.

There is no pain at first. Only the sudden shock as the first drops of water strike. It feels as though you are being smashed over the head with a baseball bat. You instantly lose all mobility.

Remember the "Kangaroo Leap"?

Suddenly the others were awakened, not by Curly's usual gay gurgles, but by an ominous "thump-thump-thump." Racing into his bedroom, they found the tiny Curly blue and rigid, his head thrown back, his eyes rolling, his right arm flailing convulsively against his mate.

Picking up a pad, Curly's mother scribbled, "Curly Arméd likes tomato juice with his hamburgers at lunch." Curly gazed at the sentence, then repeated it word for word, a few dry droplets of spittle shredding his lips as he struggled over the unfamiliar words.

"He must have memorized that," his father gasped. "No," said the doctor, "Curly Arméd has started to read."

"But he is only a week old," his mother gasped.

"And that's why daddy has a big fat tummy," said Curly.

Even so, writing is a tricky business. In "Shooting the Moon," one may get six times as high as usual and be off the ground so long you begin to tumble, eventually landing on your ear.

No one laughed. It has been reported by analysts that sarcastic people are subject to cannibal desires. We may find this out for ourselves at any time, should we so desire, through the use of a number of drugs outside of medical auspices.

For example the word "sarcasm" derives from a lunar base which originally meant "to tear the flesh from dogs." Further, it is well known by now that that type of writing known as "Shooting the Moon" has unconscious motivations related to late toilet training and oedipal erotic sensations.

There are, however, absolutely no withdrawal pangs. "Shooting" is even easier than you may expect. Your taste is not at all affected, other than that it may be broadened. Nor will your cravings be removed, though they may be changed slightly, as has been noted in the tribal records of the Minniecongas, a now defunct tribe of Indians which vanished in the early part of this century from the Dakota hills.

These men and women are now pioneering in your ears with a new voice which is more than likely your old one.

But what a man really needs is something to hold him down; so that his busy body does not fly off the handle at every tiny wriggle of the pen.

And in fact, this very need is being filled even as you read these words. The Research Department in a great American University has now developed a tiny white pill which they have tentatively called a "Lunar Gravity Simulator." At this very moment all over America writers are carefully unscrewing the tops of their pill bottles.

Suppose you want a Lunar Outlook in your works, what then?

You lose your voice. After a few weeks a new voice wells up in your throat. Much better voice. It is much more clear and stimulating. However, with it you must first give up smoking entirely, a clean break. Then do everything over again. A surgeon can't very well operate with a cigarette dangling from his lips. You don't see a lawyer addressing a jury with a cigarette in his mouth, do you?

People sometimes automatically smoke less.

Watch their eyes. Are their pupils expanding? These people are "Shooting the Moon." Their feet are resting in space in such a manner that at any given moment only one-sixth of their body's weight is still at the desk in the laboratory.

It's a tricky business, writing, sometimes resulting in a throat as red as a maraschino cherry. "I'm going to have a look at that throat when we get back to NYC."

Fortunately I have a secretary who is a wonderfully resourceful girl. She has been blessed with impeccable taste, poor girl, resulting in a tendency in her, indeed I might even say a compulsion, to tear the flesh from dogs. Doctors generally regard such a fetish as a genuine cry for help.

Now, because we want to know just what is going on in a baby's brain we monitor its brain with a brain wave recorder. In this particular treatment, Brain Damage is cured through application of a chemical compound which goes under the name "Cris."

Doctors in Germany have invented a technique in which "Cris" is injected into the baby's brain while the mother is still in labor. By measuring the content of the baby's brain at birth we will then be able to know in advance when Brain Damage is pending. Thus we will be prepared to deal with the pending emergency as soon as the child is born.

In fact, this very need is being filled as you read these words.

"Writing" is a very strange experience. You feel as if you are not writing the words at all, and yet you are. There is pressure at the seat of your pants. What a man needs, he added reflectively, tugging at his left earlobe, is something to hold him down.

Writers, imitating certain activities as described in the tribal records of the Minnieconga Indians, a now defunct tribe, have taken to grinding up and smoking the leaves of the blue Loba plant, the famous moonstone flower. The powder thus extracted is a first cousin to Lobeline Sulphate, which is a lunar gravity simulator. The lobeline acts against the sulphate, thus displacing completely the feminine element in the psychophysiology of the smoker. This causes the writer's masculinity to fall into question. For, now that his anima, or feminine element is removed, the writer is entirely masculine. As such his interests and desires now focus completely upon the masculine side of life, that is, he desires only masculine activity, and only in the company of other males.

On the other hand, watch that writer's eyes. If the pupils seem to be contracting, he will suddenly be tearing at the seat of your pants. You will actually observe him get smaller as he writes. For this man, the only hope is "Cris." He has brain damage. It is a point of recorded fact that six out of every seven babies undergo brain damage at birth.

Once the injections of "Cris" have been administered, we must begin at once instructing the patient, Curly Arméd, in that technique of brain rehabilitation known as "The Kangaroo

Leap." First, place your tiny body at a 9 1/2 degree angle above the space bar on your typewriter. Rest your tingling feet on the ancient walkway. Allow your restless hands to hover gently over your keyboard.

Now, jump.

E. J. BERRIGAN, M.D., PH.D., D.LITT., O.E.D.

NOTE ON JIM BRODEY'S POEMS & HIM

BRODEY'S POEMS HAVE always been good and involved. I have always, as have many other young poets of the first-string New York early twenties & thirties, been fascinated by their unique "weight" and puzzled by the amount of rumination he has taken aside from himself's to produce them. Brodey seems intent on erasing everything (images) from sight, then bringing them back completely transformed (see: Prophecy) into something else. He does this, remarkably, right in front of yr eyes. Not just word/nerve/combinations, but, flowing structures to amaze the gloom of lower Manhattan! He has, I know, passed through Pound's & Williams' & Olson's Breath Unit Home Study Course. The discipline inherent in Kerouac's locomotive meditations (which look so easy when read), is fed-back to him, but in mad over-dubbing stanzas. Even Whiteman-Melville-Washington Irving ghost taking leave of senses, is blown through this poet's every cellular re:phrase. But Brodey is highly original! His stanzas stem from re:wakenings at the toss of some revolving Sky Mandalas & hungry angel in the cortex divinity. I've been personally awear of many of these works, herein, for quite some time. I even once or twice have tried to explain their beauty at length but was unsuccessful, because of all one has to HEAR in these poems, in what you read. Brodey has three other manuscripts (unpublished poems, and a novel, *The Horrible*), which I hope some editor will grab to make print. His zigzag, is unearthly, sometimes. This book is full of unpacked bombardment devices. *An electric book of ordinary roses!* A Flying Horse of wild Crab Language served up by a poet already well-versed in how a poem walks.

2:10:67
N.Y.C.

186

INTRODUCTION FOR TOM CLARK
AT THE FOLKLORE CENTER

THE FOLKLORE CENTER
321 6th Ave

TOM CLARK LIKE the song says was "born in Chicago in 19 and 41." Not the least of his many other accomplishments was the winning of the Hopwood Poetry Award some years later at the University of Michigan. (Frank O'Hara is one other winner of that prize.) Between then and now Clark became poetry editor of the *Paris Review*, in which post he almost single-handedly brought into public focus a broad picture whose details on the pages of that magazine reflected the broad changes in Academic American Poetry. "The Academy of the future is opening its doors." I do not mean, however, to imply that Tom Clark is the doorman to the academy. On the contrary, he is perhaps closer to being the somewhat shady cab-driver who knows exactly where the Academy doors are in any town. His adroitness has been well demonstrated in his remarkable interview with poet Allen Ginsberg, which recently graced the pages of the *Paris Review*. Now, after many months at Essex, Brightlingsea, Tom Clark has returned in triumph to America, happily ensconced in his position as editor of the second-best avant-garde poetry magazine in the world, bearing for all to see a garland of copies of his two mercurial pamphlets of poems, *Airplanes* & *The Sand Burg*. The Folklore Center is privileged to bid Mr. Clark, "Welcome."

POETRY READING   SUNDAY, March 9th, 1967

JIM CARROLL

JIM CARROLL HAS to be the biggest thing arriving in heroic culture right now. "How does it feel to be a famous poet?" "It feels _____." No, no more. It's beginning to feel famous? & half the population is under 25. The poems for the singing voice that pour from radios and record players, are turning kids on, and turning them on to poems for the talking voice, too. There are so many fresh and exciting and amazingly talented poets under 25 now, and what a pleasure they are! Thanks, beatniks! Thanks, Beatles!, and thanks, Bobby Dylan! Or at least I think thanks.

Jim Carroll is beautiful. He says, "I was forewarned about the clocks falling on me, so all I felt was 8 colors as my wrist watch flew into the sky's cheek. Watches are very symbolic of security? They remind me of Frank O'Hara. Frank O'Hara reminds me of many wonderful things, as does the vanilla light . . ."

He's 20 years old, stands 6'3", and has a body like Nureyev (or would have were Nureyev Clint Eastwood). Across a party, or a poetry reading one sees above a black swatch of leather, Jim Carroll's brilliant-red Prince Valiant cut quietly nodding.

He is saying, "My family lives in Inwood. My father owned an Irish bar, and I went to lots of Catholic schools until this queer basketball scout Mike Tittleberger got me a combined scholastic/athletic scholarship to Trinity." (Among other famous alumni of Trinity may be listed Humphrey Bogart, Truman Capote, Billy Berkson, and Aram Saroyan.)

"I'm also impressed by the various pets everyone is concealing under their clothing."

Jim Carroll first appeared in my life as a huge white paw hung purposefully from the near end of a long brown corduroy arm. It was late one Wednesday evening, in front of Gem's Spa, the corner at 2nd Avenue & St. Mark's Place, in the Spring of 1967. A slight grey rectangle blocked my further view. I stopped short, although none of this is the least bit unusual at Gem's Spa. But the giant who materialized behind the hand certainly was unusual. It seemed to be saying, Pay attention, and I did so. "I'm Jim Carroll," the giant said and became a very interesting person. "I've just had this book of poems published, and I'd like to give you a copy to read." "I'd love to read it," I said. (That's what I always say.) So I took the small pamphlet of Jim Carroll's poems home to read.

The Outside cover read: *Organic Trains*, below that, "Poems by Jim Carroll." Inside, on the back of the outside cover, there was a brief note, handwritten. It said: "Please reply, I'd like to show you more." And then: "Fuck the spelling in this book—it was printed in New Jersey."

Organic Trains is a tremendous experience. Most of the poems in it were written when Jim was 14, 15, 16. I've never seen anything like it. I can say Rimbaud, but that doesn't bring in how American Jim Carroll is, and a critic might, and probably would, say, O'Hara; but Frank O'Hara never wrote anywhere near this well into his 20s. The poems in the book are now, and they are now (still). If there is to be another *New American Poetry*, and there is, as the fine dust settles over the *New American Poetry 1945–60*, Jim Carroll is the first truly new American poet. His imagination is as natural to him as the evidence of his senses, and, in fact, its light transforms that always slightly belated information directly back into right now; no greater pleasure!

Anne Waldman, who should know, says, "Jim is a born star. He's so tall and beautiful, and he probably knows a lot. I love the way he talks."

"I could listen to him for days."

"You're in a house. It's a good house. Babies breathe in this house. Go to the mirror. Comb my hair down straight. Put on the Velvet Underground . . . . Put on my silver ring . . . everything fine . . . Check to see how much is left . . . Giant beds with everyone I know. No sex."

"One is not searching for blind significance, only for a shelter from thousands of inverted footprints, which are those of many erotics in deep gorges of wonderfully green humidity . . ."

"There is an 'enjoyable fabric' which slips beneath me every time I pass by warmth."

"but everything has worked out fine, not like the weather, which is dark as a laundry closet in a very 'cheap' hotel."

"On a day like this, I feel like I'm indoors," says Ron, walking to the subway.

"Jim's poems really move me—it's as if Jim were right there, taking your hand—'We'll explore this place together.'"

"What can you say?" Anne Waldman said. "To be in two places at once gives you a real buzz. 'A little buzz' as Jim would say."

("Right now I'll settle for you, with your bra unhooked (under a tree) on the Staten Island Ferry.")

Once when we were walking to Julian's Billiard Parlor Jim said to me, "When I was about nine years old, man, I realized that the real thing was not only to do what you were doing totally great, but to *look* totally great while you were doing it!" Basketball, he meant. Jim Carroll has been an all-star athlete since he was seven years old. He pitched a no-hitter in Biddy League baseball, and was All-American in Biddy League Basketball. At Trinity (High School), Jim was three times All-City as a high-scoring guard on the basketball team. "How did you get into Poetry?" I asked. "Well, by the time I got to Trinity the straight Jock trip had begun to wear a little thin," Jim said. "I still had as much charge, but I simply began getting off into new directions, like pills, sex, drugs, booze, and the *New American Poetry*. I had been keeping my basketball diaries since I was 12, and so when I got turned on to poetry at Trinity, writing it just came naturally. I read *Howl* first, I guess. Then Frank."

"I still love to play ball," Jim says. And evidently Jim Carroll can still play ball. The Rhinelander Newspaper, for March 13th, 1970, reports: "The Rhinelander Seniors played their best game of the season yesterday against the bearded weirdo's jacketoff team of poets and painters. It was strictly no competition. The only player the Rhinelanders couldn't handle was the guy in bleached dungarees and a blue beret. His name is Jim Carroll, and he was High School All City a few years back. His favorite shot was a left-handed double-pump jump shot. It surprised everyone at the end of the game when he took his beret off, and long sweaty flaming red hair fell to his shoulders."

I guess what I like about Jim Carroll's writing, all of it, the poems and the *Diaries*, is just about the same as what I get to like off of Jim. It's that, given alternatives, Jim Carroll does what he feels like. And he isn't necessarily packing alternatives. The rest of what I like is easily seen. It's in the poems in *The World*, the *Paris Review*, *The World Anthology*, and *Organic Trains*. You'll get to see it in *Living In The Movies*, a book of poems due out in the Fall from Cape Goliard; and in the big selection from his remarkable work, *The Basketball Diaries*, to appear in the next issue of the *Paris Review* (no. 49).

Plus, "Class." Jim Carroll has "class." It seems to radiate from within, just naturally, and Bill Berkson recently wrote that Jim Carroll, with his naturally casual tough classical grace, seems to be making sweetness once again a possibility in poetry. It's true. His presence makes something new clear: that poetry is now, here, and everywhere, not just "there."

ANNE WALDMAN:
CHARACTER ANALYSIS

IT TAKES ENERGY to go places, and you have plenty of it. Difficulties seem to give you more strength. Your enthusiasm is great and draws people to you who want you to be their leader. People love to call you up on the telephone and tell you their troubles. Little do they know that when they hang up you say, "What a jerk!"

You are as stubborn as a goat and twice as active. Your pioneering instinct is strong and you go plunging ahead with hardly a thought to what is in front of you. This is great! It gets you to places where nobody else is yet. By the time they get there you are slightly bored and so they sometimes seem to have more fun than you do. But you are so great at having fun that you just have fun a little harder and so you have just as much fun as everybody else! More fun! Action is your key desire and strength and energy your two best characteristics.

Believing that a good front is necessary, you are particular about your appearance and meticulous with your dress. You always look neat and fresh, and you always have the appearance of a person who threw away what they wore yesterday. (Into the closet.) When you step out in the evening you look and act like a person with authority.

Your sympathy knows no bounds. You are a great reformer and champion of the weak, many of whom are among your close friends! If you do not like something, you do not throw it away without a second chance. On the contrary, you keep it close by in your private basket. You love to be first and start things, and you have a positive genius for disappearing out from under by virtue of blinding speed, without hurting anyone's feelings. This makes you a little nervous but you are a positive sort, and adept at finding little ways of temporarily dispensing with nervousness. You just save it up. You put it in a basket! You have many baskets! What a great person you are! I can hardly believe it!

Later: You have a terrific ability to get sidetracked by concentrating on hundreds of things at once. This makes you less mean, thank god. You have a quick temper but it can't keep up with you. You tend to underestimate others and overestimate other others and then switch but who doesn't? You have a bold nature, you are extremely independent and you think you are really great and so does everyone else so you love them (even before!). You hate criticism and wish the person criticizing you would shut up since you already knew everything they are saying ten years before it even occurred to them they are so boring. But that critical person is obviously a jerk. The sun is out, it's Tuesday, I can see a number: it's nine.

—The Great Constella

MAYA BY ANSELM HOLLO

ANSELM'S POEMS, MANY of them, are deceptively simple. They, like the poet himself, are exceptionally civilized. By "civilized" I mean genuinely civilized, that is, with no proportionate loss of spleen. The hits in the poems take place in your head when you read them, but the poems are not a head trip. The head speaks out to the head connected to the heart. There is no bullshit in these poems. The voice we hear is Anselm Hollo speaking, gracious, courteous, tough-minded. Everything else, history, culture, and poetry proceed as a matter of course. What the poems seem to be about is how to live in terms of doing so.

Anselm's poems are very mysterious, they will catch you by surprise without seeming to be doing so.

A FEW HARD WORDS ON TOM RAWORTH

I THINK OF Tom Raworth as a shy & sensitive man. Like many such men, he is tough as nails, something plainly seen. I like the way he talks: like Chaucer, Shakespeare & Keats, to name three others, his middle is at the middle. This makes him a gentleman, by writers' definition, a thing I just invented, & it is of the essence of what makes him one of the three best writers (poets) writing in England today. (The identity of the two others is none of your business.) I also like the way his silences, those times when he may be "sleeping on the wing," command respect and even admiration. It is one thing to be somebody, a man, when you are on the go; it is quite something else to be no less when you are stilled or going too fast (it's the same either way, in any case).

I like the way Tom's poems are absolutely straight. His feelings, his thoughts, are as complex and as lofty as practically anyone's; nor is he any less-simple-minded than the rest of us. He just writes the poems down when they come, that's all; or goes after them when they hold out.

& his poems are not afraid to be beautiful, & they are not afraid to seem clever. They are *clever*, quite often; clever with so much muscle, so much intensity, they can't help but be right. & that's very important, I think, for a poet: to be *right*; when it's a question of that.

Tom is as straight as an arrow; he is as useful as a bow is to an arrow. He is *true* because he has the necessary moves.

I speak of the man & his poems interchangeably, because that is how I know him. We've only met two or three times, despite "knowing" one another more than five years now. I find myself consistently being moved by the man, his presence, in his poems. I recognize the voice, by now, & find myself looking forward to its ring in the magazines & books that come to America from Britain. He's as good as we are, & rude a thing as it is to say, we don't expect that, from English poets today. (I wonder, is he better?)

He gets the poems turning round, & they are right there all the time, high enough in the air to be read with both one's feet on the ground.

When I read the best of Tom Raworth's poems I feel proud. They are a human accomplishment, a poet's.

LONDON, OCT 1ST, 1970

194

IN TIME: POEMS 1962–68, JOEL OPPENHEIMER

(BOBBS-MERRILL, $5.95)

JOEL OPPENHEIMER'S COLLECTION is a pleasure. The man speaking is no boy, nor is he anyone's uncle. He's an American, a worker, lives in New York City, in a neighborhood with other people, is sociable as a man should be, slightly cranky as any man has that right. He has his cares among which he finds his pleasures, ordinary pleasures, as they should be. He works, he supports his lovely buxom wife and baby son, he likes to drink, to read, to argue, talk, and be among his friends. He writes poems and he does so with extraordinary care. His poems are mostly songs, for the speaking voice, as is our way now, in America, and they include nearly all kinds of songs such a man might make. Love songs, wry & straight, laments, beautiful anecdotes, pictures of his life as it is lived, which is honestly, passionately, shrewdly, more or less patiently lovingly and drunkenly alert, or quietly & forcefully sober. The book is testimony.

The poems are in the manner developed first by William Carlos Williams, out of his own American necessity, but they are in no sense anyone's songs but Joel Oppenheimer's. He has found his own natural voice in the making of it, and he speaks always as directly as what is to be said allows. A man's voice has a music which sings as truly as he speaks, and when he speaks truly the music gives us that man, and it does the same when he speaks falsely. Our pleasure is in the first, like the pleasure of knowing how to get there.

Joel Oppenheimer has been writing poetry for half his life, at least, and he has always done so quietly and with pleasure. His work, and I am speaking now of what is seen by another poet, is as perfect as it can be. He knows he can make a poem, and he does not make one when he cannot. Every poem in the book is a true poem, and so there is little to say about them. They take place each in their proper time; they will not date for nothing alive dates. They are informed by the streets of the city, the channels on the tv, the columns in newspapers and the comics, movies, the works of friends, the politics of how to live, the stubborn graceful dealings with how to be a man.

Joel is clear, & he knows all there is to know, for him. For me, Joel Oppenheimer, along with Paul Blackburn & Frank O'Hara, are the poets of New York. These are men who loved

195

(and still do) the city they live in, with the kind of love that only a city like New York can call forth. With it come an eye for the details, a sense of both big and small, speed, energy, humor, plenty of spleen, & whatever it takes not to be a liar. I mention this because New York will lie to anyone, and delight in doing so. But it does not lie to its lovers, for there is no reason for it.

This collection is labeled *Poems, 1962–68*. It is by no means a collected works, & as the works of Joel Oppenheimer have mostly appeared in rather limited editions, one hopes that this collection will inspire someone to bring out all the earlier books as well as the many uncollected poems written in the fifties. This book will, I believe, make obvious Joel Oppenheimer's place in American poetry as one of the first new American post-World War Two poets; as solid and as rewarding, and as necessary, as the poems of Ginsberg, Creeley, O'Hara, Ashbery, Koch and Blackburn, to mention just a few.

THE QUIET BLUES

fresh coffee will not
destroy us, tho it won/t
help anything either

other than you/ve done
it, made it, maybe even
washed out the pot

which are the simple, yes
the domestic acts.

JOEL OPPENHEIMER

TEACHING WITH THE
SCHOOL TEACHERS

FIRST SESSION

IT'S A BEAUTIFUL day & I'm on my way uptown, to 2 Central Park West, where the Ethical Culture Society awaits me. Today I'll "teach" a seminar on "Teaching Poetry in the Schools," or some such subject, to a group of NY school teachers. Ok. So, I do so.

But what do I do? Well, I know I'll do *something*, & by the way of preparation I *have* had a chance to read the diaries, notes, journals, or what-have-you writings by my two predecessors, poets Ned O'Gorman & Adrienne Rich. The three of us, all poets, are sharing a nine-week course, one session a week, with each poet teaching three sessions in succession. On the way uptown I contemplate the notes of Ned & Adrienne.

Ned, who did the first three, seemed a trifle discouraged at the end of his portion of the job. He had wanted to talk about language; he felt that what was wrong with most poetry involved language being exploited for idea, & hoped to illustrate that point. He assigned the teachers poems to read, by Hopkins, Yeats, etc., & also asked them to see a movie in town, *Claire's Knee*. He also read the teachers' own poems, & their students' work. He didn't like most of it, & couldn't find it in his heart to spare them the truth. One lady liked the whole thing, wrote with spirit, & was fine. Another hated Robert Frost because Frost used women as sexual objects (presumably in his poetry). This lady left after the first session to never return.

Adrienne also assigned the class a movie to go to, called *Ramparts of Clay*, & they all talked about how it differed from *Claire's Knee*. (Alas, I had seen neither, & didn't want to, either, so, haven't.)

Adrienne assigned the class many books from which to read pages here & there, books such as *The Art of Poetry* by Valéry, & astounding others. (Happily, I had read lots of these books, just in case.) She also had the class read poems by Wallace Stevens, which were then discussed. I think, from her diaries, that she had her teachers write a sort of paraphrase of

197

at least one of Stevens' poems. Her idea, she wrote, was to get them away from the idea that a poem had one fixed paraphrasable meaning. Adrienne seemed to like her sessions, & the teachers; so, I gathered, had they liked her. About Ned & his reciprocity I couldn't tell (from his diary).

Now, here I am at the Society. Up I go to room 514. It's 3:15, so I am early. There are about eight people, both sexes, ranging in age from maybe 25 to 100 (no, make that over 60), waiting. One man introduces himself. "I am Howard Schlock (or something)," he says. "I blank blank blank for the academy." "That's fine," I say, "nice to see you. Do more people show up?" "Oh, yes, lots more," he says. "Good," I say. "We'll wait."

I drink about six cups of delicious coffee. The room is a fine spacious airy room, very pleasant, everything nicely prepared, chairs in a circle with a big Samuel Johnson chair for me at the top of the circle.

By 3:40 about 22 or 3 people are there, tho I notice most don't sign in. I sit in my Dr. Johnson chair, wearing my Allen Ginsberg hair & Charles Manson beard, & say,

"Hello. It's nice to see you all here. My name is Ted Berrigan, I'm a poet, I'm sure you've never heard of me, but I don't know you, either, so, let's do something about that." I give them my who-I-am routine: "36 yrs old, Korean vet., married 2 children, taught at Yale, Michigan, Iowa, etc., taught 8th grade once, read in High & Jr. Highs all over God's creation, have 5 books published, blah blah." Then I say, "Who are you? How many teach school?" Nearly all do. OK. One is a young black student, 18 or so, there with his teacher. One lady who just wandered in likes poetry & wants to save the trees in Central Park by handing out a poem she is writing right now, that is, writing it right now, but handing it out next week on tree day or something, in the park.

The teachers are all open, friendly, seem interested in the whole proceedings. I tell them of my various experiences reading to High School & Jr. High kids, how I got the kids' attention, how I would try to assure holding it, how there were sometimes difficulties.

We all talk about that. How to get the kids to turn on to poetry. Because that seems to be the central issue. One very bright younger woman remarks that she had finally realized not long ago that it was not important that the kids like what *she* liked, that that was not the most important thing at all. I agree completely. We all seem to agree that the issue we want to cover is, basically, how do you get the kids interested in this thing called poetry, the writing of it, the reading of it, the listening to it. How to get them to care.

I suggest ways, out of my own experiences, & those of Ron Padgett, Ken Koch, Dick Gallup, Don Hall, etc. We discuss mostly two things: the kids writing poems themselves, & the teachers delivering poetry to them.

To take the second first, I make some assignments to the teachers, asking them for one thing, if, during the coming week, they will all try to find records of poets reading their own works, & listen to them. Libraries have plenty I say. I suggest that they listen easy, just for pleasure, & when they hear something they like, to try *reading* that poem later, from a page, & hearing the voice while they do so. I say that next week I'll bring in tapes of now poets (of which I have a collection), for them to hear, & one teacher graciously volunteers to bring in a cassette. I tell them that some poetry is mostly for grownups. That a kid is rarely interested, especially at first, in reading a poem, however great it may be, in which a fifty-year-old person speaks as if to a fellow fiftier about how it feels to be them. Later for that.

I tell them some poets the kids, the white kids, might like. Brautigan, Patchen, Koch, myself, Ginsberg, etc. etc. I name some black names for them, Don Lee, Langston Hughes, Roi Jones, my own favorite David Henderson, the PR poet Victor Cruz, the Rumanian American poet Andrei Codrescu, etc.

I warn them that there is no bullshit in poetry, that they can't read kids stuff they think is trash, just to get the kids interested, that they themselves will have to search out the poems. I tell them Lawrence has poems the kids can dig, WC Williams, lots of older poets, too. We all start naming poets, & we like this and get excited. The teachers talk to each other, & share the experiences they've had that have been successful with readings to the kids.

I also ask them each to write me a short note, a few lines telling me what they'd like to learn here in these classes. I say they need not sign the notes, but that I'd like to know, & that if they don't know, but simply came because something might come out of it, that was perfectly valid.

I asked how many write, not necessarily for professional careerist plans, but just wrote poems, ever. Nearly all did. I said I'd love to read their works, altho I wouldn't criticize, but I would tell what I liked, in their works (& just about any poem has *something* to like in it). I said that all they had to do was keep on writing for ten years, & then they could criticize their own poems, as all poets do, and as no one else can really do to much extent.

I said that to me, a poem was anything anyone called "poem." I didn't care to worry myself about what was poetry & what wasn't. All that interested me was whether or not it moved me, surprised me, delighted me, bored me, etc. &, I added, a poet is simply a person who writes or has written poems: even one poem. Those definitions were not relevant to what we cared about, I thought.

All this seemed to make the atmosphere loose & easy, everyone participated plenty, tho I did have to tell the tree lady that she couldn't read her tree poem right now, tho she could read it after class to those who wanted to stay.

Then, as for the kids & writing poems, I told the teachers about "The Teachers & Writers Collaborative Newsletter," gave them the address, & suggested they subscribe, and ask for back copies. I told them about the Academy co-ordinated & sponsored program for getting poets into the classrooms. I told them of Ken Koch's book, *Wishes, Lies, & Dreams*, & of some of the ideas in there.

I said that next week I would give them leads on getting the kids actually writing in class. That I'd tell them other writings where they could get those leads themselves.

I promised to read a few of my poems, & asked them if each would volunteer to read aloud a poem, preferably not by themselves, that they liked (next week). They said they would.

Believe it or not, we also talked about a million other things, drank lots more coffee, & had a good time. We actually ran overtime, & I didn't get out until 5:45, nor did anyone leave, tho I told them to leave anytime they needed to.

I loved the session, & these seemed like fine people. I wish I had about six weeks to spend on the project, and could also visit their classes. I wouldn't mind being paid more, should that ever develop, by the way. I need a car.

What I'd like from the Academy, if possible, & I'm assuming it is, is, 1) about 25 copies of the most recent "Teach.&Writ.Collab.Newsltr." & 2) about 25 or 30 xeroxed copies of the diaries of Ron Padgett from his experiences doing this same seminar downtown, which I have had the good fortune to get a copy of from Ron (his only copy), & which I feel contains a wealth of useful information for the teachers.

OK. That's it for notes on my first session. Next notes will hopefully have some enclosures (poems written in class by me & the teachers in collaboration, etc.).

& finally, let me add, I'd like very much to be paid right away after the third session, like the next day, for example, because I have to leave NYC right soon afterwards.

YOURS IN ETHICAL CULTURE,
TED BERRIGAN

MEETINGS WITH THE TEACHERS: FINAL SESSIONS

I'm not feeling well today, so, alas, this will be brief.

After the initial session it was my feeling that generally we all understood what we were at, myself and the 20 or so teachers.

Naturally, this kind of assumption is always premature. At least half of the second session was consumed by the usual kind of either insanity or inanity that takes place when people talk with a "poet."

One lady, a retired teacher who now subs all over god's creation, wanted to read her own 19th century terse melodramatic moral nature poems about every five minutes, to either prove or disprove anything being said.

Another gentlemen, a young man, wished to discuss at length his personal and well documented theory that the new Romanticism is now over and the new Victorian period already begun. As far as I could determine, he meant in life, & poetry to him only proved it.

Others wanted to discuss how much they love poetry as compared to how much they labored at teaching etc., etc.

I fell into a narcoleptic daze at all this, & allowed it to go on far too long. At 1st I thought, wow, what's going on?

Then I said, no more.

Then, we went on from the previous week.

Those of the teachers willing to read poems of their choice aloud, did so. One gentleman of middle years surprised me by reading "Suzanne Takes You Down," by Leonard Cohen. It did not faze him one bit to omit a stanza, the central one at that, because he didn't like it. I mentioned this point gently.

One teacher asked to read "The Eve of St. Agnes," by Keats, which is about 9,000 pages long. I said, "Excerpts?" No, all. This was the gentleman with the theory of Romanticism. No, I said. Another lady read excerpts from "Song of Myself." Another, despite my stipulation that the poems not be their own, read one of hers. After one I said, no more, but thanks. The final poem read was one by Denise Levertov. We all sat through this, I liked it, & so did each person reading while they were reading. Most of the rest were bored most of the time.

I pointed this out, & said that is how the kids feel during poetry classes. Why?

An interesting discussion followed, and the major conclusion reached was that while the readers were *doing* something the other had nothing to do, no copies of the text, hadn't written the poems being read, weren't involved.

(These the teachers of poetry, o muse! These are English teachers, not poetry teachers.)

So.

More discussion, coffee, etc., etc. & time is up.

In the final session (& I must point out again that 3 sessions are not enough, since everyone is 20 minutes late and loquacious), we got a lot done.

Three teachers handed in papers with notes on what they hoped to learn from the seminars. (I had asked all to do so, but said none had to.) Basically, they didn't know, but hoped it would be something.

We then discussed methods of writing poems, esp. methods of getting children to write & like it. The truth is:

THESE TEACHERS SEEMED TO FEEL THAT THEY WERE THERE TO WRITE AND LEARN TO WRITE AND SHOW OFF THEIR OWN WRITING, and had little sense of the sessions involving their students, themselves, & poetry.

I told them about Kenneth Koch's "I wish" idea for a poem, and we tried it. Each teacher wrote one line, beginning with "I wish," on a piece of paper, I collected them, then read them at random but one after another as if one poem. All of us were delighted.

This was the real event of the whole session(s). Then I read to them some similar "I wish" poems written by students in various grades, from KK's book.

I told them that poets were available to come to their schools, I thought, at least once, that they should contact the Academy through their principals about that.

I read to them from the enclosed Book of Methods, which they seemed to enjoy, and told them how to get a copy.

Then, at a request, or rather because of many requests each time (I suspect they wanted to see if I really wrote poems, & if any were good), I read about three of my own poems.

They seemed to go very well. We broke up, many thanked me, while one boy, the Romantic/Victorian, followed me all the way downtown on the subway telling me his theory. Also, before we got out, the lady poet read me about six of her poems while I was trapped in my chair. It was an exhilarating experience.

TED BERRIGAN

NOTE ON ALICE NOTLEY, NOT USED, FOR *165 MEETING HOUSE LANE*, PUBLISHED BY "C" PRESS IN 1971

"C" Press Currently
                is inbetween stops. Address
                        inquiries to Ted Berrigan,
            c/o Schneeman, 29 St. Marks, NYC

*

ALICE NOTLEY WAS born on November 8th, 1945. She grew up in Needles, California, leaving there after High School because of Barnard College for New York City. In New York she wrote her first stories, received her BA, then moved around, gradually crossing America, until that self at last set sail on a Yugoslavian Freighter for, eventually, Morocco. She spent nearly a year there, "being in Morocco," an interesting contrast to her previous year when she was "being traveling." From Morocco she made her way to Iowa City, to study at the University of Iowa, the Writers Workshop. Her first poem was written as a direct result of being at a reading being given by Bob Creeley. At Iowa she earned an MFA, partly through a special study project which involved the writing of a group of imitations of mostly New York School Poets, which when finished was praised highly by George Starbuck, who declared that she had not only showed him what the NYC thought they were doing, but had done it, and done it beautifully, which was more than he could say of the NY School. Miss Notley was pleased, but not sure he hadn't simply been "carried away." In any case, after her MFA, and since, she has lived in Ann Arbor, in Manhattan again, in Buffalo, NY, in Southampton, NY, in SF, California, in Bolinas California, & in Pawtucket, R.I. At present she is totally homeless and has no idea what is next, nor even what the hell! She is quite prolific, and has written very many beautiful and unique poems the past four years. Besides *24 Sonnets*, she has in unpublished MSS state a number of other completed books, among which are *Love Poems* ("I love them," says Tom Clark). *Imitations* ("inimitable," exclaimed Ted Berrigan). *Shape Up!*, a study in impatient waiting for a dopey male to come to his senses & see ("RIGHT ON!" said Bill Berkson). & *Collected Complete (Other) Works*, whose variety is perfection, whose unity is insistent, and whose quality is of a standard few men can or even will see in a girl poet. Alice Notley, Bernadette Mayer, these two poets are here, & I'm delighted. It's about time. However, many many poets and poetry watchers are about to look silly & be confused so much as to never recover their own senses, at the publication of the forthcoming *Ranking List* of the National C Poetry Assn, Ruling & Stats. Div. I can tell you this much already: when the regular poetry world is busy digesting the ranking of Berrigan, Padgett, & Clark in the top ten, they won't even notice that there are no girls in the Top group, (again), BUT, in the second, & "fast-coming" ten, right after 10 come a bevy of pigeons wide awake on the wing: Miss Mayer, Miss Notley, Miss Anne Waldman, & the veteran, Joanne Kyger. (P.S.: then, among the young and best, many are found who can see that girls, who are not like men, are just like them, and vice versa, and, *how*. Among those seeing clearly and so getting direct feedback are Harris Schiff, John Godfrey, Merrill Gilfillan, Andrei Codrescu, Tom Weatherly, Tom Veitch, even Lewis McAdams, all these beginning to see what girls have, and so how to take, which, incidentally, the veterans Creeley, Whalen, Blackburn, O'Hara, Schuyler, the new pros, Clark, Padgett, Berrigan, and the dark horse sideriders, Mike Brownstein, Bill Knott, Anselm Hollo (actually Anselm, were he to legalize his obvious nationality now, American, would be right there with the three younger men, at the very least in the ratings).)

So. Given all this, Alice Notley is someone you'll know for the rest of your life, after now. Many already have seen her in *The World*, or the *Paris Review*, but here, now is a first extended view. She has realized where to start, & goes straight for the top all the way, in whichever way is *the*, & *the only* way. Look out! She sees a way, to get there, & you'll miss getting what you have to have, which is that part only in her. She won't care. She's just there, & may be had for the asking, if she hears you, and so can see you're there strictly for her, you are really you and she can see she can easily take you in hand without ever forgetting you see who is and what shows needs must be given for free.

SENSATION BY ANSELM HOLLO

I LIKE TO think that I can read, and I wouldn't like to think that I am blind. But it is only the past five years that I have been reading with eyes wide open the poems of Anselm Hollo, and what a great pleasure it is to do so. I would claim without any hesitation for us, i.e., that he is an American poet, were there any question. But for all that, he may be a Chinese poet, or a Finn. His poems have been going by your eyes in the magazines of our world, lately with even more frequency, and they are available in books, too. *Maya*, a collection of ten years' work, is available from Cape Goliard/Grossman in America. *Alembic*, a recent selection is published by Trigram Press, England, and can be had in bookstores or at least ordered. Finally, there is *Sensation*, or the book called book, which can be ordered from the Institute of Further Studies, Box 482, Canton, N.Y. 13617. *Sensation* is a small masterpiece of a collection, and I would wish everyone to have it. Some of these poems, as some poems will do, have changed my life, "not heavily," while all of them have informed it with sensation, delight, for example. Here are three:

AT THIS POINT, THE MOON STARTS
TO TAKE ON A LITTLE BROWN & GRAY
AS OPPOSED TO BEING SO VERY BRIGHT
AS IT APPEARS FROM THE EARTH

up in the andes
an old peruvian
in a featherwork mantle
sits listening to his god

his god is playing looney tunes
on the organ of novelty

while down below in iowa city

a small dane is freaking out in a drugstore
shoving & beating on the other customers
yelling this is my drugstore my drugstore
get out get out

the proprietor calls the cops
& they take him out
because it isn't his drugstore

a large unclear device explodes in alaska

furious hurricanes sweep through the banana fields

old man in featherwork mantle
knows the innate beat of all things
he is engaged in expressing unobservable realities
in terms of observable phenomena

a great body
of tender & intimate works
to sleep beside him
later
like a large friendly lioness
who loves me
the old peruvian

ON GOPHER HILL

for george & colette butterick

at times it seems merely a question of how to abdicate
gracefully to those wide-eyed brothers & sisters
who dwell in the earth
but then i am gripped by tender desire
tender desire has me by the balls again
o wide-eyed
human sisters & brothers

it is merely a question of how to abdicate gracefully
to your embraces
& let them wait yet a while

AFTER TU FU

drinking some cheap but good wine
after tu fu
two-thirty a.m.
using all this potential

not one minute of my life have I wasted

you drunkard poet uncles
i like you a lot
my nephews don't

they tired of the twang
you been puttin out

but here, have some wine!
have a good cry

FROM *THE AUTOBIOGRAPHY OF GOD*

"I HAVE ALWAYS been intrigued by the investigations of Lamarck and of Darwin. They were on the right track, but they did not go far enough. Then, I got interested in a priest at Brunn in Austria who was working along lines similar to mine. His name was Mendel. We exchanged ideas. He was the only man in the world who could appreciate me, but he could not go all the way with me. I got some help from him; but, doubtless, he got more from me.

"I will explain the essence of the mysteries of heredity to you in as simple language as possible, so that you may understand the purpose you are to serve.

"Briefly, there are two types of cells that you inherit from your parents—body cells and germ cells. These cells are composed of chromosomes containing genes—a separate gene for each mental and physical characteristic. The body cells, dividing, multiplying, changing, growing, determine the sort of individual you are to be; the germ cells, remaining practically unchanged from our conception, determine what characteristics your progeny will inherit, through you, from your progenitor and you.

"Heredity may be controlled through the transference of these genes from one individual to another. The genes never die; they are the indestructible absolute—the basis of all life, and they carry the promise of immortality.

"I have carried on many experiments with genes. Young men and women on drugs have interesting genes. Corpses in Westminster Abbey, such as Henry the Eighth, have genes. I keep samples of all genes, noble lords and ladies, scientists, rapists, laboratory technicians, gorillas.

"Men are hateful. They are bigots, hypocrites, ignoramuses. I hate them. By means of gene transplants, I have enabled gorillas to become the enemy of man. They poison the food of men; they shoot men with poisoned arrows that anesthetize them. Then I remove their genes."

(The strange creature seemed warmed by some mysterious inner fire as he discoursed on this, his favorite subject. The man and the girl listening to him almost forgot the incongruity of his cultured English diction and his hideous, repulsive appearance—for he seemed neither beast nor man but rather some hybrid born of an unholy union. Yet the mind within that repellant skull held them fascinated.)

"For years I transplanted the genes of men in my gorillas," he continued. "Eventually I commenced to note indications of greater intelligence in my gorillas. Also, they quarrelled more, were more avaricious, more vindictive—they were becoming more and more like men.

"Soon the young gorillas began using English words among themselves—words that they had heard me speak. Of course they did not know the meaning of the words; but that was immaterial; they had inherited the minds and vocal organs of their human progenitors. They were ready. I sent these first anthropoids out as missionaries and teachers.

"As the gorillas learned and came to me for further instruction, I taught them agriculture, architecture, building skills, and poetry—among other things. The queer ones made the best poets, oddly enough. Under my direction they built a city, which one of the poets named London, upon the river another poet called Thames.

"I gave them laws, naturally, because I was their god. I gave them a royal family and nobility. They owe everything to me. Ha! Now some of them want to turn on me and destroy me! They have become ambitious, cruel and treacherous—almost men.

"Perhaps you do not realize that god has troubles, too. For example I was not always immortal. No, even I was subject to my own law of life and death. But since life was not perfect, I did not wish to die until I made it so. So, I segregated body cells and transferred them from one individual to another. I used young gorillas of both sexes, no queers, and transplanted their virile, youthful body cells to my own spiritual body.

"I achieved success in so far as staying the ravages of old age is concerned and renewing youth. But as the body cells of the gorillas multiplied within me I began to acquire the physical characteristics of a gorilla. My skin turned black, hair grew on all parts of my body, my hands changed and my teeth; some day I shall be to all intents and purposes a gorilla. Or rather I should have been had it not been for the fortunate circumstances which brought you two here."

"What do you mean?" said the girl.

"With the body cells from you and this man I shall not only insure my youth but I shall again take on the semblance of man."

God chuckled.

"You will be serving a noble purpose—far more noble than as though you had merely served the prosaic biological destiny for which you were born."

"But you will not kill us," said the girl. "You took cells from the gorillas without killing them. When you have taken ours, you will let us go?"

A sad light shone in the blazing eyes of god. "You do not know all. I have not told you all that I know about rejuvenation. The new body cells are potent, but they work slowly. I have found that by eating the flesh and glands of youth the speed of metamorphosis is accelerated.

"I leave you now to meditate upon the great service that you are to render mankind through science!" He backed toward the door. "But I will return. I will return and eat you! I shall eat the man first; and then, my beauty, I shall eat you! But before I eat you—ah, before I eat you!!"

Chuckling, he backed through the doorway and closed the door after him.

THE NY JETS

A MOVIE

Scene 1:   The Miami Airport
    Son: Gee, Dad! imagine us winning a trip to Miami to watch the Jets-Falcons game!
    Dad: The kids at home should see you now!

Scene 2:   The Hotel Swimming Pool
    Son: (thinks) I never played football in a hotel pool before—and with the Jets!

Scene 3:   A Famous Restaurant
    Son: Wow! eating in a famous restaurant with the Jets!
    Dad: You're like one of the team now!

Scene 4:   On the Field
    Son: Thanks for the football tips! I'll try them out with our team.
    NY Jet: Maybe you'll be a Jet one day!

Scene 5:   In the Stands
    Son: Boy! the Jets play great football!
    Dad: And our special seats are great, too!

Scene 6:   Down on the Field
    First NY Jet: Enter now! win a trip with us to California!
    Second NY Jet: Don't forget! to play like a pro, you have to eat like a pro!—Eat "H-O," it's the breakfast of pro Champions!
    Third NY Jet: It's the official breakfast of the NY Jets!

The End

Cast for Movie

Son:	Vincent Katz
Dad:	Alex Katz
NY Jet:	Red Grooms
2nd NY Jet:	Norman Bluhm
3rd NY Jet:	Mike Goldberg

All other parts can be played by fill-ins.

THE LIFE OF TURNER

YOUNG TURNER FIRST saw the light in Maiden Lane, in 1775. His father was a barber, whose chief characteristic seems to have been a keen eye to the main chance. "Dad never praised me for anything but saving a half-penny!" Turner once was heard to remark. His mother was a gloomy and morose woman.

There was nothing in Turner's parentage to account for the artist's remarkable genius.

His parents noticed right away that their only child was no ordinary boy. They sent him to school when he was ten years old. He was not proficient at his books. Inapt at the dry bones of draughtmanship. But he adorned the walls of his classroom with drawings & filled every scrap of paper upon which he could put his hands.

His teacher told the boy's father that, in perspective, he could make nothing of the boy.

Turner colored picture-books with crayolas, and made many drawings of his father's Barber-shop windows.

He was of a reserved, almost morose disposition, inherited no doubt from the shadowy figure of his mother.

He made two friends only. One was Dr. Watson, of whom nothing has survived but his name.

The other was Girtin, a bright sociable young fellow of a character totally unlike that of the ordinary man. Together Turner & Girtin wandered about in the meadows by the sweet Thames, & together they earned many a half-crown and a good supper.

Girtin once tried to persuade Turner to join an Art Club, but he wouldn't. The society of other painters gave him a pain, he said. Turner preferred to work alone.

Girtin died at the age of 19. "If Girtin had lived, I would have starved," Turner said, many years later. No other man was ever admitted to his intimacy.

In 1802 Turner became a member of the Royal Academy.

He was often charged with being unable to love or admire any other person than himself. "I would have given one of my little fingers at any time to have been able to do so," Turner is reported to have remarked.

Turner never forgot the Dad who had taught him economy. When the Powder-tax of 1795 ruined the elder Turner's Wig-Shoppe, Turner's old man went to live with his son. He was soon put to work stretching canvases, varnishing pictures, & looking after the unsold paintings. The two men, father & son, became chums, & Turner bitterly mourned the old man's passing.

Turner never married.

Though he owned three fine houses, Turner died in cheap lodgings in Chelsea, after having composed a will so intricate as to be indecipherable. Consequently his large estate went to his second cousin, once-removed, whom Turner did not even like.

He left his pictures to the Nation, stipulating that they be hung next to pictures by Claude.

From living men Turner learned nothing, but he seems to have learned a lot from Claude.

"Crossing Maiden Lane" is generally considered his most important early work. Of the middle period, "Ulysses deriding Polyphemus" seems most representative. The exquisitely poetic "Rain, Steam & Speed," is his finest later work.

Towards the end his sight failed him completely. By then, it didn't matter, total blindness failed to hinder the artist. While stone blind he produced his finest painting, the strangely incoherent, "Queen Mab's Castle."

The trammels of conventionalism which had so long fettered imagination had been broken at last, & originality was no longer looked upon askance.

From: *Lives of Representative 19th Century Painters*

WORDS FOR JOANNE KYGER

19 November 1971

Dear Joanne,

happy birthday, love! "May you be happy in the wintertime, & in the summer, too; & may the weather play you fair, & make you happy every day."

Nothing is very new here. Alice just said, "I wish I had some side slits right now. I am wearing big rubber boots with yellow laces because of the rain and the mud."

Adrienne & Ned (I don't think you know them) are not here right now. God knows where they are. But we are, and I, especially, am thinking very hard of you. (Alice is too.) Of is my favorite word often, because it tells what (*the verb*) means. Thinking.

I've been living so seriously with your birthday (almost like living with you, but you off on a trip), that the other night I woke up from a sound (valium) sleep, maybe 3 a.m., & wrote these words down. I forgot them completely til today when the piece of paper they are written on fell out of HOKE CITY, a book I'm currently reading. These were the words:

> *JOANNE, a fragment*
>
> Joanne is not always amused by poetry readings
> not always amused by poems, not even (not always)
> by poets.
> Like all terrific people, she *is* easily amused: but
> since she is so much a poet, poems, poetry & poetry
> readings (by poets) often seem to make her walk around
> in little circles, muttering, or, look under the chair,
> constantly, if she is sitting down.
>
> —16 Nov. 71

215

Isn't that something? No girl has ever made me do *that* before. Alice says that Tom Clark once said that when the Lonesome Traveler had to give a public talk to lots of men & lady school-teachers, "he can find it in his heart to spare them the truth." One lady liked the whole thing, wrote with spirit, & was fine. Another hated Robert Frost because Frost used women as sexual objects (presumably in his poetry). This lady left after the first class to never return.

Adrienne also assigned the class a movie to go to, called *Ramparts of Clay*, & they all talked about how it differed from *Claire's Knee*. (Alas, I had seen neither, & didn't want to, either, so, haven't.)

Adrienne assigned the class many books from which to read pages here & there, books such as *The Art of Poetry* by Valéry, & astounding others. (Happily, I had read lots of these books, just in case.) She also had the class read poems by Wallace Stevens, which were then discussed. I think, from her diaries, that she had the teachers write a sort of paraphrase of at least one of Stevens' poems. Her idea, she wrote, was to get them away from the idea that a poem had one fixed paraphrasable meaning. Adrienne seemed to like her sessions, & the teachers, so, I gathered, had liked her. About Ned & his reciprocity I couldn't tell (from his diary).

Now, here I am, at the Society. Up I go to room 514. It's 3:15, so I am early. There are about eight people, both sexes, ranging in age from maybe 25 to 100 (no, make that over 60), waiting. One man introduces himself. "I am Howard Schlock (or something)," he says. "I blank blank blank for the Academy." "That's fine," I say, "nice to see you. Do more people show up?" "Oh, yes, lots more," he says. "Good," I say. "We'll wait."

I drink about six cups of delicious coffee. The room is a fine spacious airy room, very pleasant, everything nicely prepared, chairs in a circle with a big Samuel Johnson chair for me at the top of the circle.

By 3:40 about 22 or 3 people are there, tho I notice most don't sign in. I sit in my Dr. Johnson chair, wearing my Allen Ginsberg hair & Charles Manson beard, & say,

"Hello. It's nice to see you all here. My name is Ted Berrigan, I'm a poet, I'm sure you've never heard of me, but I don't know you, either, so let's do something about that." I give them my who I am routine: 36 yrs old, Korean vet., married, 2 children, taught at Yale, Michigan, Iowa etc., taught 8th grade once, read in High & Jr. High's all over God's creation, have 5 books published, blah blah. Then I say, "Who are you? How many teach school?" Nearly all do. OK. One is a young black student, 18 or so, there with his teacher. One lady who just wandered in likes poetry & wants to save the trees in Central Park by handing out a poem she is writing right now, that is, writing it right now, but handing it out next week, on Tree Day, in the park.

The teachers are all open, friendly, seem interested in the whole proceedings. I tell them of my various experiences reading to High School & Jr. High kids, "How brig brig the damasked roses" and all like that. You've been through it all yourself many times I'm sure. Well, the main thing is to get through the days.

I'm beginning to feel delirious. & all because I wanted, in fact, *had* to write for you, on *this* day. *Your* day in my life, though you are *in* my life for all my days.

"more than you know, more than you'll ever know . . ."

& that's how it goes (a song) for me & for you.

Go well, stay well,

love,

Ted

SCORPIO BIRTHDAY

for Phoebe

Love,
Ted Berrigan
(November 1971)

SCORPIO

ANALOGIES

The dog, the serpent, the wolf, the wild boar, the rat, the crab, the apple, the turnip, the watercress, the leek, the rhubarb, the dandelion, the gladiola, the earth, meat, rust, the donut.

Slaughter-houses, furnaces.

Soldiers, hunters, butchers, pirates.

The audacious, the cruel, the angry, the irreverent, the perfidious, the arrogant, the vociferous.

The generation of vipers.

STONES: Garnet, Jasper, Porphyry.

METAL: Iron.

COLOR: Bold Red.

FLAVOR: Strong & Sharp.

PERFUME: Heather, Sandalwood.

RESONANCE: Drum, tambourine.

FAMOUS SCORPIOS: Boileau, Lyautey, Danton, de Moltke, Barbey d'Aurevilly, Rodin, Picasso, Forain, Léon Daudet, Giraudoux, Paul Valéry.

SCORPIO   loves Taurus, is in harmony with Cancer and Pisces, is in accord with Capricorn and Virgo, does not love Aquarius and Leo, and is not in accord with Aries, Sagittarius, Gemini and Libra.

EMBLEM: A man gutting a wolf.
           Courage & steadiness of purpose and coolness in action.

           The elementary nature of the Scorpio is reptilian. Scorpio represents the great pro-
creative power, intra-atomic energy, seminal energy and sex. The strong sexuality and passions
of the Scorpio are indicative of his venomous sting, but two other symbols of Scorpio are less
known: the eagle, and the dove, which may be understood this way: the first, the taking wing of
the mind (in its inaccessible places); the second, the Holy Spirit. It is in this second house alone
that Scorpio becomes human and is no longer afraid.

    Scorpio is a source of life and death. Its dispositions are extreme and contradictions. Its
spirit is revolutionary, making use of its destructive powers to later rebuild and be stronger.

    A symbol of Scorpio is Silver.

QUALITIES: Logic, Power, Resistance.

DEFECTS: Cruelty, jealousy, intransigence.

           An instinctive nature, passionate, implacable, spontaneous, and never disheartened.

           Single-hearted persons who do unto others as they do unto themselves.

           A sense of reality, of matter, as tangible. Not given to philosophy, revery,
           contemplation.

           A conscience which is primitive, but solid. Operators.

           They are not ideologists, but activists.

           They are masters of themselves, and without anxiety. Their emotions have little
           outward effect upon them, and do not show on their faces.

           Their disposition nevertheless is (sometimes) very irritable. There is always some-
           thing aggressive in the manner with which they regard you.

           They are capable of leadership and of command. A great influence over the psy-
           chology of others. They know how to talk to their inferiors.

Their instinct is very powerful.

They have a vivid sense of good & bad (up & down) and right & wrong (right & left).

They are a quick study & they don't lose track of the way.

They have a tendency to scorn or make fun of those whom they fail to understand through defects of their imagination. A tendency to confuse the limits of their under-standing with the limits of nature.

"His intelligence," says Balzac, in describing a Scorpio, "is capable of conducting itself well at any point of a circumference, while lacking the capacity to encompass the compass."

They have little of pliancy and adapt themselves with difficulty to circumstances.

Brusque manners. Language rude but direct.

Plenty secrets in their affairs.

They have great ambitions and great intensity.

They are capable of extraordinary resistance. They are quick and headstrong. They never surrender. Not one thing.

They persist in their projects for better or for worse.

Elegant and Proper.

The gaiety of a child.

Never give an inch.

They stand inside their quietness when taken.

The lady Scorpio often is like the Praying Mantis who eats the male after fucking, and sometimes before (and during), (Nuns, vestal virgins, amazons, South-
American ladies, sexy and impassible ladies, Spanish women: whores or nuns).
There are some fierce Scorpio women with eyes like razor blades. The Scorpio
woman is the most peevish of mothers and the mostly deeply sexual woman of
all of the signs of the Zodiac.

PHYSICAL MALADIES: Priapism. Genital afflictions. Epidemics. Pestilences. Pustules.
                       Pimples. Chills & Fever. Hemorrhage. Frenesy.

MORAL MALADIES: Intransigence. Irrespect. Impiety.

Face open with angular features, of a brownish hue, a little cadaverous. Forehead wide &
high, uneven, with hollows and bumps, sometimes crossed with long lines. The eyes are penetrating and brilliant, their regard is rude and assured. The upper eyelid hides under the socket.
Nose straight and short, with a large spine, very blunt at the end. The voice is high and sharp.
The maxillaries pronounced. Hair blue black, thick and rich. Members, massive. Walk, cocky.

Their strength is in the hand. And in the forearms.

The BOOK OF SECRETS says:

They will be handsome, graceful, they will have shining eyes, small & wry; lean cheeks,
drawn and emaciated.

They will have an inclination to contradiction, to bad as well as to good.

It is said of those born of this sign that they will not be of any one sex, but rather be as much
the female as the male.

Would make a good crook.

* * * * * * * *

Addenda

FIRST DECANATE: from 21 October thru 31 October

CAPRICORN, MARS, SCORPIO

Wretched styles. Humble spirit. Graceful, with a big nose and wide eyes. The genius of Caliban, if any. Good-natured, a non-stop talker. Arrogance expressed in the form of complaints. To resist them demands a colossal effort which they resist. They are difficult to know with an air of not being what they seem. They offend constantly. Hasslers.

SECOND DECANATE: from 31 October to 11 November

AQUARIUS, LEO, SCORPIO

Luxurious. Great talkers, moody. Perfidious under the guise of friendship. Braggers. A Spy in the House of Love.

THIRD DECANATE: 11 November to 21 November

PISCES, VENUS, SCORPIO

A kind of humility which expresses itself as politesse.

Silence, and then all at once, a phenomenal babbling. A joker. A lecher. Straight.

TAROT CARDS corresponding to the DECANATES OF SCORPIO:

FIRST DECANATE: from 21 October to 31 October

DEUCE OF CUPS

Realization of expectations of the heart after coming through the obstacles of others.

SECOND DECANATE: 31 October to 11 November

KNAVE OF SWORDS

Symbol of dangers.

Perils through iron and through fire.

Active hate, fierceness (tenacity) always exposed to being hurt.

THIRD DECANATE: 11 November to 21 November

DEUCE OF PENTACLES

Happy realizations in affairs.

Stabilization of acquired riches.

Death, not dying.

BY MAX JACOB & CLAUDE VALENCE
—from *Miroir d'Astrologie*

TRANS. BY TED BERRIGAN

THREE BOOK REVIEWS

Air by Tom Clark (Harper & Row)

RAIN IN AIR

1.

The sweet peas, pale diapers
of pink and powder blue, are flags
of a water color republic

The soft bed, turned back,
is a dish to bathe in them

This early in the morning

We are lying
in it. We have soft eyes
Too, to separate the parts

Of angels from their garments

Here, where the sky is blue

           Cobalt
           Lupin

2.

Thank you
Now bring me a hamburger please

          and a cup of coffee
          the way I like it

      dressed   with you in the rain and the wind
out to lunch
        hair on top

              shoe on the bottom
   not dead and gone
                I mean outside
                        like mud
No, in your clothes
           I know there's someone
      singing there
              inside
for example   the honky   in the nude

& sassy pants   aren't they?

Take them off please   & start all over again

3.

I didn't mean to use you
           I just summoned you

     knowing this
    is a joyous experience
       for me
    gives you endless pleasure

You are casual when the others are only easy

You go directly toward your own thought

like
    the inside of the surface

    You didn't even try

              "about"

  up and down
  lie about
  say something

4.

It was 80 degrees
                            around
    a white butterfly
                      dancing albino speck
                tiny honky swiss

    there in the entero-system I imagine it cool

pale sweet pea snows   wild radish lakes

A CABBAGE MOTH

on a day like this your thirst is easy to identify "with"

at 5 o'clock   eighty degrees

humming bird   goat bell   bluejay feather

5.

I had it my way

Way off, it had come
Had I had it?

I'd had my way
Had it   it

6.

        frogs

mud   February

    "in mothballs"

Ah, me!

7.

Fucked mind, then
we see 3 raccoons by the door

They're exactly Jessica's size

They're very out front
it's all I can do to get behind them

                    what next?
                    or for that matter
                    what now?

8.

Space   Still another Early Morning
much the same   the window, broken
me with a head-
                    and the bed cold

        writing on the wall

      expanding
                        prayer

          ahead of the fiery tracers
    toes   tiny
                    the enemy
                    fucking with the controls

          miles below you
        down there on the ground

9.

that 40's character in the fedora
who works in the meaning room

and programmed this September morn
moonlight to be you
                          I don't know him
a carrot
           burns   as it spins

10.

the butterfly   opens itself like a fist

      dividing into wings   and drifting off

              I forget to remember
              The Pentagon

Dreamy   I lay out

     and listen.

I look up at
famous persons

             Buddha
             Bob Dylan

         Mother

Meadow garden atmosphere   sky   pill

             Little Milton

11.

sponge bath
Spice cake   coffee
sky blue china cup

clouds
bits of soap
a bowl   blue water

A happy baby
a silky wife
a lovely body

A leaf
The leaf's a roof
a flower

Everything
that breathes
Air   in the world

12.

There is alternating current
In your head   a light   a bud
a glass bubble   a wire
the wire does all the work, speaking
It reads the book to you   you provide the light

You drive your truck   all of the night
Its frozen song you place at the foot
of the day   beneath a pine tree
where needles are sweet and do warm

You let your hand stray over
soft colorless fuzz like dust
while an olive covers its head not to see

We make out OK, I'd say, I'm for you
(and you're no olive) you just you, me just me

13.   CODA

I write it for the paper, see
Trade it for bread, hand it out free

Friends call us up, come over for tea
Stay a few days, here by the sea

With us. They have a nice time, leave
A kiss on your cheek, a smile a small talk for me.

JUNE-JULY 1971. PROV.-SF.

The Poetry Room by Lewis MacAdams (Harper & Row)

NIGHT AND DAY

to Phoebe

"you are the one . . ."
                                    Cole Porter

There is a green light
Right now, near the sofa
animals are stiff
in amber light
We all need you, tongue
in this   bowl

we move to put on clothes
or vice versa, you know
        let's fuck again
                        Now
        A skier signals
We are in the sun
Do you ever move?   The sun
goes down like a boat
The sky undergoes
the grace of these children!
who call from the ocean door:

        this trance
        is filled with the juice of the sun

"We'd never get home without you, friend!"
A thousand friends wave in the head lamp
They disappear in the frozen tower
A man alive the perennial tongue cuts up
from beneath the tower

Sometimes I can't stand it
There is breath rolling
among Americans
NOW raving
as the snow cuts the power lines
in the flow   trees
"Man, we was swamped."
and it's time   suddenly
in the parking-lot for playing doctor
night ropes your body

Helplessness revolves
and everything circles the globe
If you look for you'll get
The glue of fear
Puns fall out of my mouth
Excuse me, perfect Lady
In your faith we go on
Don't throw your love away
in your sleep
She is the natural elimination of the mind
She hands me the moon
She's the pussy

Pocket, your cage grows that geared you
if you aim at a little more trouble
Dry eyes that water will go down

It rocks us to the dawn
in this room. Joy is dark.
As it slips away tonight.

We are secure in this boat
Help! The breakers bring me what I need
doves, hawks, warblers, cooling
pills, love, the mother, earth; ring
of ocean round this quiet room

Land like us toasts in the enveloping air
Taking it easy: about time: the light is now orange
Crazy music in your hair, mine

JUNE-JULY 1971. PROVIDENCE

Great Balls of Fire by Ron Padgett

NOTHING IN THESE DRAWERS

Back to dawn by police word to sprinkle it
Over the lotions that change
On locks

To sprinkle I say

In funny times
The large pig at which the intense cones beat
So the old fat flies toward the brain
Under the sun and the rain

So we are face to face again

Nothing in these drawers

Which is terror to the idiot
& the non-idiot alike
A snob in a skirt rolls past
The thought centers shoot out
Through the doors that open

It's true we use our muscles
Being so friendly
But at the same time Clearing the Range
Walking down the street

                      How do you do
How do you do
         Gillyflowers   Buttercups

Someone
My God!   My God!

is screaming at me
This I guess is my abiding problem
Others more transient swoosh by
knocked out all night   through mist and rain
knocking my head against the bed softly weeping & crying
If only   If only
we could all live in contentment   as you do
some of the time
                            Seurat & Gris
Gillyflowers   Buttercups
                                        Unlike you
we live in perpetual torment and pain

Drawn aside like music to show the notes glittering quietly
inside

Are you okay?

I'm not only okay I'm in a perfectly stupendous ape!

I am in fact the excellent careless shape

NORTH   WHITE   HEAD

to arrange everything so that everything is totally great

For example
                the lady and her newspaper
a headline which trembles

            FIREMEN CHOP THEIR WAY THROUGH SHED

But that was in the dim past
in the middle of my reveries
and turning I was face to face with the old man
a very old man

The old man shuffled away
I don't know why but
  I was so upset that I had to stand up
sit down
I disregarded the rain that never seemed to go away
It was all I could do to keep myself from bursting into tears
So
now I sit
a soda bottle in my hand
shaking
and making
fizz
spare moments of inspiration
which you don't want

the sum of all you love

There now there's a pig

the music oinks along

But who cares
about now
which if I'm right I'm beginning to feel

"Who has no home cannot build now."

Orange and blue
chocolate
is what I think
as I sit just outside the light
Evening is so small these days
It is something very much like your own heart
The same one I feel as if I mentioned a moment ago
  whose proper domain is
radiant fungus whose pictures I sent you
already, sent it as a compensation
for the money I owe you

and to hint that you need no longer
pursue the rain
with your magnificent intelligence
fizzing loudly
across restless hog bulk
no wonder
I only gave him a piece of paper to eat today
the way that will make any difference in the long run
you won't mind

If I send him to visit you sometime

But now there is the tremendous reassurance of being
The "fertile lowlands" you chalk it up in orange
& blue
to forget the angel of logic
not logic
This was the choir boy's dead
moved up a row

What could we have been left out?

A vicious song
leaped out of the frying pan
over the sarsaparilla-colored lake and the searchlights
which reveal
the gentleman lawn reclining in a gesture of crassness

The sin of the hearth had made him handsome
The lice looked up to him in astonishment
The neighbor thought it over
On the altar of girlhood
But off the bumper crop of fumes

The shadows
The wild and sleepy eyes
that are not silver or blue
tonight

The delicious crunch
Through fifteen heads
of this needles
the electricity that is not really mine
My dream to raise the breeze
on either side of you
you know and you know

The rain is rolling off the buildings
and bouncing off
and the roofs keep the rain from getting us wet

I am lying in my bed
head near the window
aware of all this

sitting

I think I'm smoking too much too many cigarettes
watch a string
broiling
smoking   an odd situation
I'm going to stop
though I love to smoke
and Dick is smoking and
it makes me want to smoke and hit someone
in the heart
and while Virgil stands at the door
and takes notes
You are pushing the bright new shiny buttons of your machine

Autour d'une histoire féconde

A history that wandered off into the swamp
beneath raving
I too can hear it at night, often, before I go to sleep
ricochets
in prune fields and a prune now shakes

the dust particles off
in one of which a medium sized one
100 white sandals peddle up
to offer you a puzzled rose
worry

Rose . . . . but I know nothing of this rose
beginning
to move and dance
lines and circles going through us
the landscape
whose clouds are really
sails spinning into water

It is night

A dog barks outside the window
A loud "Oink!"
now indistinguishable from the fog against the poles
backyards, dreams, washing, machines . . .
And the large peanut that has come to be civilized

At dawn I find an example of what I mean
an active human being other than a baby
i.e. either a very large baby or
a corpse
perhaps a bed-ridden invalid
tilted at a 45 degree angle
bent horrible monsters jump out and bite him

The next step is to know that this fuzzy angle is true in your heart
flowers gushing out
extension cords
ladies washing the street below pigeons
I don't think I can stand it
the birds swooping down
in a police car in the skies
as we turn ourselves around

The toy sailboats go round the artificial pond
as similes spoken by an insane person
start back
toward the deep green velvet
that makes sleep possible

Then suddenly my view of things
either enlarges or contracts incredibly
And all I can see is the two of us, you
with your long hair, me
looking at your dark hair in this small kitchen
bed
shot into place with light
And everything is gone forever

But enough of this my head.

The sun is now going up and down so fast I can hardly keep track
of what day today is

I'm wearing the same clothes, smoking the same cigarette, the
temperature is the cigarette

One hundred fashionable yachts are burning remind me
of yachts
I see break down
in The Boulevard of Broken Dreams St. Germaine

She was sobbing horribly
and I felt like
the traffic light
my bus had stopped at.

JUNE 1973.

INTRODUCTION TO *FRESH PAINT:*
AN ANTHOLOGY OF YOUNGER POETS

AN INTRODUCTION IS exactly what this Anthology is. There are many new and mostly unfamiliar names appearing in the countless poetry magazines now being published all across North America, and above a surprisingly large number of those names appear some startlingly genuine poems; the real thing, like they say. It is easy enough to keep in touch with what Robert Lowell, or Robert Creeley, or Robert Duncan is doing these days. Because despite the general failure of the large commercial presses to do anything about contemporary poetry, other than publish one or two token volumes a year per house, the small presses have taken over where once Grove Press, to name one, actually seemed excited about poetry twenty years ago. In the late '50s and early '60s there was a feeling that if you wrote well, and "improved," like they say, and persisted for seven years or so, Grove, or later Bobbs-Merrill, or even Random House, would pick up on you and publish at least a book or two. So, Grove published Koch, & O'Hara, & Olson, & Duncan, & McClure, & Blackburn, & myself, generally letting the books go out of print after one or two small printings. Likewise Bobbs-Merrill published Oppenheimer, and Waldman, & Random House published Schuyler and *An Anthology of New York Poets*, etc. Most of those books went out of print in editions of less than 4,000 in a year or two, and were not re-issued unless the poet died, as did Olson, for one, and Frank O'Hara, for another. New Directions continues to publish poetry, but their newest direction tends mostly to be, for example, the Gary Snyder, Jerome Rothenberg direction, some ten years after the fact (though the fact, in these cases, of course, continues).

The next step, after the great going to sleep of the major houses, would seem to be the coming to birth of presses such as, early on, Corinth, under Ted Wilentz, which has an impressive list, but is sporadic in its distribution energies. Ted keeps the books in print, but they get harder to find. A second smaller house, one much in sight today, is John Martin's Black Sparrow, which through its publisher's instinct for what is in the wind publishes nearly everyone you might think of, and so produces a lot of valuable books and at the same time a lot of silliness and worse.

But the point being made here is this: that even down to the smallest of name houses, the poetry being put out by publishers is the poetry we know about. We are glad to have it collected in book or booklet form, after seeing much of it in magazines, but a vast area is being left untapped. For whatever reasons, there is a tremendous amount of very good poetry being written and circulated right now. It is difficult to find only because of the proliferation all over America of magazines and of poetry reading series devoted primarily to poets between the ages of 18 and 32 (both arbitrary limits). Nearly every major city, and a good number of off-city areas, contain within themselves sometimes, two, three, or more widely disparate clusters of poets who are doing good work. It is practically impossible to keep in touch, and one does like to keep in touch if one can. The work of younger poets such as Creeley, Dorn, Wieners, et al. was of great importance to Charles Olson. In Manhattan in the sixties Paul Blackburn and Allen Ginsberg, Frank O'Hara and Amiri Baraka are only a few of the names of poets who were in touch with the younger poets, who came to readings, read the magazines, stimulated and were stimulated by the generations coming after them. Paul Carroll and Gwendolyn Brooks in Chicago, Donald Hall and Robert Hayden in Michigan were others. Spicer and Whalen & Duncan & Rexroth in California likewise.

In the past few years the proliferation has become such that it has become no longer possible to know the one or two places to go in the three or four cities where poetry was happening. Now poets in the same town barely know about one another. Which is why this anthology, *Fresh Paint*, is such an important step in the right direction.

Manhattan Island is not a large place, and here, with some (considerable) effort, it is at least in part possible to be in touch with what the younger poets are doing. Here, by attending the Reading-Performance series run by Ed Friedman at St. Mark's Poetry Project on Monday evenings; the weekly readings at Dr. Generosity's, presided over by the indefatigable Marguerite Harris; the readings at the Anthology Film Archives Center downtown; by subscribing to the Poetry Calendar, compiled by Sara Miles, Bob Holman, Susie Timmons, Jeff Wright, et al.; by listening to Mike Sappol's nighttime poetry programs on radio WBAI; by tuning in if you can to the ongoing poetry programs on Cable TV; by going on Sunday afternoons to the readings at the Greenwich Books series; and by keeping in touch with the series that spring up and disappear, such as Neil Hackman's series at the late Sobossek's, or the readings at such places as the English Pub, the Locale, the Tin Palace, the Clocktower, and on and on; *plus* by reading the Mother of Them All, Maureen Owen's *Telephone* magazine, and its many offspring, including, to name a few, *dodgems*, *The 432 Review*, *Personal Injury*, *Out There*, *Roof*, and the slightly bigger biggies (*Big Deal*, *Big Sky*); *while* not failing to catch any of the poet's play productions directed in various locations by the ubiquitous Bob Holman and his casts of poet-actors; *then* you can generally be pretty well in touch with what is happening and happening dramatically and forcefully on one small island.

That is pretty much what these two gentleman editors Michael Slater and Yuki Hartman have been doing over the past two years or longer. The result of their interest, excitement, and combined energies is what you have in your hand.

Fresh Paint is names, poems, some prose, some biographical data and some information such as the names of booklets you may want to search for, magazines you want to try and find.

This is a marvelously unpretentious anthology: there are no biases, neither political, not sex(ist) nor not not sexist, not even regional, though most of the poets in the anthology are at least presently working out of New York City. The costs of publication have been met by the editors out of their own pockets, their motive seemingly only to be to want to share with you as much as possible of what has been very exciting to them. They are quick to admit that space limitations due to cost prevented them from providing larger selections by many of the poets, and equally quick to admit that for the same reasons poets who might have been included were not. *Fresh Paint* presents 24 poets. In my own opinion a dozen more could have been included, from Manhattan alone; equally there may be some you will not care for. But, in reading carefully through these pages a good number of times, and given as well that in many cases I was reading work by people I did not know, in some cases even by people I had never seen work by before, I see that I have checked off at least one page by nearly all 24 poets that gave me great pleasure. I am not going to make a list of my favorites, you can do that for yourself, nor tell you my personal dislikes; but I will go so far as to recommend that you take in very closely Maggie Dubris' strong and singing piece "The Infant of Prague," and Jeff Wright's gorgeous "Malaise in Malaysia." They were the first two poems to command me to total attention, on first reading, and they continue to do so.

It is the editors, Yuki Hartman and Michael Slater, and not I, who have made this introduction, by making this anthology. I thank them for it, and you will too.

5 JULY 77
NEW YORK CITY

LARRY FAGIN

HIS WORKS ARE like those of Jack Spicer, in that they are above all completely serious. They are open to the point of self-revelation approaching enigma. By that I mean that they are never confessional, being always the hoax-paradox which is truth. They are often a shambles, whose formal concerns are powerful, whose elegance is self-effacing, and whose conclusions however disastrous are always accepted. "You are lovely / I am lame." His poem, "Last Poem," is rich and beautiful, being funny, touching, and, happily, typical. In fact, his best poems have the high stylist's trademark, that of always seeming typical. I don't know of any other New York poet who truly is an admirer of Spicer's work, not that it is disliked, but simply that it goes unread. Larry had the good fortune to come upon Spicer and his poetry before becoming a New Yorker. Nor do I know of anyone else with whom I have been able to really talk about poetry, my poetry, his poetry, anyone's poetry, in as complete and enjoyable a fashion as with Larry Fagin. He admires William Empson, and he has written a lovely, painful and funny poem "after" Robert Creeley. I like the way he sees poetry, and can say what he sees. It is inspiring. He is not an innovator, nor is he a formalist, but like every good American poet, he invents a form each time he writes a poem. His formalism is superior to that of more celebrated formalists, because he is not dry. His freshness and audacity are not due to thin manneristic effects but to the surprising satisfaction of elegance. "A balloon / is going up / filled with problems." I don't care to write criticism, as you can readily tell, but I do care to think about Larry and his writings. I would like to have a giant book of his poems to read instead of my head.

LITANY

LITANY

Babe in the Woods. Memory Babe. Babe Didrickson.
Zacharias. Babe Herman. Babe in the Manger. Babe in Arms.
Babe Ruth. Vito "Babe" Parilli, Sweet Kentucky Babe. Quattrocento
Babe. I'm with you, babe. Babe of the Fathers of the Church.
Heidelberg Babe. Child of the Lost Generation, babe. Childe of Olde
New England, babe. Puritan Babe. Pearl. Babe of Old New York
Manhattan. Whitman's babe. Newborn babe. Mother, Wife, Woman,
Female, girl, babe. High School babe, sing to him for me. Tell
him that I see. And I will sing to her for thee. Well, I believe
in the Communion of Saints, and so, I would say, does she. I speak
of what I believe, not she. Ask it of her yourself. Why should you
ask me. All I know is what I read in the papers.

15 Nov. 77

BERNADETTE MAYER

Poetry.   Ceremony: Latin.   Moving.   Memory.

Studying Hunger.   Eruditio ex Memoria.

Dear Reader.   Piece of Cake.

She spoke with the pens of men and angels. She speaks with
the tongues of men and angels. "Behold thou hast made my days
measureable." She storeth up. And she knoweth not for whom
she shall gather these things. "that I may know what is wanting to me."

*

"thou hast made me a reproach to the fool."

*

Because I was silent my bones grew old. I spoke with my tongue . .
. . . to sing with the psaltery . . . to make a new canticle . . . to sing
well . . . so as to live, not forever.

*

Because thy hand was heavy upon me,
                to not cry out all the day long, I
        turned
                and because my substance
        is with thee,
                I turned, I spoke,
                        to sing well.
                My hope . . . . to give
                        To give praise
        to Him.

_____

*

Whatever a girl tells me to experience I must experience

*

Send me the tone that sings

*

It is all ritual.

*

"Me, Bernadette, your family."

———————————————

*

"I like to address someone."

*

"There are no works of art without sentiment."

*

"They will be lies if I don't have an audience."

*

"I have difficulty continuing to write syntactically. I just
get bored."

*

"My love is greater than yours." (an observation)

*

"I like to write something big all at once, in a few sittings, or
       a few months, the Kerouac school, I guess."

*

"In the last few months I find my vocabulary
       concentrating on a few words."

*

"Vague words include: case, instance, nature,
	character, condition, and degree.
		Never use them."

*

"The English translations (of the Maigrets) are always
	much better than the American ones."

*

"he implied . . . (that my book MEMORY) . . . was cold and unemotional
	but he meant it in a good way and I still don't really
		understand that."

*

"these are opinions so I don't have to be fair . . . ."

*

"William Saroyan is good."

*

"The New York Times travel section etc."

*

"I think it is more interesting to read Civilization & Its
	Discontents as a novel . . . . the character of Freud, as the
		person writing the novel, already known to us, is much
			more interesting to us during the reading of it as
				the main character, than so many novel characters
					who ultimately have no secrets."

*

"I don't like cynical writing either."

"Even Nathaniel Hawthorne had a bottle of gin
in his closet which he would sip on cold
evenings."

———————————————

*

"Dante.   Shakespeare.   Hawthorne."

*

"I'm trying to think if there's a writer who makes me laugh."

*

"What's wrong with good writers with funny personalities
is . . . . that they aren't running for their lives . . . ."

*

"Nathaniel Hawthorne speaking — I offer to you as my own
opinion of something."

* *

"The One does not know him or herself, it passes over into two."

* *

"The verifiability of my angel, all else is forbidden."

* *

a beautiful swirl on the paper

* *

Social life is necessary

* *

The family roles of children are permanent roles

* *

Peer contact increases aggression

* *

"The act of a passing generation produces good or evil
later on and there's no avoiding it."

———————————————

*

Philip Whalen: "There *is* no ultimate authority."

*

We are against the said into the have and hold.

*

What is the psyche doing here, what is a spiritual height.

*

humility, while assumed, nevertheless remains
the unknown quality

*

A young girl is walking home. Many things are current.
She speaks of more things than are dreamed of in your philosophy.

*

There is no idea except itself to sing. And sometimes it is sublime.

*

Literature will save the world.

*

Each voyager had a name. This voyager has no name. My name
is Bernadette Mayer.

NYC 15 Nov 77

THE FASTEST TONGUE
ON THE LOWER EAST SIDE

Light and Shadow by Simon Schuchat. Vehicle Editions, 238 Mott Street, New York, N.Y. 10012. 1978. $3 paperback.

"Here I am walking into the ocean
                                        the sky
which is an ocean—and the most beautiful
                                        of many

        chilly in jersey
        the one I'm wearing

and also chilly in New Jersey

                WITH A HARD ON

and the political implications thereof
                born under the conjunction of
        the lion and the crab

I've got the fastest tongue on the lower East Side

        Ripe
in the heat sink of summer, what else can a poor boy do?

        Mine eyes have
        been seen as blue

I think they're gray
or 'nondescript'

They're nothing
Compared with yours

Saint City, seated in the occident
las casas in the pale linda blue radiating

on the calle de la noche

deep   melancholic   light & intense   lunatic

piercing into the steam, the
luxury of steam

Escuche the tearing of the stupid action

confused your dog so furious in rage
pain just below the ribcage
body remagnetized
by heat closing in
and the heavy progressive breath

incomprehensible to the eyes of
the incomprehensible

City so nauseous, green mold on green acres

Der dichter says to you, 'you look great!'

rushing and rolling inside

words zip out
'Take this, you Motherfuckers!'

Crying under the lightbulbs

         of the streetlamps
            by raggedy walls
                most sinister
      along Love's muddy path
                  AFTER DANTE

(but also after Rimbaud)

     And my heart's in the fucking distillery
     As pain such as this hath ne'er before been tasted
My heart mired in distance and BAD AIME

      The sky beautiful gravy
     I was limping down the road

     It was bad   and I couldn't run
     from whomsoever wasn't there

     (so) in the last ebb of light
     I drew a mass of arrows

     at the adventures of a silver pigeon
     who was my favorite of all my youth

     There a Zombie from the body
     devoured by rain white as dawn

     round as flesh, that showed me how to walk
     at right angles in a place where the highest

     silent self rests, pale & fit for flight,
     and I know what this means this time

I wouldn't lie You weren't there but it was raining
when I went upstairs

To be here now forever
Up all night writing

from disappointment shame and disgust
Your heart beating six, seven blocks away

I might weep, but you were not invented
And a voice once locked in the ground now speaks in me."

It says all that, which seems to me quite beautiful, very moving, and also true. There is, of course, a lot more to it than that ("3 Graces" is a considerable achievement). In scale & ambition it is the opposite of petty, which is grand. At this point your reviewer couldn't be more pleased.

NAROPA WORKSHOP NOTES

Preliminary: a poem is a personal and
             measured communication (tho it
may be at the same time a cri de
coeur, or a found work, such as a
paragraph from a newspaper article
on the current gold market and its
economic implications re: the cost
of milk per year for the average American
family & it in particular sections of the country.)
It is still "who is speaking, what is that
or person like, why are they talking at all, telling,
(meaning) (?) and to whom
do they think they are speaking."

Thus what "learning about poetry" is
is learning how to read — witness:

                         . . .

         Of who we and all they are
         You all now know. But you know
         After they began to find us out we grew
         Before they died thinking us the causes
         Of their acts. Now we'll not know
         The truth of some still at the piano, though

They often date from us, causing
These changes we think we are. We don't care

Though, so tall up there
In young air. But things get darker as we move
To ask them: Whom must we get to know
To die, so you live and we know.[1]

---

1. "The Grapevine" by John Ashbery

10 JULY 78
NYC

10 FAVORITE BOOKS OF 1980

A Year or So with Edgar, George V. Higgins
The Virgil Thomson Reader
Gore Songs, Rosemary Mayer
Vols III & IV of the *Olson-Creeley Corres.*
Basin & Range, John McPhee
The Selected Letters of Ernest Hemingway
Collected Poems of Frank O'Hara
Freely Espousing, James Schuyler
Themis, Jane Ellen Harrison
Robinson Crusoe, Daniel Defoe
Histories, Herodotus
We Always Treat Our Women Too Well, Raymond Queneau
The Drums of Space, Steve Carey

OLD AGE AND DECREPITUDE

I DO BELIEVE that even I couldn't outcamp Eileen Myles' ministunner in *Newsletter* #80 (the "February 1981" issue). "I Submit My Favorite Books" is a title only Bob Rosenthal should be able to conceive. And by implying that borrowing, stealing, or the receiving of gifts (from less impecunious friends) is her s.o.p. with respect to keeping hip to it all reading-wise, she effortlessly maintains her *I Cover the Waterfront* role even while laying down that cool (if slightly breathless) Danny Richmond NEW DIRECTIONS under CITY LIGHTS rap-on-your-door, she has Rocks in her Heart; requited love doth never bore.

It's true. & just the other day I said to Alice, "You know, if you know enough people, sooner or later some son-of-a-bitch will give you a terrific book to read!" For example, I taught a class at the Kerouac School (Naropa) last Spring which met on ten consecutive Friday evenings, and whose name I remember only as "my novel class." Michael Brownstein had invented it & usually taught it. I adored the books we read for it, and then discussed, often heatedly & at great length. They were, *On Us* by Douglas Woolf; *Heavenly Breakfast* by Samuel R. Delany; *Fat People* by Carol Sturm Smith; *Who Is Sylvia* by Tom Clark; & *What's for Dinner* by James Schuyler. FYI, the students, including Annie Witkowski & Liz Fox, liked but didn't entirely understand DW; found "Chip" Delany to be banal, superficial, boring, annoying, and without any redeeming qualities; had mixed feelings about *Fat People* ("I don't think I *cared* very much about her," said Liz Fox, meaning the heroine); were rapturous over Jimmy Schuyler; & despised Tom Clark, despite having to admit his book met the requirements ("oh, it's a work of art, but that's about all," my favorite student said, pointedly). We finished with *The Street* by Aram Saroyan, which all agreed wasn't much. That was my Spring in Prose; each book was perfect, in its own way, & all were beautiful. Woolf was very powerful, Delany brilliant, provocative & spooky/hilarious; Carol Smith was wonderfully moving & resonated with courage, which is no small thing. Tom Clark was a scared novice black-magician who wisely declined offer of a permanent position, while James Schuyler was naturally, a knockout, & outrageous. Aram had it all covered, & one could never say to him, "You lack charm," though he offended Clark who hated him forever, and despite getting his facts wrong, he pleased me, tho in doing so made my best friend hate me even more than he does now, tho not more than I hate him. A

Scorpio's notion of perfect revenge (poetic justice) is, when someone you love, in cold fury for some "reasons," fixes a steely pair of eyeballs onto you & says, carefully, "Don't ever speak to me again," comply.

As preparation for this assignment by Greg "Sheila Graham" Masters I made a partial list of books read during 1980. The list as compiled from memory, with help from Alice Notley & Steve Carey, is incomplete in that A) It consists only of books I liked, in one way or another; and B) after 327 titles & authors Greg called and asked to pick up this piece, which I had told him days ago was already finished. Given two more days I'd have remembered at least a hundred more (that I'd liked) which means 950 or so books read during 1980. This seems less than I had recalled other years, when less pressing events left time for recording books read in journals, but of course we did travel a lot (Boulder, Needles, SF, Providence, South Attleboro), and I did get sidetracked by teaching the Spring term at Naropa, and the Fall at Stevens Inst. of Technology in Hoboken. Then, too, we had NEA Grants, which needed to be spent, there was Woody Guthrie's house to be visited in Okemah, Oklahoma, with Allen; and then, of course, the Great Naropa Poetry War briefly engaged most of my attention. As I knew the Federation (my self's own head) would require of me a full report, I had to imbibe (through my armpits) a great mass of conflicting documents, sub-texts (e.g., *Slinger*), and even one great never-spoken statement, part credo, part political exegesis, part Chief Joseph Update ("I will fight plenty more"). Next came microscopic scrutiny of the major participants, followed by depth interviews with same, and finally, the great Naropa dinner, drinks, dope, white stuff & extended shouting match between myself as non-neutral, & General Andy "Old Hick" Jackson, the Opposition leader. Well, nobody won that, thank god! so after de-briefing Rabbi Martin "the fag" Boob, President of Poetry and Party-leader of the party-in-power, who only wanted to know exactly what was going on, I was able to submit my report to nobody, and leave. It was only June, but I barely remember the rest of the year, except as titles & authors in bed.

        I did read a little poetry, too. *Triangles in the Afternoon* is, not heavily, as bleak a series of pictures of current actuality as ever elicited a shrug, an apologetic look, and a fervent "oh, darn!" from any poet just finished reading what he had written. Ron Padgett, of whom I always assume mistakenly that it is clear to everyone as it is to me he is a far better poet than Gary Snyder or Mike McClure, let alone Robt. Bly & Mark Strand, like the United States, owes no apologies to anyone. In this book, even more so than in the past, he speaks of experience and emotion, his own, clearly and directly, with no technical distortion. I gleefully & bitterly envy him this one. Anselm Hollo's *Heavy Jars* killed me. He is Wild Bill Hickok facing down Death, father & son & blue-eyed ghost. *Finite Continued*. *Morning of the Poem*: I can't put down Jimmy Schuyler's new book. At third reading last week it was still being almost all anyone could ever want. Bob Rosenthal's poems in magazines inspire like Jimmy, from a different country. Bob wants to get it all, and so do I & he makes it so I can't forget &

to try *this* way. Eileen Myles is better than the rest of you, so eat your hearts out! I'd never dare tell what I like best in her poems! Last but not least (I'd never not "take the responsibility"), Alice Notley is even better than anyone has yet said she is.

But if you'd rather just have something wonderful to read (rather than me), I recommend *The Letters of Evelyn Waugh*, worth every dime, and *Tales from the Texas Gang* by Bill Blackolive, which Allen Ginsberg got in the mail & loaned to me. Send $5.50 to TEXAS GANG ENTERPRISES/ PO BOX 5974/ AUSTIN, TEX/ 78763. It's the sleeper of 1980, & so am I.

GEORGE SCHNEEMAN
AT HOLLY SOLOMON

WITH HIS THIRD show of frescoes in three years, Schneeman's place among the most accomplished painters now coming to the fore makes itself obvious. The 23 paintings included were mostly small, though by no means diminutive, and their variety, arrived at through formal means (size, shape, dispersal of subject matter) made walking into the gallery a great pleasure.

Schneeman lived with his family in Italy, near Siena, from 1959 to 1966, and did some fresco painting then. During succeeding years in New York he painted mostly figures, on fairly large canvases in acrylic—friends and family both clothed and nude. These remain marvelous pictures, done in his characteristic manner of "un-handling" the paint (no brushstroke virtuosity), with drawing and painting often taken to mean the same thing. Highly admired by a few, this early work nevertheless brought the artist little of the notice or success that should have been his.

Schneeman's first show of frescoes, three years ago, consisted of some 75 small examples, each 7 by 9 inches, mounted on 2-1/2-inch-thick cinderblocks. They were paintings of flannel lumberjack shirts in three-color plaids, flattened on wire hangers and depicted dead center on an eggshell white background. The show was a success, all the paintings were sold, and reviews were admiring. His show last year consisted of over 30 more frescoes, similar in size but of heads this time, and while loved by admirers, it was only a modest success. (Who wants a monumental object: that cinderblock, with the face of someone you don't even know on it?)

This most recent show was a knockout from any point of view. There were four of the familiar shirts, on silver hangers this time and done in relief. They are perfect. The four window paintings, a shade larger than the shirts (9 by 8 inches), are almost equally accomplished, their kitchen-window curtains—also done in relief—opening out onto remembered Tuscan landscapes that the dazzling white window mullions divide into quadrants.

Also included were four landscapes, all complete winners. Three are rectangular, one recapitulating the famous Veneziano John the Baptist landscape, minus the saint. The fourth, my candidate for most charming picture in the show, is round, mounted on a rectangular white base, and slightly recessed so as to emphasize its distance from the viewer.

Finally there are the figure pieces, which are *not* portraits per se, but people sitting for paintings. Two such single-figure works are based on Piero di Cosimo's "Profile of a Young Woman." The first, "Anita," is of a ripe beauty; the painting is round and has been given a white mounting resembling a Duchamp rotorelief. It is all innocence and light, truly delectable. The second, "Alice," is rectangular and dark, with storm clouds curling behind the woman's dark chopped hair. Her knowing but unspeaking face is paired with a sensual, womanly body that is all about earth and outdoors. A third painting, "Britta," of an individual against landscape, is one of the show's real standouts. In front of a rough Tuscan landscape, in profile, is an implacably made-up European (German) head, with red hair tight across the forehead, and red lips.

The highlight of the show was a painting of the kind referred to in quattrocento talk as a "Sacra Conversazione." "Three Figures/Landscape" gives us three men in the foreground, the figure on the left turned into the picture, the figure on the right (who, I ought to point out, is myself) turned slightly outward. Behind them a third figure wearing a straw hat looks straight at you, smiling in a blissful awareness of stage center. The artist has used landscape to pull the picture together, and also to disguise the seams. (Frescoes dry so quickly—within three hours or less—that only one figure can be painted a day. Next day, or session, more plaster is applied, and another figure may be added, etc.) Two of the figures have Hawaiian shirts on. The sky is a triumph, the figures are poised in attitudes befitting their countenances, the colors are serious—something portentous is at stake.

ON FRANCO BELTRAMETTI

FRANCO BELTRAMETTI IS a serious man. This is not so common a thing as one might assume. Also, as a visual artist he has an eye, he has a touch, and he is a man of feeling. Right now his instinct is toward paper and ink. (He is, not incidentally, a fine poet in at least two languages, American and Italian.) He looks at the paper, the feel of it to the eye, the whiteness, and then he makes a line. He knows the liquidity of the ink, he sees the way it takes to and is taken by the paper. He likes the blackness of the black on the whiteness of the paper. He makes another line, then a whole series of different kinds of lines. They are wavy, or bent, not baroque, but straight, which is American slang for "honest." He is a beautiful artist. One wishes to take what he makes, and place it on one's wall, and look at it, often. That is art.

NEW YORK CITY, SUMMER 1980

3 REVIEWS

Am Here Books Catalogue #5, Edited by Tom Clark & Richard Aaron

A sociological document of the first order, this Montgomery Ward-type catalogue (alas without pictures) is well worth the $10 price simply as Americana, let alone for its evidence on the condition known as The Economy. It's an alphabetical listing of materials for sale by authors ranging from Abbott to Zukofsky, at prices that almost make you believe you are a cultural asset. Every item is numbered and priced, and throughout this large-sized paperbound basic text are sprinkled comments on particular books, penned in his best absolutely straight and informative manner by a very astute Tom Clark. Clark on Dorn, Clark on Roy Fisher & Jim Burns, Clark excellent on Dick Gallup, Clark incisive on Robert Creeley, and the manners are impeccable. Dennis Cooper adds his comments here and there, showing his own biases endearingly. Do you need every book ever written by Anselm Hollo? I do. You won't want to buy them from this guy, for these prices, but the list is useful, and to see the size of Mr. Hollo's oeuvre is to be told. TC is not useful on AH, one of his rare lapses. Again, do you need $7,500 worth of mss. by Janine Pommy Vega? You have come to the right place. *Am Here #5* is salted with a one line per page text by Mr. William Burroughs also, and is prefaced by a penetrating & telling list poem by Mr. Clark which is in fact the best thing in it. Kudos to Tom Clark for Marcel Duchamping it into this particular mirage.

The Early Auden by Edward Mendelsohn (Viking Penguin)

A massive tome which might have better been titled *The Poems of the Something Auden*, in which, without benefit of anecdote, drollery or light touch, the coming to birth of hereafter dominant themes (it says here) in Auden's Corpus, including extensive documentation of genesis and maturation via helter-skelter, entropy, eccentric practice and the chemical life (Benzedrine by day, wine & martinis at even, seconal for sleep) marches past the eyes of hundreds of pages, insomnia's perfect enemy . . . . . "Lay your sleeping head my love / human on my faithless arm" . . . . .

Paris Review #79, The 25th Anniversary Issue

Let's hear it for Hi-jinks & decorum. The Paris Review Gang, tho they never did come up with a Hemingway, nor even a John Maynard Keynes, did have fun in their day, and still do. Especially the brilliant Harold "Doc" Humes, the appalling but lovable Terry Southern, and someone wonderful named Patti Hill. The 25-year memoirs by assorted hands, woven together by George "The Bogey-Man" Plimpton, should be read. Believe it. This issue also has plenty of poems, many terrible, but first-class works by Clark, Padgett, Ashbery, Koch, Schuyler, and probably somebody else. Also amazing nonsense by Kinnell (ye gads!), a rare tired poem by Philip Levine, who generally confounds by being good, and some really awful unknowns. The Interview, with Rebecca West, is not to be missed. She is perfect. "Leonard (Woolf) really had such a tiring mind . . ."

BUSINESS PERSONAL

POET JAMES SCHUYLER, quite recently, had the unfortunate experience of discovering that during the course of this past summer, a good number of valuable personal items had been removed from his files, including among other things, letters from Frank O'Hara, W.H. Auden; Mss. of published books of his own small art works, and working notebooks including among other pages, unpublished & incomplete poems. Most of these items had been taken for the purpose of resale to dealers, & private individuals, and through the generous cooperation of dealers around the country, much of this material has been recovered. Still missing, however, is a working Notebook, approximately 6" x 9" in size, with a Green Marble-ized Paper Cover, & a red leather spine. Among other hand-written poems and assorted writings contained in this notebook is a hand-written, revised version of Schuyler's poem, "Korean Mums," which appeared in Mr. Schuyler's recent Pulitzer Prize winning volume, *Morning of the Poem*. Anyone having this notebook in their possession, or information as to channels it has been and/or is passing through, should contact Mr. Schuyler, or Ms. Helena Hughes, c/o The Hotel Chelsea, W. 23rd St., NYC, NY. (tel. 212-243-3700), (ex. 626) in order that its return can be negotiated.

for Greg Masters

for Jim & Helena & Tom's
engagement notice,
best, Ted Berrigan
Oct 81

THE ORAL HISTORY SERIES COMMUNITY DOCUMENTATION WORKSHOP

Blending into the Life; *Working at St. Mark's*; *Long Road from Lares* — David Perez; *Making Mud* — Merle Steir; *Full Time Active* — Sara Plotkin; *Changes* — Nora Lugo; *Between Wars*; *Starting Off from the Dead End* — Michael Donahue; *Fishmerchant's Daughter* — Yuri Kochiyama (all $3 available from the Community Documentation Workshop, Arthur Tobier, Director, St. Mark's Church 10th St & 2nd Av NYC 10003 also distributed by Teachers & Writers Collaborative 84 5th Av NY NY 10011)

"The Church," as we call it here in the neighborhood, for me, to name at least one of its members, is, in fact, the Church in my life. It has been, and has been the *only* Church in my life for over seventeen years. Its name of record is, I think "St. Mark's Church in-the-Bowery," &, as many readers & subscribers to this journal know, it sits at the corner where Second Avenue & 10th St. meet, in Manhattan 10003. A designated landmark building, it is equally a "place d'importance," as Ron Padgett might say it, because one wooden leg & all of Peter Stuyvesant's bones are interred in a vault in its south east wall. Stuyvesant, for a fistful of cash-value stuff to the amnt of $24.00, purchased Manhattan Island from certain Indians, who claimed themselves to be either its owners, or parties empowered to act for said party, or parties. Time flew, & Petrus Stuyvesant, intrepid Dutch sailor, died. More time passed, & life, until one day The Church, a/k/a Petrus Stuyvesant's Grave, consecrated May 9th, 1799, looking at and around itself, found itself to be a still beautiful, not dying, but considerably rundown personage, still a living being, also still of considerable stature, but wanting. Its Parish equally had been through changes, some, at least, trying ones.

The streets & avenues at whose center The Church long had held pride of place, always a melting-pot village of major league proportions and activity, included among its residents a large non-voting power bloc of loosely allied groups of children (people between 11 & 32); these were, and are, the children of those who had recently moved out of the neighborhood, & children of those most recently arrived, of the still arriving. Among these were Blacks, Ukrainians,

Russians, Puerto Ricans, Portuguese, & lots of Poles, with Cubans, Koreans, Vietnamese, and etc. arriving fast. Ripping open gravestones, tearing down its fences, breaking into & removing contraband, and general site-transformation toward Disaster Area, constituted one of the major recreational activities of these kids, easily the cheapest, and often surprisingly rewarding.

In the Spring of 1975, via landmark designation, new spirit & small amounts of procurable cash, people fond of The Church, and notably Stephen Facey, first and continuing Director of what became the Preservation Youth Project, conceived of enlisting members of that same generation of kids, same kids no doubt some of the time, into paid job-holders, very much unskilled workers in terms of past job experience, and doing something about the poor old rundown easy mark Church and its grounds, which included yards, playground space for the very small, and The Church itself, inside & out. A book, *Working at St. Marks*, put together as documentation, in part to help with fund raising, was made & organized, under the direction of Arthur Tobier. Eight members of the Preservation Youth Project, Arthur Tobier, & Steve Facey met over several consecutive Saturdays in The Church itself, to talk over the experiences of growing up on the Lower East Side and taking on the responsibility of being a worker. It was all taped, and in the final compilation, who said what, i.e., names, was left out; brief remarks by Muriel Rukeyser, the poet; or Brecht; or John Berger, were placed apart as fitting, and fittingly; and the result, *Working at St. Mark's, "Preservation Youth Project," An Oral History*, emerged as a remarkable document, with sheaves of striking testimony, self-evidently truth, in a round of voices making a Round of American, a song, that is history, plain story, plainsong, plain talk, and everything anyone anywhere needs to know if only in order to be aware of today's date, let alone its obligations, pleasures, tasks, rests. I'm glad I live nearby, and didn't miss out on its availability. Now it is available again, together with the nine other pamphlets, at least, that grew from the doing of this one.

The Church, the neighborhood, people, parents, children, lovers, school, the old and their stories of 50 or more years of change, the world as it is, here, in this United States we call so easily America, is in these books whose central speakers, by now identified by name, ages, all the several occupations & changes, and it is a telling you are hearing while reading. Seeing through ears. (There are beautiful photographs as well, of Second Avenue et al., old days, nowadays.) A young secretary, Nora Lugo, whose mother came here from Fajardo very young tells stories; there is a painter, & an actor, Sara Plotkin, whose history begins, "I was born in a very little town in old Russia"; her story has been named for her book, *Full Time Active*, and it is a treasure. *Between Wars* is Depression Lower East Side; read it and compare, I implore you. And above all don't fail to read the series' first authentic classic, a natural work of art by a natural, terse, but open, story-teller: I mean, Michael Donohue, whose (An) Oral History, called *Starting Off from the Dead End*, is 60 some years of Irish to Irish-American, by a full citizen of most of those sixty years of the Lower East Side. Fireman, Painter, Union Organizer, Singer, lover of his own city, now this one, ours, Manhattan Island, Donohue begins with Cromwell as living presence, covers street-workers, the world of coal robbers & kids, cops, ward politics, family & all that might mean, and he is naturally frank while equally naturally reserved, the result being simple sentences sometimes devastating in the revelations about human survival technique:

".... after my mother died . . . I lost my exterior edges on both ends—to anger and to joy— . . . We protect ourselves by pulling in on both ends. Never go extremely to one end or another. We watch ourselves, even when we're laughing."

. . .

"Maybe I'm wrong," he said, "but I've always placed emphasis on doing the job and then leaving and then not coming back."

These booklets, 5" by 7" in size, and near 40 pps or more usually, should be in every library and school and anywhere else people want to open a book and experience other humans going on telling the story. The story that is the one story and the only story . . . that people lived, are living, do continue, also die, are sick, change, vanish, become successful at whatever, tell about it. Here is some of that story.

RUNNING COMMENTARY

"Now it is autumn and the . . ." is a kind of poetry I have always loved but *not* "and the days dwindle down . . ." because the days go by and it all always is falling in, it always does all fall in. For example, Olsonian syntax becomes a waitress. Young girls' letters is now the newest formal idea around (poems). This book, *5 Aces & Independence* (from Tombouctou), by John Thorpe, is about all the "issues" (money, war, marriage, tribal separation) in that it is person(s) experiencing them. No one else is writing like this. It is a stunning read . . . and searing addition to its predecessors in the world, *Matter, & Cargo Cult*, difficult to find but still extant John Thorpe texts (books). He is present and holds himself accountable.

Meanwhile, in Norman, Oklahoma, Madison Morrison has taken time out from his alchemical laboratory, in which he has been for some while conducting provocative & just possibly significantly important experiments with the application of *condensare* to the cosmological epic, to assemble *Sleep*. ("I want to think of the nether elliptic, and the sun, pausing by the streams of Glacier Creek to regain composure.") *Sleep* willingly fails to contain a high degree of risibility and (at) distractions, and it is clean & white & cool, like sheets are in the land of Will Rogers & Kerr-McGee, where Woody Guthrie was born, and Karen Silkwood's fate predetermined. I'm fascinated, you may be too. "And if thinking of that makes you want to give up thinking, relax. You know, it'll all disappear whether you think of it or not, so why not enjoy it."

In England what is to enjoy, this Indian Summer, is *Birds, Cattle, Fish & Flies. Lamb* #1, can be had cheaply from Nick Kimberly's, 11 Lambs Conduit Passage, London WC 1, England. Ralph Hawkins, a new presence in English Poetry, is presented in large-scale miniature in this small collection, which serves as issue #1 of Anthony Barnett's 3 x 5 mag. *Birds, Cattle, Fish & Flies* is 4 poems in which Resurrection is pondered one Monday morning, while not gone off to work. Nature on earth, in the air, under water, and at table (ah, Easter Sunday dinner!), yields up her reflections in long sinuous lines full of word-love, informed seriously via tone of voice. "hello to what's inside this outside and vice-versa / mincing the chicken with pork, adding cream, / cloves, mace and plenty of seasoning

/ skipping to you in a blue dress . . . it's all about distance and survival / dust wind and flare / it's to do with each day / what's after this I always ask?"

Whatever it is, at this point in my head, I'd rather be reading a book. A book you can read with delight once more, with feeling, is *Footloose*. Irving Stettner wrote the stories in it, and a long time ago he was a Chocolate Soldier in Tokyo. It was a few days after Japan surrendered, and what Japan got in return was a 21-year-old American phenomenon from Brooklyn, who became their first genuine tourist in years. He was a marvel, and the Japanese gently showed him how it is possible to live one's dream life, to draw and paint, & write, & fall in love, & see, & speak, get drunk, & be disappointed & never really surrender except totally, and grow up to be Irving Stettner, author of *Footloose*, poet, painter, reader, peripatetic philosopher-king, mildly pleased. He did it, and I did too.

MILLENIUM DUST, JOSEPH CERAVOLO

LITERARY TIME FALLS away and "history" too & place as *only* local, and one is where one is, which is here, in geological space/time: Joseph Ceravolo lives and has lived all his lives in that this which Charles Olson is now legendary for having given name to in our own cosmos. Millennium existing. Which is why Ceravolo is, so clearly, the purest, most classical lyric poet of body-mind intelligence writing today. And which is also why, given the no less important considerations of talent, technology (technique), sincerity, eloquence, it has continued to seem to me, since first seeing poems of his over twenty years ago, that of the poets that have come into appearance since the landmark Donald Allen anthology, *The New American Poetry, 1945–60*, Joseph Ceravolo stands among the finest, as first among equals.

In this book, his fifth collection, and largest to date, the gathering of poems gives, for the first time, I think, a full sense of the person, who is their voice, and their maker. I love the (his) knowledge that "the face of the mystic" can change. He is a religious person, like Dante, his ancestor, and like William Carlos Williams, his grandfather. There is (his) lovely remorse at such self-involvement ("I am sorry I'm being the most central one here since you are, too . . ."), a remorse which he disposes of quickly, in the first 12 pages, so that naturally it is always there not anything to ever be a main cause of being "upset." Body-mind intelligence is geology reality, which recreates soul as tangible reality, & he can use the word soul as easily as pebble. He "would give up his soul to the salt; though what good is that? the universe being so all alone . . ." Ceravolo is visionary. Visionary in that he gets a real vision of himself inside time, geology (universe), universe; real vision in that his language is a person in places, not not-literary, but not in prophetic tone (tone is words), not in trade language, i.e., science talk, or class talk, whatever, but in "person," who knows as well as himself birds & dogs and sandy beach, pebbles, their own dreams.

Lovely again his sense, Catholic, after Dante & before, that we I mean I his I therefore ours, mine, is capable almost of doing the cosmos a disservice.

He writes love, and the word marriage doesn't intrude, even though its lineaments get delineated. He is just as much a sucker for a good sound trick as anyone. He makes good riddles (you can solve them); the spaces between the words are constant & true, so that verb phrases are talk but for a moment it's Clark Coolidge, James Schuyler, Stein, Petrarch (breaks the line after the preposition is one way, example). Master of making a phrase, e.g., "wiped out" look (work) like it's part of this oh so lyric beauty. And then, there is his amazing You, being the loved one, the beloved, mate, daughter, sister, girl friends of boys and of person. He, that voice in songs there, singing, is real animal male person; it's himself and other person, persons; and because it is real time real space it's a real predicament, it's not ideal: it's a predicament, not something to *realize*, to make you glad!

Millenium Dust: Book of History of Universe as one person might know it right now.

NIGHT FLIGHT BY LITA HORNICK

LITA HORNICK'S NEW book, *Night Flight*, is further good news from this remarkable and valuable woman. She goes to the heart of the matter that is American poetry and painting through the '60s and '70s and still continuing, and she brings us information that is direct, plain-spoken, and self-evidently true. Writers as far-removed from one another as John Wieners and David Antin are brilliantly served in *Night Flight*, by Ms. Hornick's presentations of their in-person answers to her on-target questions as to what they think they are doing now, how they think of themselves, to whom have they looked for inspiration. And her quotations (notably the ones from John Wieners) make you want to have those writers' works in your possession immediately, if you don't have them yet.

In *Night Flight* she has extended her inquiries into the world of painters and paintings and the results are stunning. Al Held, Joe Brainard, Alex Katz, are forthcoming about their own work and its intentions, each in clear, precise statements, far beyond any previously recorded comments. And it is equally clear that it is Ms. Hornick's achievement that they have done so. Her methods, and finally her writing, in which she shows in every sentence her more than basic, open questioning and appreciation of paintings, as it did with poets and their poems, makes for illuminating discussion of painting and ideas, of particular paintings in terms of ideas, in some way that is both new and all her own. What were you doing, she is able to ask. Is what I think I see really here? (that's a question we would all like to ask a painter); and the answers from Jack Youngerman, etc. etc. etc. are wonderful.

Not everyone knew what to do with Ms. Hornick's first volume, *Kulchur Queen*, when it appeared. Was it a memoir, or artifact, was asked. After all, Ms. Hornick has been a close viewer of the new in Art for a considerable while. Now, with this new book, *Night Flight*, one may see clearly that we have in our presence a gifted person, a talented and intelligent writer, who herself lives in the world in which poems and paintings exist, who partakes of their existence, not unquestioningly, but in that particular manner any artist hopes for from the audience of one. That is, with enthusiasms, with doubtings of both self and art, with nerve, with inquisitive even impertinent affection, with love. Put *Night Flight* next to *Kulchur Queen* on your bookshelf. Take them both down and re-read them often. Keep them where your children will be able to get at them. Tell your friends about them. They are useful, *and* a pleasure, like friends.

THE BEEKS

THESE ARE THE BEEKS: four guys in their twenties, from four different parts of the United States, who have come together in New York City to make music that goes straight for the heads *and* the hearts of the listeners. TOM CAREY, singer-songwriter from Los Angeles, California, is the lead singer. MARK BREEDING, composer & guitarist, born in Texas & raised in Hollywood, California, plays lead guitar. JON ALBRINK, from West Virginia, is the bass guitarist & sings vocals. The drummer is BILL WARD, who grew up in Cincinnati, Ohio. Bill Ward also does vocals, tho his main job is to play "a whole lot of drums" at the heart of THE BEEKS, which he does, and he does it well. These terrific musicians make a unique and extraordinary Rock & Roll sound; Breeding plays guitar-line in a clean, clear, and absolutely selective style. He can play fast runs and clusters of notes as well as any guitarist playing today; it is the *right* notes that he, by choice, plays. Jon Albrink's bass playing is steady and fluid at the same time; he and Bill Ward provide the platform on which THE BEEKS must stand or fall. And stand, they do.

Tom Carey's songs are THE BEEKS' stories, and they are the stories of right now. As performed by Carey, they are by turns intense, dramatic, poignant, urgent, raucous, deeply felt, and comic. When you put all four of these musicians together, you have the instantly recognizable & immediately present music that is THE BEEKS.

Already known in both the United States & Europe, for the club dates they have played here, and through the European tour they made in 1980, these BEEKS were made for you and me.

1982

PUBLIC PROCLAMATION
& ADVERTISEMENT OF SALE

Dear Editors,

    It is our unpleasant duty to report to the Community-at-large that Ms. Bernadette Mayer, until recently Director of the St. Mark's Poetry Project, 2nd Ave at 10th Street in Manhattan, has been judged and found GUILTY of reckless abuse of her office, in that she, aided and abetted by her poet-husband, Mr. Lewis Warsh, did, in cold blood, commit savage violence and brutal rape upon the person(s) of a fellow poet(s) by means of secretive and inexplicable removal of a poem, (to wit: "Motto of the Whores and Poets Guild," submitted by Ted Berrigan and Alice Notley; see below) from some 200 copies of *The World* #37, Fall – Winter, 1982. Of a printing run of 400 copies, 200 copies had been collated & mailed or distributed by editor Harris Schiff. Mr. Schiff then resigned for personal reasons (rumor has it as drugs or herpes or both), and Director Mayer then removed the "censored" poem, leaving the title page intact with its listing of Mr. Schiff as Editor. Mr. Warsh prepared a doctored page, with one side as before, and a blank page where the heinous CRIME OF CENSORSHIP took place. Director Mayer told no one what had been done. Mr. Warsh, not even an employee of the Poetry Project, likewise made like a clam. When Mr. Schiff discovered, accidentally (what else is new), the appalling and VICIOUS CRIME, he complained, by letter, to each of the 8 board members of the Poetry Project Advisory Board. Mr. Schiff was then informed by Co-ordinator Bob Holman, of the PP, that "nothing would be done," despite the fact that Mr. Schiff, like Ms. Mayer, was an appointee of the Board, not an employee of Ms. Mayer, the Director. At a meeting, in February, of the Board, despite a plea by Board Member Rochelle Kraut that Mr. Schiff's letter be discussed, the Board, in informal discussion, at a meeting chaired by Director Mayer, agreed that no notice need be taken of Schiff's complaint, thereby revoking the existence, *in toto*, of Mr. Schiff (nice work if you can do it), in the world, as well as the existence of the poem's authors, Ted Berrigan and Alice Notley. Ms. Kraut then submitted a written statement in disagreement, and against CENSORSHIP. She was told it would be included on file, with the minutes of the meeting. Ha, ha.

As Archbishop Emeritus, I felt it necessary at this point to step in (what?). Examination of the facts soon made it very clear CENSORSHIP had been committed, for no other reason other than personal quarrel (that's not good enough?), or, possibly, rampant and incurable madness due to Director Mayer's being under the control of Deadly Evil Powers, of whose existence we are all well aware.

As Mr. Warsh is not an employee of the Poetry Project, his case is being handled elsewhere. Concerning the Poetry Project Advisory Board, consisting of Ms. B. Barg, Ms. Maureen Owen, Mr. Gary Lenhart, Mr. Jeff Wright, Mr. Steve Levine, and Mr. Bob Holman, these poets have been branded on the forehead (or foreskin, whichever applies) with a livid scar in the shape of an *S*, for SHAME, and advised to go and sin no more. Ms. Jessica Hagedorn, the AB's outside observer, has observed this. Neither praise nor blame has fallen on Ms. Rochelle Kraut, for, in acting honorably, she was simply behaving like a person, which is its own reward, and not w/o grief, either.

DIRECTOR BERNADETTE MAYER, by remaining angrily unrepentant, and by to the very end refusing even to communicate the *fact* of her Act of CENSORSHIP, let alone her reasoning, proved herself beyond redemption, and beyond all human help. Consequently, by order of this office, she has been recycled into a small lampshade, and 8 tiny bars of soap. These can be purchased from the Poetry Project for $1.98 for the lampshade, and $.08 (8 cents) each for the bars of soap. Order now. The supply is limited.

> —Office of the Dept. of Final Judgement
> Ted Berrigan, ARCHBISHOP EMERITUS &
> GUARDIAN OF THE FAITH, AND THE OVENS
> Friday, the 13th Day of May, 19&83

= + =

EXHIBIT A, The Censored Poem:

*

You'll do good if you play it like you're
        not getting paid
But you'll do it better if the motherfuckers pay you.

(Motto of THE WHORES
& POETS GUILD—trans.
from The Palatine Anth-
ology by Alice Notley &
Ted Berrigan. 20 Feb 82)

a paid political advertisement

"I have come to debase the coinage."
                          —DIOGENES

THE WHITE SNAKE BY ED FRIEDMAN

Directed by Bob Holman. Sets and Costumes by Robert Kushner. An EYE AND EAR Production. April 22, 23, 24, 25, 29, 30, May 1, 2, at Dancerschool, 400 Lafayette Street, NYC.

CAST:
Boatman: Jose Rafael Arango
Blue: Debra Granieri
White: Rochelle Kraut
Syu: Titus Welliver
Yoshiko Chuma as Yoshiko Chuma

CHORUS:
Sophie Clarke, Suzu Kawamoto, Doris Kornish, Marc Nasdor, Ethan Ryman, Margery Segal, Pierre Shrady, Elizabeth Tobier; Trainer, Yoshiko Chuma

Music by Vito Ricci.

The magic of the theater clicks on in that anticipatory moment when the audience goes silent as the play is about to begin, as it will when "something is about to happen," in this production of Ed Friedman's *The White Snake*, & never once diminishes through all the tricks, tangles & turns director Bob Holman, in collaboration with the designer/painter Robert Kushner, and the choreographer/dancer/performer Yoshiko Chuma, constructs to bring to life once again in 1982 a 12th Century Chinese Folktale, reborn as a 20th Century Peking Opera.

Friedman's fast-talking song & dance re-presentation of his source material sparkles with liveliness; and his near-geometrical economy in rolling out a many colored but single-strand ball of yarn which remains abrasive enough to stimulate the phagocytes to head-shaking amusement and unflagging attentiveness, while throwing up enough tender-hearted tough-talking optimism in the face of the world muck, is a miracle in that it all remains so simple, just like life. "You had to run downhill in your sink to take a shower," White explains, of former living quarters.

The White Snake is the story of a White Snake Spirit (White) and her companion, a Blue Snake Spirit (Blue), who return to earth in order that White may pursue an ordinary mortal, Mr. Syu, with whom she has fallen in love. This pursuit begins by the shores of West Lake, continues on a boat which the ladies and Mr. Syu board, piloted by an astonishingly deadpan half-sinister, half-cretin Boatman, and culminates in Redondo Beach, after a boatride through a storm. At Redondo Beach action resumes inside a Winnebago camper, evidently the home of Blue & White, which is driven around for a good while, until after some thorough "trying it before you buy it," White and Mr. Syu marry. The wedding is followed by a Kung Fu Honeymoon, consisting of a beach party and then a battle, in the middle of which all freeze, and a shabbily dressed happy pitchman pitches *White Snake II*, which, he says, will appear in the next season; Coming Attractions are highlighted in speech, and what has been seen & heard so far is described as "a story of people's liberation, depicted as a knockout spectacle . . . & an educational experience." "He was a mortal who couldn't make up his mind. She was a White Snake, or was she?"

That was merely the story. What the audience got to see and hear was a dazzling progress of stories which ranged from sight and sounds of a pride of lions to the appalling wisecracking and crude fornication of a nest of ninnies. It was all never less than heavenly, and never more than earthbound.

First came wisecracks, insults and American graffiti, out of the mouths of two beauties. The shining-eyed, radiant, world champion sex-midget, White, was played with heartwarmingly shocking insistence by Rochelle Kraut, who delivered her foulmouthed lines in a desperately funny rollercoaster Swedish accent thoughtfully provided by Mr. Friedman, who wrote much of the play in phonetics, necessary also for Blue's Mexican accent, and Syu's Indian accent. Debra Graniere, a big broad, played Blue as if she were Walter Matthau playing Garbo, and surrounded the demure White with whirling currents of electricity and thunderclaps. Blue's accent was indecipherable, sounding more coarse Rumanian peasant than Mexican, but her speeches were clear. Rochelle Kraut wore White's Swedish accent like lipstick put on in the dark, fetching, and perfectly shaped, but marvelously off-target. Titus Welliver's Mr. Syu spoke mostly in an accent-accent, slightly "down," but very there, as if someone had told him his legacy was of the highest order, i.e., ordinary. Jose Rafael Arango brought his own distinct accent to the role of the Boatman. He was by turns ponderous, unhurried, vulgar, and devastating. All of the words, Mr. Friedman's, were made, by judicious pace & staging by Bob Holman, to float over the action; thus it was truly an eye & ear production. Mr. Holman does this wonderfully well, as those who saw his production of Edwin Denby's *Four Plays* last year can attest. In *The White Snake*, the final magic was made possible, very obviously, by Yoshiko Chuma, from both on and off stage, and by Robert Kushner, in absentia.

I can hardly go on, but believe it or not, literally dozens more things & events to see took place. There were the songs, sung first by a mindblowing chorus of attractive androgynous (only at first) young people in black and other colors; with small songs by the major players. There was a fashion show in the Winnebago, during which Mr. Arango quietly and off to one side went through a half-dozen vividly real portrait appearances, each time by means of adding or subtracting a few pieces of clothing that had been dumped onto a party, courtesy of Mr. Kushner. Arango appeared, while sitting up very straight and rarely moving, first as an old man, then a young rake, then a dancing girl, then a sheik, then a sissy, then the devil. Very possibly he was the devil.

And finally, there was the ever-present Yoshiko, who, clad in dancer's workaday costume of tights and stockings, played a kind of robust Tinkerbell, who never spoke, but at each seeming lull strode purposefully over to the nearest players, made a few abracadabra hand-gestures, and set off something new happening. She, like the chorus, was in constant league with the audience, winking, grinning with satisfaction, or knowingly, as she animated all of every change. There were 16 scenes and in Act One, nine of them were signalled as beginning and ending, by Ms. Chuma, and at each ending a large piece of vari-colored fabric was rolled out across the action, like roof to floor scrolls, coming from far downstage left, right up to and past the audience. When the stage was entirely divided into foreground and behind the curtain by Mr. Kushner's panels, it was the end of Act One, and the Chorus came racing out belting out the song "You've Got to Move." After lining up facing the audience, and directly addressing them in wonderfully natural and intimate but large-scale flirtatious movement, they raced off. To the great delight of the audience, Ms. Chuma then did a slow half-strut "dirty" dance across the front, and sang in perfect (almost) unaccented American, "you got to move," bawdy and suggestive to the point of making one feel faint, and clean, at the same time. She also made it very clear that she was to be taken literally, and so Act I ended with the audience quite naturally getting up, carrying their chairs to a specified location behind Mr. Kushner's curtain, which had completely bisected the room, to find themselves in a lobby they had half made themselves, to stand or sit in during intermission.

In Act Two, behind the curtain, where the chairs had been moved to, the three lead players, Blue, White, and Syu, entertained themselves, did "it," which Blue had already done with Boatman, and discussed love, death, the terrible condition of the city and country, reprised discussion along similar lines from Act One, and finally, Syu & White had a wedding. All players, including Boatman, who was still around, and was soon to be a Kung Fu Teacher of different name, went off, to reappear as a wedding party, bride and groom, for the ceremony. When Mr. Syu entered again, with Ms. Chuma on his arm, wearing the bridal gown, she seemingly having become one with White, everything seemed to fall into place, like magic, and one finally "understood." What was understood? Everything that had passed before one's eyes, and in (& out of) one's ears: life was real, all was illusion, everybody is hopeless, and you got to move. Who could ask for anything more.

This truly was at least one kind of "poet's theater." It was poetry, and it was theater. Neither would have come alive without the other.

HARRY FAINLIGHT:
IN MEMORIAM (D. 1982, LONDON)

"Many great dears are taken away."

MAY NO FATE willfully misunderstand me, but . . . . Duration, durability, being something I have never questioned in me, it is just so that I am not, cannot, be surprised that Harry is dead. For it is that fate, Death, early and still late, that Harry had so unquestioningly taken as his own from before I met him. Speaking with Ron (Padgett) over the phone earlier tonight, I heard Ron once again say those words, *poète maudit*, and was struck by with how little severity one could hear and even use that phrase; something I only first realized twenty years ago upon reading Allen Ginsberg's fulsome praise of John Wieners, in an account of first hearing a tape of Wieners' reading. Allen himself indicated a difficulty with the bare text of Wieners' *Hotel Wentley Poems*. He didn't "get it" at first, for it was in the music. With Harry, too, it was in the music, and in how achingly beautiful the lyric is in the hands of someone who makes it in the throat. "A lamp / creates a glade." is one of Harry's great couplets, from a selection of his, arranged by himself, that I published in *"C" Magazine* in 1964. The whole arrangement was titled by Harry, "Ah, London," and the reader was referred to a sister selection from *Fuck You (A Magazine of the Arts)* entitled, "Oh, London."

    In 1963 I moved back downtown, to 630 East 9th St. in NYC, and into the rush of the days of the underground movie explosion, the heydays of LeMetro Coffee House as the center of Poetry Readings, Allen's return from India, and the emergence of Ed Sanders' *Fuck You* gang, the "C" Magazine crowd of "soi-disant" Tulsa poets, and the ongoing pursuits of the Kelly/Rothenberg Camp. Harry Fainlight circulated through all of these, appearing as even I did, into LeMetro from the street, there to be brought together, perhaps by Gerry Malanga, whose importance as someone who brought people together was central, as a crowd of new, young, nearly certifiable poets, the regulars ranged in age, in 1964, from 17 to 30: boys and girls, black and white, queer and straight, a new class, drawn from any other, the class of '65. Harry and I met like two boys in a John Buchan novel: a Yank with no connotations other than friend on that word, and a Brit, one who as it turned out had American citizenship by birth, but had grown up entirely in England and was Oxford London to the core, so much so that he was even half-Jewish, and so, of course, cosmopolitan, urban rather than urbane, and not one bit Middle Atlantic, as say Bill Merwin was (and Anselm Hollo would not be). We liked one another from the first, like they say, and spent long hours and nights in Ratner's, comparing maps of the worlds of poetry, our world, as we had boyishly taken it to be, each. Harry was a serious, intent listener, with great handsome sweep of brow and piercing nose above long sensitive lips. I thought he was beautiful. He could blush, and his laugh, part full, part giggle, cracking like a croak of a raven in the middle, encouraged one to greater earnestnesses which still now do not seem extravagances, as they didn't then.

Gleefully earnest we discussed like shopgirls everyone: Allen himself (and Harry recounted to me his own saying to Allen, "I want your power," and Allen's cheerful reply, "you can have it"); Peter Orlovsky no less (Harry recognized further depths than he knew when he came upon them, and further sheer physical strengths); John Wieners, virgin daughter of Mother Mary's sorrows (Harry was severe with John only, for he recognized his own fate and its dangers, and was audibly heard to tsk, tsk, when John would veer beautifully close to playing the role that was each of theirs for real, in a poem at a reading) & Frank O'Hara, John Ashbery, and Kenneth Koch, whose banners small as they then were, Ron and I carried as we rode our donkeys into the fray. Harry found Frank's cheerfulness distressing (Irish, I said) & his strengths, disconcerting, and after careful brooding consideration, found it necessary to confront Frank, at a party, and alas, all because of me and my insistence, I'm afraid. For Harry was vanquished with a smile, by a courtier with self-evident friendliness. Approaching Frank, while Frank was in conversation with Bill Berkson, or John Ashbery, he said abruptly, "Frank, I've been reading your poetry, a lot, and thinking about you a lot, and I've come to the conclusion that it's not all that great!" And waited. And Frank without missing a beat, turned a sun of a smile on him and said to him laughingly, putting his hand on Harry's arm as he did so, "Oh, stop it!" with rising inflection. There was no malice, there, no patronizing, only recognition of what play we were all in, maybe. Telling me of the incident a few moments after it happened, Harry was rueful, but not chastened. "I was actually wittier than he was!" he complained to me, and I've always loved him for treating me equal at that moment, and always loved myself and Frank and Harry and all of us there in that room, for being there, in New York City in 1965.

Harry was watching, as Harry was always there, seeing, watching, when Paul Blackburn came over to me in LeMetro in early 1964 and asked me if I thought I would like to have a Wednesday Night reading of my own, in a month or two; and he was glad, glad for me, and glad to have been there to see it, and glad to be able to say to me some minutes afterwards, gleefully, and warm, and boyish, and radiant with friendship and comradeship both, as indeed there is a difference, "I saw him do it. I saw him thinking it, and I saw him get up and come over and ask you!" I was glad, too, and though we didn't embrace and laugh, as it was neither the time nor the place, I embrace you now, Harry, Goodbye, old friend.

October, 1982, NYC

PUBLICATION INDEX

'60s Journals (*Shiny*, No. 9/10, 1999)

Some Notes About "*C*" (Unpublished, May 1964)

Art and Literature: An International Review, edited by John Ashbery, Ann Dunn, Rodrigo Moynihan, and Sonia Orwell (#1, March 1964, $2.00) (*Kulchur*, Vol. 4, No. 15, Autumn 1964)

Lines About Hills Above Lakes, Jonathan Williams (Roman Books, $3.00) (*Kulchur*, Vol. 4, No. 15, Autumn 1964)

Lunch Poems, Frank O'Hara (City Lights Books, $1.25) (*Kulchur*, Vol. 5, No. 17, Spring 1965)

Poems from Oklahoma (Hardware Poets) and *The Bloodletting* (Renegade Press), Allen Katzman (*Kulchur*, Vol. 5, No. 17, Spring 1965)

Poems: Aram Saroyan, Richard Kolmar, and Jenni Caldwell (Acadia Press) (*Kulchur*, Vol. 5, No. 17, Spring 1965)

In Advance of the Broken Arm, Ron Padgett, w/ cover and drawings by Joe Brainard ("C" Press) (*Kulchur*, Vol. 5, No. 17, Spring 1965)

Nova Express, William Burroughs (Grove, $5.00) (*Kulchur*, Vol. 5, No. 18, Summer 1965)

Art Chronicle (*Kulchur*, Vol. 5, No. 19, Autumn 1965)

The Anxious Object: Art Today and Its Audience, Harold Rosenberg (Horizon Press, $7.50) (*Kulchur*, Vol. 5, No. 19, Autumn 1965)

The Doors of Stone, Poems, 1938–1962, F.T. Prince (Rupert Hart-Davis) (*Kulchur*, Vol. 5, No. 19, Autumn 1965)

Pavilions, Kenward Elmslie (Tibor de Nagy, $2.00) (*Kulchur*, Vol. 5, No. 19, Autumn 1965)

Saturday Night: Poems, Bill Berkson (Tibor de Nagy, $2.00) (*Kulchur*, Vol. 5, No. 19, Autumn 1965)

New Directions 14, ed. James Laughlin ($1.65) (*Kulchur*, Vol. 5, No. 19, Autumn 1965)

Peace Eye: Poems, Ed Sanders (Frontier Press, $1.50) (*Kulchur*, Vol. 5, No. 20, Winter 1965)

Desolation Angels, Jack Kerouac (Coward-McCann) (*Kulchur*, Vol. 5, No. 20, Winter 1965)

Painter to the New York Poets (*ARTnews*, November 1965)

The Portrait and Its Double (*ARTnews*, January 1966)

Red Power (*ARTnews*, December 1966)

Sentences from the Short Reviews (*ARTnews*, issues February 1965, March 1965, April 1965, May 1965, Summer 1965, September 1965, January 1966, February 1966, March 1966, April 1966, May 1966, Summer 1966, October 1966, November 1966, December 1966)

Joe Brainard (*ARTnews*, February 1965)

Red Grooms (*ARTnews*, April 1965)

Alice Neel's Portraits of Joe Gould (*Mother*, No. 6, November 1965)

Frank O'Hara Dead at 40 (*East Village Other*, August 1966)

The Chicago Report (*The World*, No. 15, March 1969)

Southampton (*The World*, No. 38, May 1973)

Bolinas (*The World*, No. 38, May 1973)

Selections from a Journal: 1 Nov 1977 to 17 May 1978 (*United Artists* #13, April 1981)

On the Road Again, an Old Man (Unpublished, Chicago, New York City, 1972–1978. A "C" Press mock-up is in the Rose Library collection)

The Arrival Report (August 3, 1974, from a journal in the Rose Library collection)

Get the Money (*East Village Other*, Vol. 1, Issue 3, December 1965)

An Interview with John Cage (*Mother*, No. 7, Mother's Day 1966)

Introduction to *In* by Aram Saroyan (*In*, Aram Saroyan, Bear Press, 1965)

Ten Things About the Boston Trip: An Aside to Ron & Tom (from *Back in Boston Again*, Tom Clark, Ron Padgett, and Ted Berrigan, Telegraph Books, 1972)

An Interview with John Ashbery (*The World*, No. 8, November 1967)

Brain Damage (Some Notes, and a Case History) (Unpublished, early to mid-'60s)

Note on Jim Brodey's Poems & Him (Introduction to Brodey's *Fleeing Madly South*, 1967)

Introduction for Tom Clark at the Folklore Center (Unpublished, delivered March 9, 1967)

Jim Carroll (*Culture Hero*, Vol. 1, No. 5, New York, NY, 1970)

Anne Waldman: Character Analysis (*Contact*, No. 5, 1973)

Maya by Anselm Hollo (back cover for *Maya*, Cape Goliard, 1970)

A Few Hard Words on Tom Raworth (back cover for *Moving*, London: Cape Goliard Press; New York: Grossman Publishers, 1971)

In Time: Poems 1962–68, Joel Oppenheimer (Bobbs-Merrill, $5.95) (Publication unknown)

Teaching with the School Teachers (Report to the Academy of American Poets, circa 1970)

Note on Alice Notley, Not Used, for *165 Meeting House Lane*, Published by "C" Press in 1971 (Unpublished, 1971)

Sensation by Anselm Hollo (*The World*, No. 28, April 1974)

From *The Autobiography of God* (Unpublished, circa 1972–73)

The NY Jets: A Movie (*Slice*, February 1967)

The Life of Turner (Unpublished)

Words for Joanne Kyger (*Iowa Review*, Vol. 3, No. 4, 1972)

Scorpio Birthday (Unpublished, November 1971)

Air by Tom Clark (Harper & Row) (Unpublished, June–July 1971)

The Poetry Room by Lewis MacAdams (Harper & Row) (Unpublished, June–July 1971)

Great Balls of Fire by Ron Padgett (Unpublished, June 1973)

Introduction to *Fresh Paint: An Anthology of Younger Poets* (*Fresh Paint: An Anthology of Younger Poets*, Ailanthus Press, 1977)

Larry Fagin (*Contact*, No. 4, 1973)

Litany (Unpublished, November 15, 1977)

The Fastest Tongue on the Lower East Side (*Poetry Project Newsletter*, No. 57, July 1978)

Naropa Workshop Notes (Unpublished, July 10, 1978)

10 Favorite Books of 1980 (*Poetry Project Newsletter*, No. 91, May 1982)

Old Age and Decrepitude (*Poetry Project Newsletter*, No. 81, March 1981)

George Schneeman at Holly Solomon (*Art in America*, Vol. 68, No. 3, March 1980)

On Franco Beltrametti (Franco Beltrametti Neue Werke, Edition 999, Zurich, 1980)

3 Reviews (*Poetry Project Newsletter*, No. 84, October 1981)

Business Personal (*Poetry Project Newsletter*, No. 85, November 1981)

PERMISSIONS